MEMORIES BELONGA ME

LACH TERRY

Copyright © 2025
First Published in Australia in 2025
By Morpheus Publishing
Geelong Victoria 3216
www.morpheuspublishing.com.au

All rights reserved. No part of this publication may be reproduced, stored in a retrieval system, or transmitted in any form or by any means, electronic, mechanical, photocopying, recording or otherwise, without the prior written permission of the publisher or author.

Paperback ISBN: **978-1-7640063-9-2**
Author: Lachlan Terry
Editor: Lynette Reurts
Cover Graphics: Lynette Ingles

A catalogue record for this book is available from the National Library of Australia.

DISCLAIMER
The information contained in this book is for general informational purposes only. The author and publisher are not offering any medical, legal or professional advice. While every effort has been made to ensure the accuracy and completeness of the information provided, the author and publisher assume no responsibility for errors or omissions or any outcomes or consequences resulting from using this book's content.

COPYRIGHT
All original material in this book is the sole property of the author and Morpheus Publishing.

DISTRIBUTION
This book is distributed by Morpheus Publishing and is available through authorised distributors, booksellers, Morpheus Publishing website.

COPYRIGHT PERMISSIONS
For copyright permissions or any other inquiries, please contact:

PUBLISHER: Morpheus Publishing
www.morpheuspublishing.com.au ||
hello@justinemartin.com.au ||
+61403 564 942

AUTHOR: Lachlan Terry
https://www.morpheuspublishing.com.au/authors/lachlan-terry

FOREWORD FOR 'MEMORIES BELONGA ME' FROM NORAH KERSH

Thank you Lachlan, for sharing your story. In more isolated parts of our country there are few people to write with authenticity about life out there. Your account adds to a history that too often is lost.

Lachlan grew up on Elton Downs, the eldest child of Rupert and Monica, followed by six siblings. Life on Elton Downs presents the whole spectrum of outback station scenarios. Along with the good times come the dry times, the big wet seasons, the bushfires, all helping to produce resilient people. The Terry family – adventurous, resourceful and interesting – exemplifies this.

Further along the track Lachlan, with a family of his own, contends with a debilitating condition, Primary Lateral Sclerosis (PLS), for years undiagnosed. His doctor advised that there was no medication or operation to improve the situation. Lachlan's response was typical: "I was a jump ahead of a lot of people in that I was in no pain and it was a slowly progressing condition". So he just got on with it.

Family values are dearly held. Like his grandfather, John O'Brien, who travelled great distances to keep in touch, Lachlan has taken his children visiting relatives and also to far-flung places camping on the way

– as he says, "to give them a broad scope of interest". Most Australian children would only dream about such a gift.

Further hurdles to negotiate have been the heartbreaking loss of brothers Eddie and Byrne, in different tragic accidents.

As a child growing up in western New South Wales, I thought of Queensland as a sort of mythical place. Visits from Uncle John O'Brien (my father's brother) were anticipated with excitement. Years later, we were to raise our own family in this mythical place, north-west Queensland.

Lachlan refers to the Hughenden Show as one of the highlights of the year for children. Soon after my family settled at 'Bora Station' in the Richmond district, Monica invited us to the Hughenden Show and down to Elton Downs for the night. We sat around the table till all hours rocking with laughter as Rupert told story after story. Lachlan's mother too was a raconteur extraordinaire. It is in the genes.

Lachie, I am inspired by your words: "You can only play the hand that you have been dealt". I believe your story 'Memories Belonga Me' will inspire many.

PROLOGUE TO MEMORIES BELONGA ME

These are technically not my memories, but after some research, as well as a lot of family oral history over the years, I will briefly fill in the gap from the beginning of the settlement of Australia to the settlement of western Queensland. My great-great-great-grandfather Thomas was born in London in 1793. He was a transportee to the great southern land of New South Wales and arrived in 1812 aboard the 'Guildford'. He married Ann Crouch (also a transportee) in Parramatta in the year of 1816. They had two sons and two daughters, with their youngest child, a daughter, being born a few months after he was killed in a wagon accident in 1823. That daughter also died in infancy.

Their third child Thomas, who entered this world in Campbelltown, married Margaret MacDonald (sister of JG MacDonald, the noted Queensland explorer) and they eventually in the 1860s settled on the banks of the Murrumbidgee River in the Hay district. Initially he had some business partnership with his brother-in-law William Rudd at 'Howlong Station' on the northern banks of the Murrumbidgee River, not far from the small township of Carathool. He and Margaret later owned 'Rudd's Point Station', a holding not far away.

It was on the southern banks of the same river that they raised their eleven children, and where they also operated a hotel, 'The Wool Pack Inn'. It was their eldest son, AJM Terry, who ventured north to Bowen in

Queensland working for his uncle JG MacDonald in the Bowen district, becoming the first Queensland connection. Their eldest daughter Margaret married a teamster John Bethel and they also raised a large family, eventually moving north and settling around Chillagoe and Mareeba.

AJM Terry married Rosemary Angela Byrne, and they owned a number of properties in the Bowen area, first 'Etonvale', then 'Blenheim' and finally 'Kirknie Station' on the banks of the Bogie River. For a number of years they also ran a butcher shop in Bowen. While all this was going on they raised their family, and it was their three sons Tom, Alexander and Leslie that saw the promise of the western plains and made their move in that direction around 1910.

Legend has it that they attended a race meeting in Townsville at the Cluden racecourse in the early 1900s, and the bulging wallets of the western graziers made their eyes pop. The three brothers had already bought their neighbouring 'Byrne Valley' property in partnership. Two brothers managed the property and helped on 'Kirknie' while Tom conducted a droving business from many large western properties to help pay for it. It was not long before they moved west.

Together and in their own right they owned many properties in the west including 'Keen Gea, south of Torrens Creek, 'Laurelvale' near Prairie, then 'Enryb' and 'Knapdale' near Corfield. When they concluded their partnership arrangements, Tom went on to own a string of properties in his own right including 'Limbri', 'Saranac', 'Eldorado' and 'Stamford Downs' as well as others. Later on, in partnership with his sons, he formed "The Stamford Fat & Store Stock Company" which, using Westmorelands, a gulf country cattle station, to provide the store cattle, they bought more Stamford district properties to fatten their cattle on.

Mum's previous family history has not been quite as lengthy but certainly her family were not short of achievements and personal bests either. Her grandfather John (Jack) O'Brien left the family home located in Tullow, County Carlow, Ireland. The year was 1883 and he was aged

21. A few years after his arrival aboard the 'Chimborazo' he took up a small balloted block of 1070 hectares near Warren in western New South Wales and started doing the hard yards. The stark differences between County Carlow and Coonamble would not have been lost on him. They were of robust Irish stock and if you could put up with the English for hundreds of years this would be a walk in the park. In a matter of years most of his neighbours had walked off their leases which he had either bought himself or other family members had bought. Through sheer perseverance and hard work they prospered and expanded throughout the west of New South Wales.

But it was not only around Coonamble that the O'Briens were hard at work. There were droving trips involved with the buying and selling of stock to and from their properties. In 1917 they also bought Yanda station, a huge property that had frontage to the Darling River about 100 kilometres downstream from Bourke. Another family member became a very well respected doctor. Dr Daniel O'Brien served as a doctor in the gold mining town of Ravenswood in Queensland, later moving to Rockhampton and running his own private hospital there for many years. He became a very wealthy man with his astute trading of shares on the stock markets as well.

Like the Terry brothers, John O'Brien, Mum's father, had also heard of the vast expanses of grass on the plains of western Queensland. With this in mind, as a young man, he and his brother Mick, before there was ever any bitumen even in the towns of western Queensland, had ridden their ancient motorbikes on a tour north from their father's property 'Hatton'. He also saw the promise of this country and how it could benefit his future. A few short years later he married Irene Byrne in Sydney and a decade after that with 5 children in his family he was looking to expand.

He entered into a land ballot for resumed country off Marathon Station, which then was a huge property between Hughenden and Richmond. The year was 1935. He was successful. A 35,000 acre block which he called 'Terranburby' was the result. His new property was named for his two sons Terrance or Terry and Bernard but using his nickname Burby. It was about 15 kilometres south of the railway siding and telephone exchange at Barabon. So started a new chapter in the sea of grass on the western plains of Queensland. Over the next 30 years this toehold in Queensland for the O'Briens saw them expand to own a number of properties in the north west.

This is the broad back story of my ancestors in the Great Southern Land and brings us to the early years of the twentieth century which is where both my parents enter the picture. The story of my recollections began in the mid-twentieth century. Telling a story is very much like life itself, there are many fascinating threads all woven together starting and finishing as time unfolds and it is hard to stick to the one thread continuously without getting distracted by other events that happen along the way. I have endeavoured to keep it easy to follow and I hope you enjoy the story of the Terry and O'Brien families as I heard and saw it, which then enabled me to tell my story.

TABLE OF CONTENTS

Foreword for 'Memories Belonga Me' from Norah Kersh iii

Prologue to Memories Belonga Me v

1: Westmoreland, So Close To The Never-Never 1

2: Stamford Town, on the Downs 20

3: Elton And The Early Years 39

4: Characters That Made The West 59

5: Kids Growing Up In The Bush 70

6: Educating The Offspring in the Big Smoke 85

7: Life On The Land 101

8: One Task At A Time 117

9: Springtime, It Brings on the Shearing 134

10: Never Getting Bored In The Bush 153

11: The Ellenbrae Experience 171

12: Marriage, Mining, Mount Isa & Medical Issues. 189

13: Taxis, Townsville, Trials & Tribulations 203

14: On My Own Again 219

15: Delving Into The Arts 233

16: Down The Dusty Road We Go 252
17: Looking Forward, Looking Back.. 272
18: Moving On With MND 291
19: Remembering The Man That Was Dad..305
20: Dad, The Entertainer 323
21: Remembering The Woman That Was Mum 340
22: Mum, The Knowledge Gatherer and Globe Trotter 357
23: Terrys Into The Future..380
Glossary 396

1

WESTMORELAND, SO CLOSE TO THE NEVER-NEVER

Westmoreland was a lot of hard work for three boys who went there when they were still all in their teens and working unsupervised with only a team of much older Aboriginal men for staff. It was all pack horse mustering with a team of about 10 stockmen, 2 of the brothers and about 8 Aboriginal stockmen. One of the brothers always remained at the homestead. Between the end of April and September they used to try and do about 6 rounds of mustering. A round of mustering took about 3 to 4 weeks from when they left the homestead until they returned and consisted of just moving in a huge circle collecting cattle each day as they went. They left the homestead with a small mob of perhaps 10 or 15 coacher cattle to steady the wild cattle as they were brought into the mob.

The mob of cattle grew each day as more wild cattle were captured and added to their small mob of coachers. After 2 or 3 days in the mob, the wild cattle became used to the routine and being continually pushed back into the mob so in effect became coachers themselves as time went on. It followed a set course determined by where their bush cattle yards were located. Each yard was about 10 miles apart, which is about a day's mustering distance. Each mustering round was limited to about 200 to 250 head of cattle because none of the impromptu bush yards could hold any more than around 250 head. If they struck a particularly heavy concentration of cattle in an area and collected their quota in, say, two weeks, well, that was when they had to head back to the homestead.

A little bit about the bush yards dotted all over Westmoreland that they used for mustering the cattle. They did not build these yards as they were mustering; they were the result of collective years of work with some concentrated effort at year's end when the mustering was over. Usually located near a creek as a water source for their camp, but not always. I don't know for sure but my guess is that there would have had to have been possibly 40-odd sets of these yards scattered around different areas of Westmorelands. A 'permanent impromptu' bush yard was built from materials at hand.

Trees were cut down right on site and standing trees were used as the posts of the yard. The felled trees were used as yard rails by cutting them to length to suit distances between the 'posts'. The fastenings used could be No. 8 plain wire in a Cobb & Co twitch, but sometimes lengths of 'greenhide' were used. If they were to use 'greenhide', a beast in poor condition would be shot somewhere close by and its hide cut into a long strip about two inches wide to make the greenhide.

This was done by starting in the centre of the hide and, using a spiralling circle, cut around and around, until you run out of hide, ending up perhaps with a couple of hundred feet of leather about two inches wide. You would have to kill more than one beast to have enough leather to do the whole yard. When constructing the yards the rails were placed on the inner side of the 'posts' so that the posts would take the actual pressure of the cattle pushing against them. There was a deep notch cut out of the side of the tree to place the rail into and then the 'greenhide' leather strip or No. 8 Cobb & Co twitch would fasten the post and rail together.

If the greenhide was used it was wrapped around post and rail a number of times whilst wet and tied off; as it dried it shrank and tightened the rail to the post. The notch that had been cut into the tree trunk or 'post' took most of the weight of the rail and prevented the rail from slipping down and making the gap between the rails too wide. The gate to the yards was always just a gap in the panels with a number of loose slip rails left lying on the ground that were put in place after the cattle were in the yard and fastened in place with some rope or wire.

Just after daylight each day the cattle were let out of the overnight yard and away they would go. Two or three would tail the coacher mob along while one man would look after the spare horses and pack horses that had the tucker and swags on them. The other men would work out wide of the coachers and bring cattle back into the mob as they found them. These were wild cattle so it was not easy work – there was a lot of galloping involved and very strenuous throwing of 'mickeys' or bulls. Sometimes a shot through the nose from a .450 Adams revolver was used to either 'wheel' or turn a beast back to the coaches or permanently subdue any beast that proved to be too unruly. The rule was simple: if you couldn't be controlled you were eliminated, there were plenty more cattle to be found. On their dinner camp each of the mustering team would catch a fresh horse for the afternoon's mustering.

As each little mob was found, any bulls or mickeys (male cattle) of any size were chased and thrown by hand so they could be earmarked (with a pocket knife), castrated and dehorned with a horn saw and then let go. The only cattle put into the mob were bullocks that had had this same operation 2 or 3 years previously and matured. Cows, calves and any half decent breeding bulls were let go again. Cows were not dehorned so that they would be able to defend their calves from dingo attacks. Early in the year as they went around mustering they would be back-burning the country by dropping matches behind themselves all the time.

The country was still green so only the old dead grass lying on the ground would burn and every evening the dew would settle on the ground and put the fire out. You had to keep lighting the fires continuously as they did not keep burning, because of the dew and moisture, and only small and irregular patches of country were burnt. That was enough however to prevent any out-of-control bushfires in the dry end of the year. They especially made sure around the area of their bush yards that they did not get a big build up of grass and have the yards burnt down in a bushfire.

This was exactly the same practice that the Aboriginal people used for thousands of years before the white man arrived and it has many very useful advantages. For starters, it is called a 'cool burn' and does little damage to bushes and trees that are living. If you leave the dead grass to accumulate and build up to a thick, dense mat of fuel on the ground, then when there is a fire, it is a 'hot burn' and will burn totally out of control, razing any young trees and vegetation to the ground.

For the Aboriginals in the days of old, the burnt ground after a week or two would have a succulent green shoot come up which would attract wildlife from miles away, and in effect you would have a larger concentration of wildlife on a smaller area of country which made for easier hunting. Aboriginal people were wise and knew the country as second nature. Those same basic principles also applied to cattle, making it easier to muster. The added attraction for animals of any type was that if they camped on burnt country they would be less affected by ticks because of the ash adhering to their hairy hides.

After about 3 weeks of mustering from yard to yard they would be back at the homestead with roughly 200 to 250 head of bullocks. There would be a few days of branding and earmarking any animal that needed it, and then, after retaining a few coachers for the next round, all the rest would be turned into a natural holding paddock, a huge valley that was very well watered by means of Lagoon Creek. It was nudging around 200,000 acres in size and a sizable portion of it was actually in the Northern Territory. This was because the mouth of the valley which was the only access to the valley was right at the Westmoreland house. To give you a visual idea of the size of the valley, it was about 35 kilometres in length and about 20 kilometres wide with the end near the house being a very narrow neck only about 5 kilometres wide and 10 kilometres long.

Except for around the homestead and cattle yards this was the only part of Westmorelands that adhered to civilisation and had a fence on it. This fence stretched from the hills on the northern side of the valley to the hills on the southern side and crossed Lagoon Creek that flowed through the centre, which at the height of the wet season would be three kilometres wide and at least six metres deep in various channels. It had to be made cattle proof again on an annual basis. The cattle naturally prefer grazing on the flat country near the creeks and lagoons where there is plenty of water and grass rather than climbing the rocky slopes where there is not much of either. After each mustering round the captured bullocks were turned into this 'paddock' to wait until the end of the year when they were mustered and delivered to Hughenden via a droving trip that took about 10 weeks.

After each processing of the new additions the pack saddles would have been replenished, the horses changed out for a fresh plant of horses and off they would go again. Westmorelands was a very nutritionally poor country and mustering was heavy work on horses because they were always galloping, so you had to have lots of horses in the plant and you had to spell them often. There was never any shortage of 'fresh' country to muster on Westmorelands. Roughly speaking the station was about 80 kilometres square with the western boundary being the Northern Territory border and the northern boundary the Gulf of Carpentaria coastline. To the west was Wollogorang Station in the Northern Territory - it was an old station and occupied so the two stations used to do what was called a boundary muster. That means that a mustering team from both stations mustered the area of the common boundary, and after mothering branded cows with unmarked calves took what was rightfully theirs.

However to the east and south of Westmorelands was all unoccupied country in those days and the matter of boundaries didn't mean so much. As my Dad told it, you could easily get lost by 15 or 20 kilometres if there were plenty of cattle in that area. A couple of their mustering rounds each year would see them go down to the coast to muster the tidal islands which actually did have cattle living on them. They would have to get over onto the islands at low tide then muster what they could and then muster the cattle back to the mainland on the next low tide and continue mustering the mainland as they moved down the coast towards the next island. These islands were not scenic tourist destinations, just low sand islands, perhaps 20 or 30 feet above the high tide mark, covered in scrub and with lots of mangroves and mudflats around the water's edge. Yes, you did need to keep your peepers open for 'large lizards' if you were anywhere near water.

After mustering a few islands and the mainland coastal country they would then muster for 40 or 50 kilometres on the way home, repeating the process again and again all over Westmorelands' huge area until they had a mob of between 1,200 to 1,500 bullocks in the holding paddock, which meant it was time for a droving trip. Something that I have never seen, but Dad spoke of often and in wonder, were the 'Morning Glory' cloud formations that are unique to the gulf country and occur only in spring. What are they, you ask?

Imagine a roll of carpet (only it is a cloud) hundreds of kilometres long at an altitude of 1,000 metres or so and up to 300 metres in diameter. Usually they form out to sea and move in a south westerly direction for about a hundred kilometres inland where the atmospheric conditions change and they simply disappear. Sometimes it was a singular cloud, sometimes there may have been three or four clouds, one behind the other, separated by a kilometre or so. They have a movement to them that makes it appear as if they are being rolled along but apparently that is an illusory effect created by the air mass around the clouds themselves.

By the end of September the three brothers would have got enough cattle together to drove into their Hughenden properties. The other aspect that they had to consider was that if they left Westmorelands too late in the year they would be running into storms at the other end of their droving trip, which usually took about eight to ten weeks. So the first step would have been to muster that 200,000 acre holding paddock, which would have been a major job in itself. As I mentioned earlier this paddock was roughly 35 kilometres long and 20 kilometres wide.

Dad never explained in detail to me the process of how they went about it. I can only imagine that mustering such a huge area with their limited resources they went to the far end of it and spread out a kilometre or two apart and making a lot of noise, probably even firing guns perhaps, started generally pushing everything back towards the mouth of the valley. Even then it would have been far from a clean muster, there would have been some cattle slipping back through the gaps and I reckon it would have been at least a couple of days to regroup at the mouth of the valley with a concentrated mob of cattle.

There would have been a couple of days tidying up the mob, some possibly cut out for one reason or another, counting them before they left. A stock permit would have already been prepared, the pack saddles would have been readied and they would have had the horse plant selected and ready to go as well. Everything was a process with their departure date and the first week of the droving trip. The first week was always the worst. Unsettled cattle broken out of their usual routines and reluctant to be contained were always ready to rush at the drop of a hat. On top of that the first couple of weeks or so was in fairly timbered or scrubby country.

If the cattle did rush it was more dangerous and a lot harder to stop. Dad reckoned that in that first week you could always count on at least a couple of rushes. So for those few reasons they used to have 4 or 5 extra hands with the droving team for the first leg of the journey. And one other thing, they always left two or three nights before the full moon so that you had a maximum amount of moonlight each night during that critical first two weeks. If you were galloping a horse through the scrub in the middle of the night, at least you would be able to have an idea of where you were going.

Upon leaving the Westmorelands yards, they would steer south east to get to Turn Off Lagoons on the Nicholson River and then follow the Nicholson River along eastwards until they crossed the Gregory River. From there it was cross country through Armraynald Station and Floraville Downs where they crossed the Leichhardt River. Up until here the risk of a cattle rush during the night had been high and Uncle Bernard would have three or four men on night watch every night. The cattle were touchy, not liking being off their usual turf, and the country until here was either timbered or scrubby. Usually when droving there is always at least one person doing night watch on what was called a 'night horse'.

A night horse is one that is exceptionally agile on its feet and has better than average night vision. In your horse plant you would have a handful of horses that had better night vision and agility than all the others. These horses were used for nothing else but night watch. Night watch is when the men take it in turns to do two hour stretches of continually riding round and round the cattle and sing, if you couldn't sing you could recite poetry and if you could do neither you could talk to the cattle but the important thing was to always have that constant, soft, steady noise there to settle the cattle as they lay sleeping.

A rush could be caused by a branch falling from a tree, a twig snapping or an unexpected loud bird call or anything else that startled one beast in the mob; but whatever it is that causes the rush, in the space of a second you would have 1,200 animals from asleep on the ground to all up and at full gallop. I have never had the experience but from what Dad told me about rushes, they did get your adrenaline moving. The camp always had a fire in front of it to prevent a rush from going over the top of the camp and the sleeping men would immediately be out of their swags, onto their horses and after the mob. The night watch man would have let his horse have its head and be trying to get to the lead of the mob in an effort to turn the lead in on itself and get it circling. The man on the night horse did not try to control the horse until he reached the lead, if he reached the lead.

He just hung on and watched out for low branches and was prepared for the horse to jump over fallen logs or gullies. Sometimes a rush might be controlled relatively quickly during the night, usually it would be daylight and the cattle may be scattered in small mobs for miles. In which case it may take a day or two to put them all together again, count the cattle to make sure the number is right and get back on the road again.

Usually by the time they reached the Leichhardt River after about three weeks on the road the cattle had got used to the routine of marching along each day, they were tired of a night and the country was not as timbered. It was at this point that the extra men and their spare horses (each man in a droving team usually had about five or six spare horses) would be sent back to Westmorelands or wherever Uncle Bernard had borrowed them from.

From Floraville Downs they would push on cross country through Neumayer Valley, Augustus Downs, Talawanta and Donors Hill where they crossed the Cloncurry River, and from there it was only a short distance to the Flinders River. They moved upstream, passing through some of the old stations as they went, like Wondoola, Canobie, Kalmeta and Millungera. They used waterholes where they found them in the lower Flinders, but as they progressed upstream were often watering at windmills. There is a lot of water in the upper Flinders River but it predominantly has a sandy bed and the water lays beneath the sand. After they walked their way upstream as far as Richmond they left the river and headed cross country once again to their properties on the open Mitchell grass downs of the Stamford area.

Sometimes, seasonal or time constraints dictated which stock routes they followed. Once they did a much shorter droving trip to Cloncurry and trucked the cattle to Hughenden by train, and a Hughenden drover took them out to Stamford. Another year, they followed the Flinders River up as far as Julia Creek and trucked the cattle to Hughenden from there. The company that ran this operation was the "Stamford Fat & Store Stock Company", of which all the younger Terry siblings were partners. It operated until about 1956 or 1957 when they all began marrying, so the holdings were then all allocated to various ones, and the company dissolved. There was some silver table cutlery stamped with 'S.F. & S.S. Co' that I remember seeing as a kid, but it has all since vanished and just become memories of another time, probably lost to picnics and social gatherings.

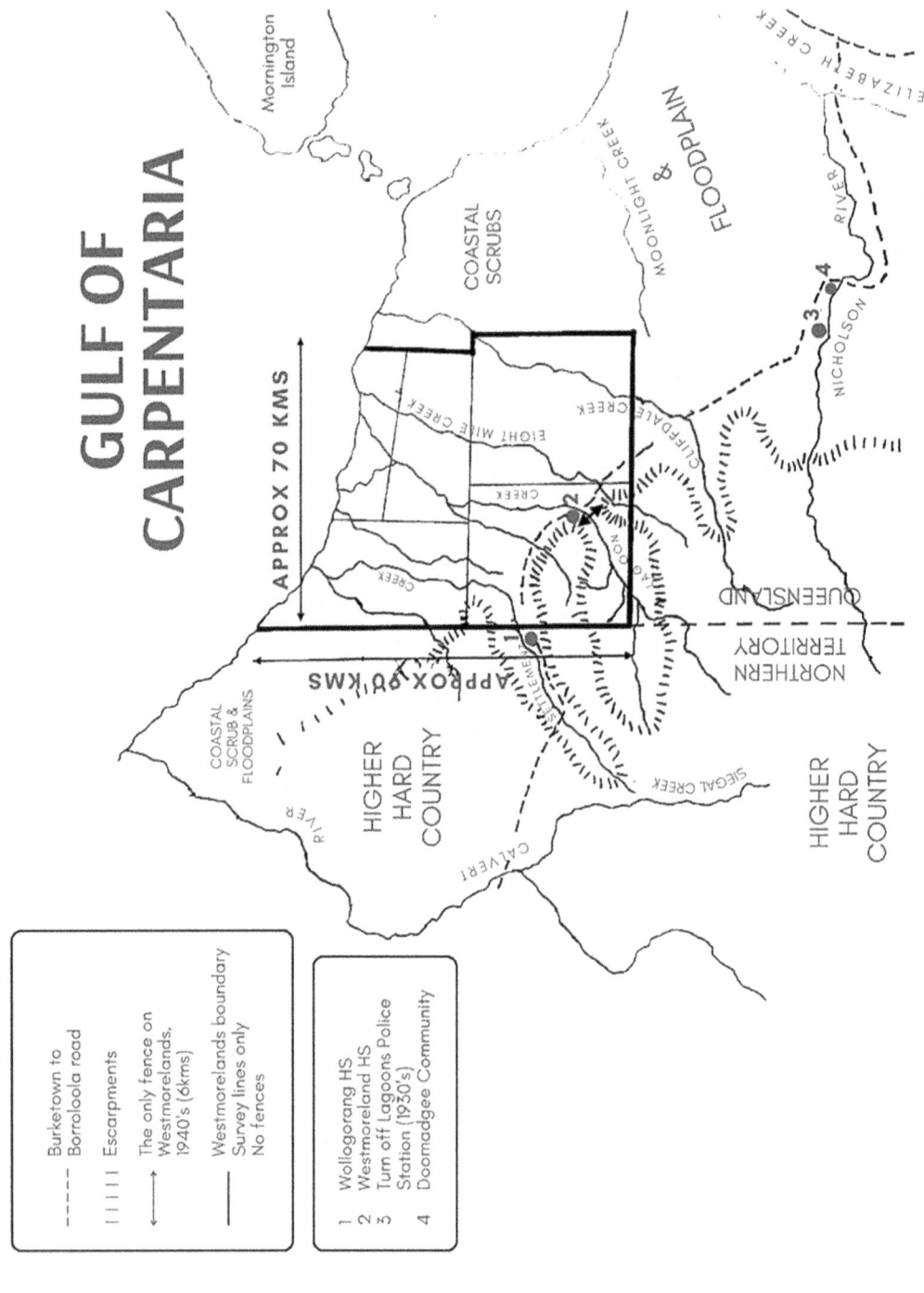

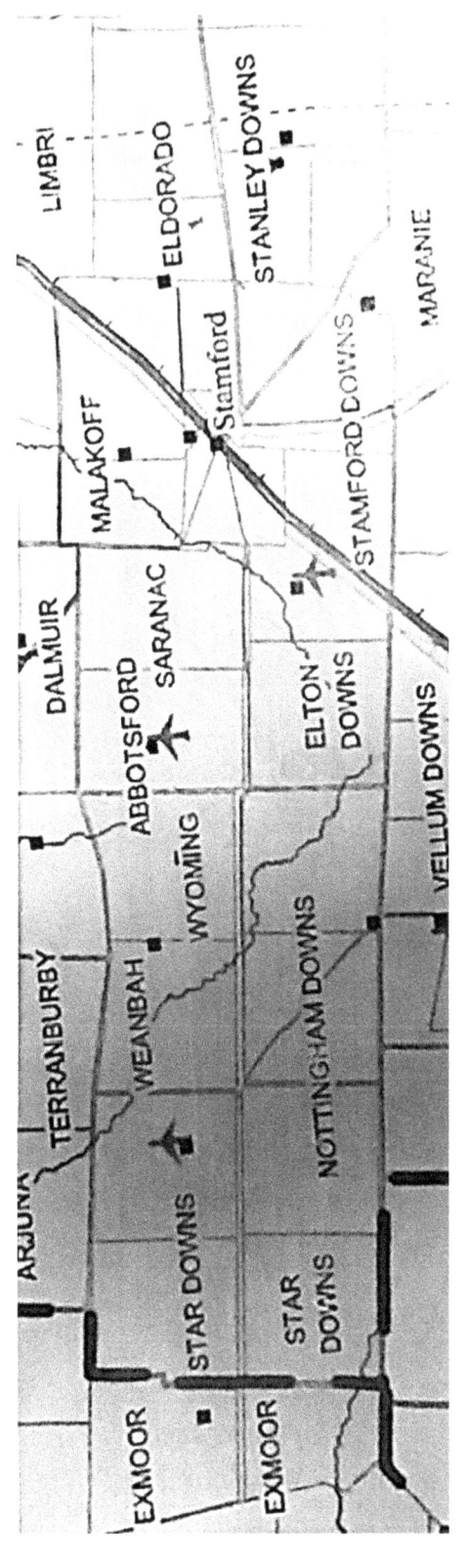

320,000 acres or 130,000 hectares of fattening country held by the Stamford Fat and Store Stock Company in the Stamford district to fatten their Westmoreland bullocks on

Westmoreland cattle yards. Bernard Terry 2nd from left with the black boys

Woolagorang homestead Northern Territory in the 1940 s. Next door to Westmoreland

Bernard Terry and unknown in front of the Tom Terrys car at Westmoreland. 1940s

Bernard Terry in the yards at Eldorado with one of Tom Terrys part Clydesdale horses

Bernard Terry on the rope horse. Bronco branding at No.8, Nottingham Downs

Cattle from Westmoreland watering and swimming in the Stamford dam

Cattle yards at the Westmoreland house

Getting the packs ready for a mustering trip on Westmoreland

Graham Terry at the Westmoreland house

Overlooking the waterholes at Westmoreland, 1940s

Refurbishing the bough shelter at Westmoreland horse yards

Rupert Terry in front of Westmoreland_ house

The boys, Westmoreland in the 1940s

*Rupert Terry taking 100 plant horses to Westmoreland.
At Turn Off Lagoons in 1939*

2

STAMFORD TOWN, ON THE DOWNS

The closest community to our property was a little rail siding called Stamford, which had existed since the railway reached the area in 1897. Before the railway, nothing existed where Stamford is now standing, and there are many tales about Stamford, some true, some doubtful and others outright lies, but all most undoubtedly interesting.

Hughenden, Winton and many other western communities had all been settled from about the mid-1860s onwards after the numerous parties sent out searching for the lost Burke & Wills expedition reported on extensive, magnificent, unoccupied grasslands. Hughenden was settled in 1863. Initially, there was nothing more than bullock teams to convey goods and news to, from and between the isolated settlements. Then in about 1883, Cobb & Co. coaches started a service to Winton, conveying goods, passengers and news from the rail head in Hughenden. For 15 years, they operated between Hughenden and Winton, but there was a change coming. Locomotion and rails were the future of goods and passengers, and as these services expanded, Cobb & Co. coach services correspondingly diminished until their final run in 1899 when the rail link between Hughenden and Winton was completed.

The area approximately 35 miles southwest of Hughenden was serviced by a Cobb & Co horse changing station that also had refreshments and accommodation in the form of 'The Coach & Horses Hotel'. It was called a hotel, but a shanty would have probably better described the building. It was also a Post Office. This group of buildings was located on the western bank of the Little Warriana Creek overlooking a man-made water hole called Burke's Tank. There are not a lot of details available but it is said that the contractor's name was Burke and he oversaw the earthworks with a combination of intrepid earthmovers when Cobb & Co first developed the route. One group consisted of men driving horse teams and drawing what was called 'monkey tail' scoops behind them. These dragged along the ground to load and the man behind was the muscle to make it dig and also to unload.

Modern earthmoving machinery can load 20 or 30 cubic yards of dirt in a single pass; these machines loaded a pitiful ⅓ of a cubic yard at a time, with the operator all the time trudging beside or behind. Then there was the other group of earthmovers that all came from China with their plaited cues topped with conical straw hats, and pushing wooden wheelbarrows that were loaded with a pick and shovel. These 'machines' carried even less in their payloads but what they missed out on in payload they made up for in numbers. There were no records kept but there could have been up to 200 Chinese labourers on this site as there was no shortage of them in the west after the goldfields had petered out in the couple of decades previously.

Now remember, this was in the decade after discovery and initial settlement of the western black soil plains and detailed records of wet seasons were still a thing of the future. Perhaps in those first few years they had light inconsequential wet seasons, which might have been the reason that they dammed what was a fairly major creek. This was a big mistake as they could have and should have dammed any one of the numerous large gullies that flowed into the Little Warriana Creek. Needless to say 'Burke's Tank', as they called this dam, did not last too long when the first 'decent' wet season arrived. It went straight over the top of it and washed both banks away in very short order. You can still see the very obvious remains of Burke's Tank today if you know where to look.

The Chinese were also responsible for building another style of water reservoir throughout the west called an overshot dam, and there is at least one of these in the near vicinity of Stamford. It was constructed basically by collecting flag stones from the surrounding area (that might be in a radius of up to 10 kilometres or more from the dam site) and placing them in a particular way across the bed of the chosen creek. Being very labour intensive work there would have been many Chinese men working on these numerous overshot dams in the west. Because of the distances involved to source the flagstones, they would probably have utilised wagons or drays.

A lot of the stones were too heavy to carry. I know nothing about the construction methods but I have been told that there were keystones in the construction of these dams to prevent damage to the layout in times of strong flows. In these dams, and there would be hundreds of them throughout western Queensland, there would be tens of thousands of stones in each dam. Each one of these stones was not just thrown in a heap but placed and positioned in a particular manner. It is worth noting that most of these dams are still there and largely intact to this day, over 140 wet seasons later.

However, getting back to the story of the burgeoning township of Stamford - it was around this time at the turn of the century that the Hughenden to Winton railway line was being built, and Stamford, which was about four and a half miles to the east of Burke's Tank, was created as the railhead at the end of the first year of construction. The 'Coach & Horses Hotel' at Burke's Tank was burnt to the ground the very same year, on August 31, 1897 (whether accidental or not is yet to be determined) and logically they built their new premises in Stamford.

For the next 12 months the Cobb & Co service connected from the Stamford railhead through to Winton. The next year, 1898, it was Corfield, about 40 miles further to the south west, that became the railhead. In 1899, the following year, the railway line reached Winton, which was yet to be connected to Longreach and Rockhampton. That would be another 30-odd years off yet. The writing was on the wall for Cobb & Co coaches, but they still connected the scraps of what was left over that the railway departments had no plans for as yet and would continue struggling on for another 20 years in various isolated places.

In the very early days of western settlement, during the 1870s and the 1880s, the stations were called 'Runs' and they were absolutely huge. Many of them would have been several million acres in size and they recorded shearings of 200,000 sheep. Between Hughenden and Winton, which is a distance in a straight line of about 230 kilometres, or 140 miles to use the old measurement, there were only 5 stations. However the country was still undeveloped with no permanent water and an extremely unreliable wet season system, which the entrepreneur lessees had yet to learn about. A station that had shorn 200,000 sheep this year and then experienced a failed wet season the following year might only shear 20,000 or 30,000 sheep in the next shearing if they were lucky. Stock losses were horrendous and so too were financial losses, and many grazing entrepreneurs were wiped out in those very early years.

Following the construction of the railway line, a lot of these gigantic holdings were being broken up by government decree, especially just after the First World War, with a lot of smaller blocks being given to returned servicemen. Often they were balloted for, with aspiring land holders putting their names in a barrel to test their luck. Even if you were lucky there were still conditions of capital and improvements that you had to do within a certain amount of time. Government departments in their wisdom had decreed that 15,000 acres to 20,000 acres would be a good living area for a family.

Even with all their arrogant, government wisdom they still had much to learn about the rugged and harsh conditions of outback Australia. Many families after 10 or 20 years of toil walked away from their properties with nothing but broken spirits and backs. You needed at least twice that area to make a decent living from this harsh and unforgiving outback environment. In this day and age, many eke out a living on 20,000 acres but usually use off-farm income such as stock dealing, a contracting business or some sort of a job in a nearby town to make that happen.

Stamford grew from nothing but long grass bending before the wind to a sizable little community in a few short years. There was a need for water for the town as well as the steam trains passing through, so a bore was put down and equipped with a windmill and a 20,000 gallon overhead tank. There was also a timber railway station and a large goods shed built, as well as a set of sheep and cattle yards for the loading of stock. After the 'Coach & Horses Hotel' was rebuilt in Stamford it operated for 10 or 12 years and once again it had been rebuilt as the simple structure of a ground level shanty, but then came the story of how Stamford came to have its very own two storey hotel.

The Stamford Hotel came about, so legend has it, as the result of some wags having a lend of the licensee of the 'Coach & Horses Hotel', a Mrs. Pfitzenmaier. A group of men alighted from the train one morning when it pulled up at Stamford and went over to the vacant block beside the 'Coach & Horses Hotel' and began banging in pegs, running string lines about and taking measurements. The publican was very interested in all the activity and wanted to know what was going on. She was told that this was where the new hotel was going to be built.

The next week she was on the train to Charters Towers, which at that time was in decline with many buildings being sold and moved elsewhere. She bought a closed down hotel, had it dismantled and brought to Stamford by train, then re-erected, and that is how Stamford, in 1911, came to have a two storey hotel. When the hotel burnt down in 1954, Tom

Terry got the blame, as he thought his sons spent too much time there. Some 70 years later that fact is still yet to be proven.

In the early years of the big stations being broken up none of the smaller holdings had their own shearing sheds, so there was a community shearing shed built just to the east of Stamford. This was built by Rooney's Shearing Contractors sometime around 1916, and I believe it was a 16 stand shed. The smaller recently balloted holdings all took turns to bring their sheep and hold them on the Stamford Reserve while their mob was being shorn. This also brought business to the hotel and butcher shop, as the shearers as well as the owners and shepherds needed accommodation and victuals as well. The community shearing shed did not have a long life, burning to the ground in 1923 and subsequently not being rebuilt.

The contractors started operating off the backs of trucks. Wool presses, classing tables, tents, beds and cooking equipment were all carried from shed to shed on the back of a truck and erected at the sheep yards of the station they were shearing on. The shearers lived in tents and the shearing was done under canvas or bough shelters. The cooking was done on open fires with the kitchen being under a bough shelter or canvas fly. The big properties had their own shearing sheds and shore sizable wool clips numbering in the hundreds of bales so there was a need for carriers and a number of bullock and horse teams were located in Stamford to haul the wool to Stamford to be railed to southern centres.

The wool boom of the early 1950s saw even the smaller stations building their own shearing sheds and investing much more in the age of mechanisation. Gone were the shearers camping in tents, cooking on open camp fires and shearing in temporary bough shelters. As the decades progressed and mechanisation became more reliable, larger and sturdier, there started a decline in the west of the numbers of employees and tradespeople peculiar to the rural industries. Smaller settlements with their post offices, telephone exchanges, hotels and railway sidings became a shadow of their former selves and today most have ceased to exist. I can just remember, as a child, Stamford being a much busier place than it was two decades later as a young adult.

There was a blacksmith shop in the very early days, then a garage and a carrying business run by the Bingley family. There was a Post Office and store operated by the Vinson family who also operated a carrying business in my time. The Station Master, fettlers and navvies to maintain the railway line in their section were a constantly changing cast of thousands. One particular Station Master that I remember was a colourful rogue by the name of Mike O'Reagan. His notoriety as a rough and ready character was legendary and there are many stories in which he features. Charlie Hunt and his family lived in Stamford, and he and his sons worked on properties or did droving of stock in the district to earn a living. Their house was beside the Bingleys and opposite the railway windmill and water tank. I can just remember it still standing in the late 1960s, but a decade after in the late 1970s it had been demolished and became the site of the Stamford District Tennis Club.

Horse and bullock teams continued to carry most of the heavier loads around the districts for a few decades after the rail went through. My grandfather still used horse drawn 'monkey tail' scoops and horse drawn fire ploughs up until the late 1940s. He bought a huge FDE Cletrac bulldozer in the early 1950s and was instantly converted to the machinery age when he realised how quickly they could build a dam compared to horse drawn equipment. Also by the 1940s trucks, although small compared to today's behemoths, had taken over from the wagons. In the early days there would have been many bore sinking contractors working around the Stamford district, patronising the services of both the rail head with the demand for drilling equipment and the associated windmill towers and bore casing.

Bores were sunk on the basis of a sheep being able to walk about 3 or 4 miles from water, so bores on average were sunk about every 8 to 10 miles apart but sometimes further. On our Elton Downs home block alone, which was 35,000 acres, there were 3 bores. Throughout the west there would be literally thousands of flowing bores and windmills providing life giving water for stock in a previously extremely dry environment. The Stamford Hotel, until about the 1930s, likewise provided liquid (of the amber kind) to all of the hardworking bore drillers, railway fettlers, shearers, teamsters, drovers, station owners and employees. The 1930s saw the beginning of the mechanisation of life generally.

The Second World War, with the American involvement in the war and huge bases throughout Australia, saw the much needed development of Australian roads in general and the beginning of large scale macadamisation of Australian roads. Initially during the war only around the larger centres, but after the war local government areas continued on with the practice, and by the end of the 1970s large portions of the Queensland road network had been bituminised.

Then there was the Hughenden to Winton 'highway'. Bitumen had crept out from Hughenden and Winton respectively about 10 miles, leaving a "no mans' land" in the wet season of 120 miles. That bitumen was only one lane bitumen, mind you, two vehicles going in opposite directions had to both drop their outer wheels onto the dirt to pass each other. The respective councils and State Government had 'discussed' sealing the entire length of the road for about 3 decades and still the dust and mud remained. No one ever thought they would see it in their lifetimes, then came the 1990s, and the action really gained traction when Queensland Rail stirred the possum.

They announced a discontinuation of the Hughenden to Winton rail service, removing the rail line completely and selling it for scrap. That really created some controversy, because the all weather access between the two towns would then become non-existent. Consequently the all weather bituminised road became a reality in the space of about 5 years. Initially because of the black soil underlying the road base there were some problems with road movement and crossings being washed away but over the course of the last two decades these problems have largely been sorted out. However when there is a major rain event the road is closed to heavy transport until the underlying black soil has sufficiently dried out.

Another humorous story concerning Stamford occurred in the mid 1960s, in a year where we had experienced a lighter season than usual and the amount of feed was starting to get a little bit light on. Dad had a couple of hundred head of cattle in a paddock adjoining the Stamford Reserve and stock route. Now the Stamford Reserve, apart from passing mobs, never ever had any stock on it, and there was grass in abundance when compared to our side of the fence. So what would you do in a situation such as this?

Our paddock just happened to have a gazetted road running through it to five other properties, and the boundary gate was accidentally left open by 'persons unknown' and the cattle had all escaped out onto the Stamford Reserve. Dad was away in Townsville when the Flinders Shire Council were brought into the situation. The cattle had only been lost to The Reserve for a few days when Mum received a phone call from the Flinders Shire Council wanting information regarding earmarks and brands about a certain two hundred head of cattle now impounded in the Stamford Railway cattle yards.

Someone passing on the main road through the reserve had reported cattle on the reserve to Bob, the stock inspector for the Flinders Shire Council, who had duly got a team of men and horses together and gone out, mustered The Reserve and impounded the cattle in the yards at Stamford. So the ultimatum was that Dad could have his cattle back when the fine had been paid. There was some arguing back and forth about the gate on this main access road having been left open by 'persons unknown' and it not being Dad's fault. However the Flinders Shire Council were adamant that the cattle would remain in the yards until they were in receipt of the monies. Uncle Graham had been into Stamford, acting on Dad's behalf, who was still in Townsville, to look at the cattle in the yards and speak with Bob. While in the yards he happened to notice that the gates were chained but not padlocked.

So that evening, Uncle Graham, Doc Collins and his nephew Kerry Kendall, who both worked for Dad at Elton, saddled up their horses and set forth into the night towards Stamford. Bob and his offsider were camped at the railway yards to guard the cattle and make sure that nothing untoward happened to 'the evidence'. Bob and his man had already had their dinner and were in their swags and fast asleep by the time that the three men arrived in the vicinity of the Stamford railway yards. The three of them stayed a few hundred metres out from the yards for a while just to see the lie of the land.

Then Uncle Graham dismounted and very quietly approached the yards, then slowly and quietly opened the gates and very gradually moved away to let the cattle quietly sense that the gate was open and slowly drift out of the yards into the night. Uncle Graham stood to one side and gently turned them in the direction of the other two men and followed the tail of the mob until he got to his horse, and then softly, softly, softly they put the mob together and reached the Elton gate about 5 miles away just before daylight. Bob and his offsider slumbered on, looking after an empty set of yards.

One can only imagine their dismay when Bob and his man awoke in the morning, stretched, yawned and then jumped up in disbelief at the sight of the open gates and the empty yard. After a quick tour of The Reserve it was decided that the cattle had not accidentally escaped from the yard as they were nowhere to be found on The Reserve at all. Bob and the Flinders Shire Stock Inspector arrived at the Elton house absolutely livid, but despite a lot of empty threats all they could do was to return to Hughenden empty handed and embarrassingly report their loss to the Shire office. Uncle Graham and his men were quietly referred to after that by many in the district as Captain Moonlight and his men. Landholders - 1, Shire Council - 0.

M.C. Fox the publican and his son on his race horse. Someone has notated at the top of the photo that this is the Coach & Horses Hotel in Stamford, so sometime between 1898 and 1911. Lorraine Carter Photo

Albert Bingleys 1910 Renault FU truck with an early ahead of its time double deck sheep crate. Circa 1920s. Lorraine Carter Photo

Another of Albert Bingleys trucks this one with a load of wool. Railway goods shed directly behind and railway ballast wagon on the right.
Lorraine Carter Photo

Bourkes Tank on Little Warriana Ck. Loaded wool wagons in the distance and the Cobb & Co changing station. Circa 1890s. Beryl Godfrey Photo

Charlie Hunt, Stamford droving and teamster family patriarch. Date unknown but the location most likely at a Stamford Race meeting. Clan Vinson Photo

Clan Vinson in about 1957 at 18 years of age. In business with his parents George and Joan Vinson and his first truck. Clan Vinson Photo

Clan Vinson in front of Stamford Store about 1945. Clan Vinson Photo

Clan Vinson with his double deck sheep crates loaded and ready for the road. Clan Vinson Photo

Clancy Vinsons truck with a load of cordwood for shearers stoves. Parked out the front of the Stamford Post Office

Fettlers at the Stamford Railway Station on a sail equipped hand operated trolley

Laurence Lee with his niece Morva Power beside one of Albert Bingleys trucks loaded with hay. Unknown date and location Lorraine Carter Photo

Looking over Stamford township towards Winton. The hotel is quite visible being the only two story building (burnt down in 1954). Low set building that is closer than the hotel was the original Post Office (burnt down about 1950). L. Carter Photo

One of the last horse drawn wagons carting wool in the Stamford area in the early 1930s. Lorraine Carter Photo

Photo of a train load of sheep taken from the verandah of the Stamford Hotel. Most likely taken by Tom Terry who was a keen photographer for his time. Probably his sheep in the rail wagons. Mrs Pat Terry Photo

Stamford Railway Station. Further down the line is the Goods Shed and windmill. Just visible to the right of the station, the left of the tree and underneath the rail is Bingleys Garage and Carrying business. Lorraine Carter Photo

The Stamford Hotel operated from 1911 until 1954 when it burnt down. Date unknown but the Licensee is still the original Mary Pfitzemmaier who married Neil Coates a local teamster. Lorraine Carter Photo

Vinson family and friends in front of the Stamford Store ready to leave for the Corfield Races. Mid to late 1940s. Clan Vinson Photo

3

ELTON AND THE EARLY YEARS

Being the eldest of seven children was my position in the family lineup, and we all grew up on a 70,000-acre western Queensland sheep property. 'Elton Downs' was just to the sundown side of where the railway line between Hughenden and Winton used to be for 90 years. I, along with my siblings, were sixth-generation Australians, the product of a mix of dispossessed English and Irish exiles or convicts and free settler immigrants. Now called Australians, they settled the vast expanses of land in outback Australia to create homes and livelihoods for their families. Fortunately for them, their genes were strong in persistence, and they were quick learners in a strange land.

My father, John Limbri Rupert Terry, was born in Hughenden on the last day of October in 1921. Consequently, his formative years were in the transitional era between horse-drawn transport and motorised transport, as well as being a part of the Great Depression. Before they were 10 years of age, his brothers and he, on the bi-weekly train days, would take a dray to the nearby railway siding of Stamford, some 9 kilometres distant, to collect the mail and perishables. As young boys of about 10 years old, they were put on horseback before the sun rose and sent out for a day of mustering on their own. My Dad's father, Tom, was a legendary hard taskmaster and didn't believe in any idle hands around him. Still, it was a childhood he had experienced himself 45 years earlier on properties around Bowen with his father, A.J.M. Terry.

My mother, Monica Mary O'Brien, was a third-generation Australian and the eldest of her family, being born on American Independence Day in 1924. Mum lived with her four siblings as a child on their parents' sheep property, 'Murrimbong', near Warren. My Mum and Dad's orbits came into contact only because in 1935, her father, John O'Brien, applied for and won a balloted block when one of the larger Hughenden stations, Marathon Station, was broken up into smaller holdings. Mum had attended boarding school at The Brigidine Convent at Randwick in Sydney until her senior year. In early 1942, after completing her schooling, she came north to help her father on the property.

Mum has recounted the fact that she can never forget her last day at school as it was the day that the Japanese attacked Pearl Harbour. Because of the war and the many men enlisting in the Army, her father found himself without staff. Within six months of finishing school, Mum travelled by train from Warren in western New South Wales via Sydney up the east coast to 'Terranburby', his Hughenden property. She stayed helping him for two years on the property and, because of that, became acquainted with most of the members of the Terry families in the Stamford district. In 1944, after two years working at 'Terranburby' with her father, Mum returned to four years of study in physiotherapy at the University of Sydney. She applied her professional training around Australia for eighteen months after that, working in Sydney, Perth and Darwin before returning home.

It was only then, in 1949, that she met our father, as during her earlier stay in the Hughenden district, Dad had been working on the remote Westmorelands cattle station that his father had bought in 1939.

It was at a clearing sale for Curragh Station north of Richmond where everyone had gathered to see what bargains they could haul home. Previously, he only returned to the Hughenden district very intermittently and briefly whilst droving mobs of cattle from Westmorelands. Even though they may have had their eyes on each other, it would still be another seven years before these two married. In March of 1950, Mum went on an already planned trip to England and Europe for a little over two years. Mum returned to Australia in July of 1952 and helped out on the family properties, of which there were three by this time, for the next two years. In 1954, when Dad learned that Mum had accepted a physiotherapist's position in Canada, her fate was sealed. He decided it was time for action, and there was a whirlwind six-week courtship, his proposal, her acceptance and then a two-year engagement.

They honeymooned in the Whitsunday Islands and around Cairns and Port Douglas, after marrying on the eighth of May 1956. They then settled down to raise their family on Elton Downs, which was about 50 miles south of Hughenden. Elton Downs and a number of other adjoining properties in the Stamford district were the result of the Terry brothers' decade-long effort during the 1940s on a very remote cattle station right in the northwestern corner of Queensland called Westmorelands. There were no improvements on that property at all, apart from a two-room sandstone block homestead, a few sheds, and a set of cattle yards that had been built 60 years before. There was no electricity, no wireless, no telephone, no two-way radio and no motor vehicle. The only communication was through the once-weekly mail run, suspended during the three- to four-month-long wet season when the country was impassable.

The property was all naturally watered, and apart from the cattle yards and a 170,000-acre holding paddock situated in a secure valley with a six-kilometre fence at one end, it was totally devoid of fences. There was no machinery or mechanical implements. In fact, on the odd occasion that they had to get supplies from Burketown, 220 kilometres distant, it was done with a team of horses and a wagon. Mustering was done by packhorse with a team of about 10 Aboriginal stockmen. They mustered for about six months of the year, during which time between 1,000 and 1,500 head of cattle were in hand, and they then drove them along the stock routes to the fattening blocks in the Stamford district. The droving trip, doing 16 kilometres per day on average, took them about six or seven weeks from the wild back of beyond gulf country of 'Westmorelands Station' to the relatively closely settled and civilised country of the Stamford district. These properties were where the store cattle would spend a couple of years to fatten on the excellent pasture into bullocks. I will tell you more details about Westmorelands later in this book.

A person's disposition and outlook on life, I believe, is all relative to the times and places they lived in during their impressionable years. When I think back on it, I often chuckle over this incident that happened many years later. While driving taxis in Townsville, I drove out to Bushland Beach, about 20 kilometres north of the Townsville CBD, one evening to collect a fare. It happened to be a couple of ladies that, I gathered from their conversation, had previously lived in Sydney, and wanted to go to the nightclub area in Flinders Street. As we were driving back to the city along the mostly dual carriageway and they were chatting away to each other in the back, one of them said to the other, "Oh, Bushland Beach is such a nice little suburb, but oohhhh, it is so remote". It was all I could do not to burst out laughing at their perception of remote, but that perception, unfortunately, is very prevalent amongst our city folk of this day and age.

When the Stamford district was in a good season, it was well-grassed and considered excellent fattening country for stock. It was still a place where extremes were normal, summer was hot day and night and winter was extremely cold during the night, not so cold during the day. As a child, I had vivid memories of the contrasts between the harshness of the end of the year and the abundance of the wet season months that ended and began, usually almost simultaneously. In the dry part of the year, the main roads were generally very corrugated and dusty as unsealed western roads on the black soil plains always are. Then, for three months of the year during the wet season, with our roads all being dirt, quite often you could not go anywhere, sometimes for up to a fortnight or even a month at a time, depending on the intervals between the falls of rain.

January, February and March were our 'wet season' months, although as I have said, they were sometimes prone to being unreliable. April and May were cooler months heading into winter. June, July and August were usually somewhere between cold to freezing nights and warmer days, but infinitely cooler than the daytime periods of the summer months. September began warming up again. The end of the year – October, November and December – were filled with a dry, furnace-like heat that began almost as soon as the sun was only fractionally above the horizon. Inside a house at night during those months could also be extremely hot because of radiated heat in the building, and because it was cooler, we often slept outside in the garden, under the stars, on stretchers.

We had floods and droughts, and we saw death, suffering, and hardship amongst our livestock.

The sparsity of grass in the dusty, undulating paddocks was reflected in the lean, gaunt condition of the sheep as they trudged in daily for the life-giving liquid that would now claim the lives of their weakest. The dams were low and boggy with numerous 'deadies' around the water's edge, along with a murder of jet black crows "ark-arking" as they hopped around through the mud, picking over the corpses, eyes first, always the eyes first, mind you. All the while, tauntingly huge clouds are filling the sky from horizon to horizon as the wet season builds up. Each day, the clouds teasingly claimed that this was going to be the day the sky burst open, but each sundown usually only delivered more dry earth. Tomorrow was the oft-repeated promise from the sky, it will happen tomorrow.

As children, we were homeschooled, and our schooling was reasonably flexible, so we were usually involved in stock work with mustering, shearing, and doing chores around the station homestead and sheds. Our eyes and ears were always cocked and tuned into whatever was happening outside the classroom, looking for any chance whatsoever to escape the confines of the classroom. I remember we used to particularly enjoy helping pen up in the shearing shed yards because it gave us the opportunity to ride the wether sheep. As opposed to the ewes, they were strong enough to support us. We used to give the rams a wide berth, however, because although they were 'polys', they were a little too energetic and boisterous for our rough riding abilities.

Our education while we were children at Elton Downs and of primary school age was done with governesses whom Mum and Dad employed. Over the years, we had three governesses; two young lasses in their early twenties were the first ones. First Rosalie Inwood from Grafton, who we had for two years. In the Christmas holidays between her two years, my brothers Byrne and Edward and I were invited to spend Christmas with her family in Grafton, which was a big deal as we had never been so far away from home without our parents. Then we had Jacqueline Walsh from around the Clermont district, who, even as kids, we thought was a stunning good-looker and had a string of young fellows from around the Stamford area wanting to squire her to dances. The final governess we had was Mrs Levis from Upper Daradgee near Innisfail. She was an older woman and a retired schoolteacher, and she was a very cranky, nasty old piece of work. Fortunately, we only had her for one year.

In the event that Mum couldn't engage a governess, she would get domestic help for the household duties, and she would teach us herself. One of the domestic help ladies was Evalyn Roddy, a Canadian lass who was travelling the world, whom Mum maintained contact with for decades. From the Primary Correspondence School, we used to receive our lessons in a sealed packet on the weekly mail run.

There were three main events that we looked forward to each year. One was the SOTA annual camp on Magnetic Island, which lasted for a week and was held in late June or early July. SOTA was the acronym for 'School of the Air', lessons done over a two-way radio in conjunction with Primary Correspondence School postal lessons. The half-hour lessons for Grades One to Seven were conducted by school teachers working out of a room in the Flying Doctors Base in Charters Towers. Each of the Flying Doctors Bases in Charleville, Longreach, Mount Isa and Charters Towers provided a SOTA service for the children in their area who lived on remote stations and could not attend a regular school.

The SOTA Annual Camp began with a much-anticipated train journey on "The Inlander", which we caught in Hughenden at around midnight on a freezing midwinter's night. It is hard to forget that cold wind whistling across the platform of the Hughenden Station as we waited for the quite-often late arrival of the train. Arriving in Townsville around 8 am the next morning, it was then to a Hales' Magnetic Island ferry to Picnic Bay and thence by the famous open-sided Magnetic Island buses. These would struggle, grunt and groan with the bus driver quite often changing all the way down to first gear to summit the crests. The young passengers all breathed a sigh of relief as the old bus coasted down the hill to the Methodist Camp in Nelly Bay.

These old and original three-and-a-half-ton tray-back trucks were relics from the Australian Army of the World War II era. They had had a canopy built over the truck's tray with roll-down canvas sides for inclement weather. Flamboyant paint jobs had been applied with novel names painted on the front. "Nippy Nell", "Flighty Flo", and "Galloping Gertie" were three that I remember. They have long since been consigned to the dustbins of history in the interest of moving with the times. They have modern buses now done up in the same style, but I can assure you that these buses don't have that same struggling character, nor do the drivers have that uniquely laid-back, casual island style of old. Some real characters lived and worked on Magnetic Island in those days. Now, corporate uniforms, business and the almighty dollar have annihilated all the uniqueness and individuality of our northern holiday island retreat.

At the camp with other usually 'distant' classmates, we attended a classroom daily to do our ABCs and our 'guzzinters' (two guzzinter six three times, two guzzinter eight four times and so on) and other academic endeavours. We went out into the paddock in the afternoons to practice our sports and athletics events. In the evening, there were games, 'theatrical productions', and sometimes a movie on a home movie projector. At the end of the week, all of the previously shy, gawky and self-conscious bush kids had meshed into a 'best mates forever' camaraderie as all and sundry packed their bags to travel back to Charters Towers, which was the home of SOTA.

The diligent daily athletic and sports training, including tunnel ball, leader ball, captain ball, relay race, egg and spoon races, various distance races, tug o' war, and others, had at least instilled a sense of team spirit and had us all running in the same direction. All the salt air, sea breezes and arduous training were put to good use over the weekend at the annual SOTA Sports Day held in the Charters Towers park of renown, Lissner Park. The following day, the far-flung families, parents and children alike, that had all melded together for a week on a tropical island, then travelled back to their respective stations, some as far as 300 kilometres apart, to continue their 'over the air' associations for a further twelve months.

In addition to the annual School of the Air sojourn to Magnetic Island, we had periodic outings and local school events. There was the Cameron Downs State School, the Whitewood State School and the Corfield State School, where we sometimes attended Sports Days. The same centres also sometimes hosted priests and ministers from various religious denominations to conduct services for the station people who lived further out of town. Different Catholic priests over the years conducted the masses that our family used to attend, which were followed by the usual social gathering with tea, sandwiches and cakes, as well as the institutional talk about rain or the lack thereof or how the feed was drying out.

As being on the land was the centre of our lives, it was quite in order to speak of it, as though each of our Dads was the central character of a poem called "Said Hanrahan". It was a poem with real Irish pessimism that I quite liked and was written by Catholic priest Patrick Hartigan, who was a renowned bush poet who wrote under the pen name of John O'Brien and was popular from the 1920s after he released an anthology, "Around the Boree Log and Other Verses". This caused me, as a kid, to think we were related to a famous author. Alas, it was just a pen name, and we were not related.

As each of us reached the age when we did our First Holy Communion, we would spend about a week staying at the Hughenden Convent, which was run by the Good Samaritan Order of nuns. The Convent building itself was the biggest and most imposing building in town, except for a couple of the hotels. The kids all slept in a room upstairs that opened onto the huge verandah that offered a magnificent view of the Flinders River approach of the town from the basalt country. From this vantage point, you could see for miles until you were interrupted from your daydreaming by a nun hurrying you off for more catechism. Keeping busy will save you from the devil, they would tell us. Staying at the Convent in town, for me at least, was very different with all the strange 'town noises' of traffic moving about night and day, as well as all the town's roosters crowing in unison in the mornings and mixing with the group of kids from the far-flung stations that used to board and go to school at the Convent School on a permanent basis. It was so different from the quiet, familiar, regular life at the station. At Elton, if we had a visitor or something happened out of the ordinary, it would be a big deal as far as we were concerned, and we would all be like houseflies around a pot of honey.

As kids on the family property circa 1963.
Billy boiling in the middle of the road

Doc Collins and Rupert Terry tar branding shorn sheep in Aug 68. Elton shearing shed

Shearers on the board at Elton shearing shed, Aug 68

Dad and I at Elton in 1958

Front yard at Elton 1964. Mary Lou, Edward looking backwards, Lachlan, Byrne, Rupert and Monica Terry holding Catriona

Elton Downs in the 1940s when the Terry's bought it and pretty much as Dad and Mum moved into it in 1956

John O Brien with Lachlan at Elton Downs, Christmas 1957

Just after building the Weaner Pdk Dam 1958, Elton. Rupert, Graham and Frank bought a Cat. D6, 6 yard scoop and a ripper between them in about 1957. That tractor each year would build 3 x 20,000 yd dams and do 1,000 miles of fire ploughing

Lachlan and Mary Lou and the pedal car. Elton 1960

Monica Terry and her brood. Apart from Lynne Terry in sailor outfit

Monica Terry at Elton Downs with Lachlan, Mary Lou and Byrne in 1960

*On the swing at Elton in 1961.
L to R - Edward, Byrne, Mary Lou and Lachlan*

Monica Terry with Lachlan at the back of the Elton house in 1958

Queenie with Lachlan Little Boss. Eldorado, Boxing Day 1957

The bride and groom, May 8, 1956

*Thomasine, Monica with Lachlan, Jack Saunders, Tom and Leona Terry.
Eldorado, Boxing Day 1957*

4

CHARACTERS THAT MADE THE WEST

"**4RK Base to Mobile Six**, do you read me?". "Mobile Six to Base, I read you, Mrs Reilly". If you heard a conversation such as this, you were within hearing distance of Clan Vinson's Mack Superliner and he would have been getting an update on road conditions or his next loading. Using HF radio, usually on the 10170 band width, Mrs Rielly kept her drivers up-to-date with all the latest in weather, road conditions and changes to any loading schedules.

Nev and Mrs Reilly were transport legends of western Queensland, their fleet of red Mack road trains crisscrossing every station track and shortcut between the gulf country and Brisbane. They carried general freight outbound from Brisbane and Toowoomba, to anywhere between Doomadgee Community in the north west, to Birdsville in the south west, regularly to Darwin, and occasionally to any location in Australia. Invariably he back loaded wool from the Queensland west to the Brisbane Wool Stores and sometimes even to Sydney. They had a great team of drivers who were used to long hours and adverse weather conditions, and were adept at solving mechanical problems with the minimum of workshop equipment if they should occur.

Nev ran a very good show and his gear was always in tip top condition. Nev didn't believe in music in his trucks; his drivers listened to the music of the engine and the gearbox and kept an ear cocked for any abnormal sound that may indicate a problem. Amongst his drivers were his son Geoffrey Reilly, Clan Vinson, who originally hailed from Stamford, and his son Greg Vinson, Tiger Stevenson, plus a few other veterans of the road. Even right up to the 1980s a lot of Queensland's outback highway network was still dirt roads where it was often as rough as guts, with corrugations in the dry or boggy and impassable in the wet.

On more than one occasion we assisted Reilly's trucks, either through the mud or out of a bogged situation, when in the near vicinity of 'Elton Downs'. In fact that is how Dad first met Neville in about 1964 with his old B model Mack. His truck was bogged in a gully with a full load of wool on, about 2 miles from our house. Dad could hear his engine roaring every now and then trying to get out. Nev eventually walked into our house and Dad went out with the tractor to help him get out. It took two days to get Neville's truck out of that sticky situation with the use of wire ropes and double and triple pulley blocks. When he had more work than his trucks could handle, which was not often, Nev Reilly would subcontract his loads to other truck owners.

Mick Hazel was manager of 'Elton Downs' when Mum and Dad moved to Townsville for a few years so we kids could go to high school. Despite his English origins he had worked in the west for a reasonable amount of time and was fairly adept at working with sheep in western conditions. He did not have a terrific sense of humour but was very loyal to a boss and resembled a bloodhound if he found something on the property that he thought was not quite right. My Uncle Graham and Uncle Bernard used to both enjoy taking a light hearted rise out of him as often as the opportunity arose. The access to both 'Nottingham Downs' and 'Star Downs' was by a gazetted and formed road through 'Elton Downs' to the main road at Stamford and then onto Hughenden. Knowing his tenacious bloodhound instincts they would slow right down (so the car tracks were very obvious) and turn off the road and travel cross country for 200 or 300 metres turning this way and that, doing a couple of big circles and eventually driving back on to the road and continuing on their way to town. Mick would come along that road at some later period, spot the tracks leaving the road and would follow them all around the paddock until they led him back onto the road a few hundred yards distant. He would be puzzled what it was all about but reported to Dad what he had found on numerous occasions. Dad knew what was going on straight away and without saying so, enjoyed the prank as much as Graham and Bernard, but later on spoke with his two brothers and asked them to cease and desist, "before they sent him bloody broke buying petrol".

Previous to his employment at 'Elton Downs' he had managed 'Stamford Downs' which was just to the east of Stamford. The fettlers and railway staff in Stamford owned a menagerie of fairly sizable hounds that on regular occasions used to wander to the east in search of some fresh mutton. Mick would find the dogs killing sheep and would shoot them with his rifle without hesitation. He would tell the railway workers what had happened to their dogs and tell them to tie them up or it would continue to happen. Of course they were most bitterly disappointed in his treatment of their hounds. The suggestion was that he should catch them and return the dogs back to Stamford. So a week or two later when he was in Stamford he yelled out to the men in the navvies huts that he was returning some of their dogs and promptly threw 3 or 4 dead dogs out of the back of his Land Rover and drove off. They got the message about their dogs and he had no further problems.

Mike O'Reagan was another colourful character who inhabited the small town of Stamford. He was the Queensland Rail Stamford Stationmaster which, when you only have two trains a week, was not a very arduous or taxing position. He would also have probably been in charge of maintaining the line in his section, but was not actually out there physically toiling. Dad used to refer to him as "The Commissioner of Railways Stamford". He was a fairly rough diamond and when he was in full uniform he might condescend to wear the navy railway uniform vest. The rest of his clobber would be a pair of old tennis shoes with no laces and a pair of khaki shorts with no belt. He might wear his railway hat on occasion.

I don't know how or where he began his career in the railway or how long his tenure had been before he arrived in Stamford. However at some previous stage he had been employed as a DJ in Longreach at 4LG radio station. As the local media 'personality' he often performed as host or compère at various public events. One particular time he was compèring a town dance and, being late in the year with some rain about, a few people were having difficulty getting in. Now Mike was late in arriving for his duties but made the pretext of having been delayed by the rain. He took the microphone and said, "I am very sorry ladies and gentlemen for my late arrival but on my way here I became hopelessly bogged, but fortunately not long afterwards I was dragged out by the balls. If Mr and Mrs Ball are in the crowd here tonight I would like to thank them very much for their assistance."

Another story went something along the lines of this. Back in the 1950s, during Mike O'Reagan's tenure as a DJ with 4LG, a lot of the back streets of Longreach were still unpaved, the same as many other western towns. It was in the middle of the wet season and of course many streets were inaccessible to motor vehicles. Mike was on the radio one day playing some music, reading a few notes from various areas around Longreach – how much rain there had been, which rivers and creeks were flowing. Then he went on to speak of the shocking state of the streets in Longreach when it rained and said, "You know, when I was a kid growing up down in the Gippsland (which was possibly highly debatable), all the small towns used to pave their streets with circular wooden blocks and it worked very well. I realise that we lack the same type of trees here around Longreach but I thought that if all the Longreach town councillors were to put their heads together we could achieve something very similar". His intent was very clear however and not viewed very favourably by the said councillors.

The end of his radio career came however, when one day he was doing a kids' show. Apparently this was a daily show to entertain the kids after school was over and covered areas like games, general knowledge, stories, sing-along games and such like activities for the younger fry. Mike must have had a bit of a rough day because apparently when the show finished Mike made the comment, "Thank Christ I have finished with those little bastards for the day". The comment would have been fine if confined to the studio of 4LG but Mike had forgotten to turn the microphone off and his comment went to air for the whole town to hear. Of course there were plenty of irate mothers ringing the radio station to report on that abominable DJ for his language in addressing their children and of course it was not long before Mike received his DCM. (Don't Come Monday)

Another character who lived in the town of Hughenden was a man by the name of Jack Close. Jack was born on 'Middle Park Station' north of Richmond in 1911. His education was provided by an itinerant travelling school teacher that he saw occasionally and he started working at a young age at the nearby small goldfield of Woolgar. His wife Barbara had been a Richmond lass, and shortly after they married in 1948 they bought a cattle property north of Richmond in the Croydon area called 'Claraville'. In a very short time a drought and then a flood got the better of them and he and Barbara sold the station and moved to Hughenden. He bought the Olympia Movie Theatre and a tobacconist shop to provide for his family.

As well as starting to 'swing a bag' at local race meetings he was also involved in the early days of the Live Export Market, dealing in large numbers of cattle, which he agisted on a number of properties around the district, with one of them being 'Elton Downs'. Jack and Dad used to get along very well together having had much the same background as young men. He was a genuine old salt of the earth fellow who had grown up in the old school of not having too much in the way of creature comforts or holidays. Jack used to come out to 'Elton Downs' every few weeks just for a drive and to have a look at the condition of his cattle.

He could also assess the quality of the grass in the paddock whilst also stopping by the house to have a yarn. He, without fail, brought a newspaper and a loaf of fresh bread with him even though he knew we didn't need it, it was just bush etiquette. Jack always had a very dry sardonic sense of humour and a quick wit much the same as Dad's. His favourite retort when asked how he was going was invariably, "Well it is funny you should ask that. I was feeling a bit unwell the other day, went to see my doctor and he told me not to buy any green bananas".

Jack could be found most weekends at a racetrack anywhere in Queensland between Mackay and Mount Isa. Later in life he limited that to within about 200 kilometres of Hughenden. His wife Barbara quite often assisted him at the track in the betting ring. The great Australian institution of gambling would not have been the same without these dedicated men that travelled every weekend on the dusty outback tracks to cater for the patrons of these small communities that hosted a race meeting. Often when asked about how he had fared at the races on the weekend, even though you knew that regularly and invariably he had done very well, the reply would always be the same, "Done me arse, done me bloody arse again". He got the name, at least locally and in the third person, of 'The Man of a Thousand Arses'.

Another of many characters that inhabited Hughenden was George Pearce, who was a well respected western windmill expert, whose skills were highly sought after by properties far afield from Hughenden. He probably would have been born around 1900, I think, as he seemed a lot older than Dad when us kids held him and his vehicle in such awe in the 1960s. Information about him is scant and I only know what Dad told me of him. He did all the windmill work on Eldorado and other properties that Tom Terry owned when Dad was a young man, and Dad was George's favourite offsider when he was doing any of Tom Terry's windmill work.

Dad used to get George to do the windmill work at 'Elton Downs' and I vaguely remember when occasionally he visited our place I was always in awe of his utility.

He was very particular with all his steel ropes and tools, with the ropes and tools always being meticulously wiped down with a cloth and kerosine. The ropes were then very carefully rolled, put in a hessian bag and stowed in special compartments on the back of the ute. Not just any Tom, Dick or Harry could pack George's gear away; it was only allocated to trusted individuals, otherwise he did it himself. Never in a rush, always slow and methodical in his approach to work, as if time did not matter. He lowered the rods and the casing with a hand-powered geared jack because using a vehicle to raise and lower rods or casing was way too fast and much too unreliable according to George. His vehicle was an old Model T Ford that had every available (in those times) gadget and convenience known to a man of the outback.

You never, never know when you might just need it one day. There was a temperature gauge mounted in the cab of his car and a rain gauge attached in a protected spot on the tray. Also mounted to the side of his tray back was a vice in case you had anything that needed cutting, hammering or screwing. During the wet season, with the difficulty of travel in the black soil, he would spend time at his residence in Hughenden, building galvanised water tanks and many other galvanised steel items in his backyard.

If the weather was on the inclement side he moved under his house and made all sorts of smaller items from tin and galvanised iron including but not limited to downpipes, guttering, galvanised carbide lamps, watering cans and buckets. Carbide lamps were a type of lighting still commonly used in the outback right up until the 1970s. I can remember Dad using carbide lamps for lighting when we camped out, and the peculiar smell of the 20 litre metal canister that the carbide was kept in over at the saddle shed.

A carbide lamp consisted of two galvanised metal cylinders about 4" in diameter and 8" in height, one of which closely fitted inside of its corresponding companion. The lower one was watertight and half full of water into which you dropped a lump of carbide which then emitted acetylene gas. The upper one had a slender tube extending from the top for about 6" and when you slid it over the lower canister the acetylene gas came out of the top of the tube which you then lit. The flame burnt with a very bright, white sort of a light and emitted a not unpleasant smell but it did leave a distinct odour in the vicinity.

Herb Wilson was another identity of the Hughenden district and he had a connection to the Stamford area as a long standing employee of Tom Terry. A keen horseman and very able with stock, he assisted Tom at 'Eldorado' and with his other properties around Stamford for many years during the 1920s and 1930s. Tom in fact assisted in providing Herb with a bride. A young woman by the name of Catherine Chambers applied for and was successful in her bid for the position of cooking at 'Eldorado Station' in the year.

Within a short time of her arrival at 'Eldorado' there developed a mutual attraction between Herb and the new cook. With a matrimonial union on the horizon, Tom Terry made mention to the manager of the National Bank in Hughenden that they would be ideal managers for Mrs Lou Salisbury, his sister, who owned 'Killarney Station' near Hughenden. Whilst managing this property for Mrs Salisbury, Herb and Catherine had two daughters, Betty and Beryl. Later whilst working for the Logans at 'Cressy Station' their son Bert was born. Later still when they were at 'Rainscourt Station' near Richmond another son David was added to their family.

The last property that the Wilson family worked on was 'Elton Downs', after the Terry family bought it in 1945. It was while they were at 'Elton Downs' and for reasons of advancing years and health, Catherine was finally able to convince Herb that a job with Queensland Rail would be a good idea. Initially Herb, as a lifelong rural worker, was unsure that he would be capable of this position, but he was very successful in his railway career working at a number of the railway sidings on the Hughenden to Winton line as well as the Townsville to Mount Isa line. Later still Herb was an interested purchaser for Tom Terry's 'Westmoreland Station' in the gulf country.

As tough a man as Tom Terry was renowned to be, he was also a man that was willing to 'give a man a fair go'. Herb Wilson was not financially well positioned to purchase 'Westmoreland Station' outright but because of their longstanding association and mutual trust of each other's character, Tom was going to close on the deal in this fashion. Herb was to deliver him a certain number of cattle each year for a nominated number of years with the result that Tom would be paid out and Herb would own a cattle station. Herb went out to 'Westmoreland Station' for some months to assess the country and learn the ropes but while he was there, a bout of ill health and the remoteness of the property caused him to reassess the situation and so eventually he did not follow through with the deal.

These were a few that were known to me but there were many characters and identities that lived not only around Hughenden but throughout the west. Every town in the era before television and the internet had their comedic characters and their unusual antics. They were resourceful, they were tough and they were funny, hilarious characters that never intended any malice, just to take a rise out of you and see how you reacted. You could write a book on these people alone and the laughs and situations that they created.

Barbara and Jack Close, two Hughenden identities. Jack used to have cattle adjisted on Elton for many years

Neville Reilly on top of his Commer truck. Loading wool at Cabanda in 1956

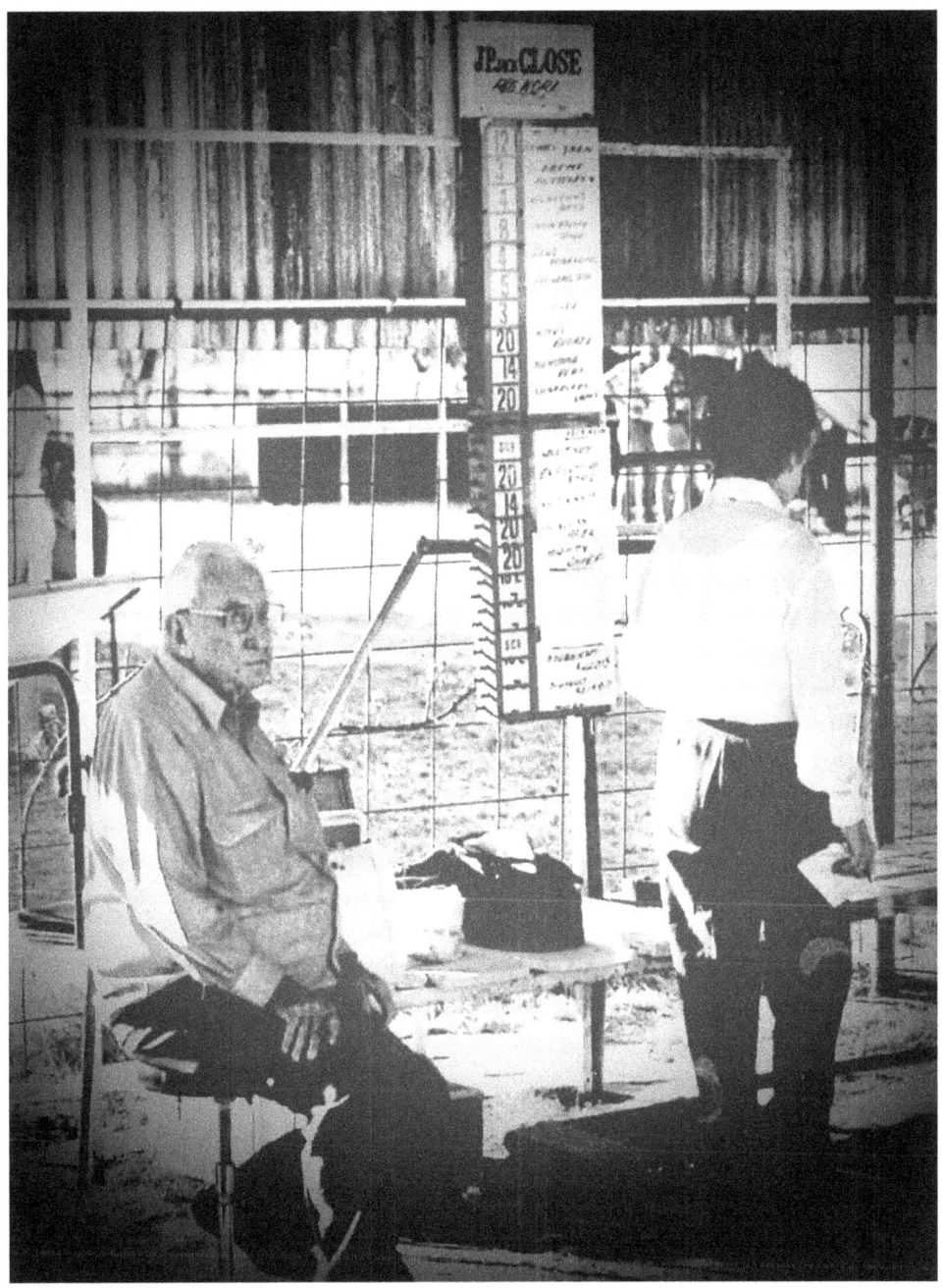

Jack and Barbara Close swinging the bag and taking bets at an unknown location

5

KIDS GROWING UP IN THE BUSH

The second highlight of the year, and a huge event in our eyes and minds, was the annual Hughenden Agricultural Show, which for us was exciting and competitive. Dad exhibited fleeces in the Wool Pavilion, Mum made cooking entries, and we children entered all manner of school projects, including handwriting, mapping, embroidery, and art. One of the pavilions was devoted to animals of all descriptions, mainly for the townspeople. You could see almost anything in the pavilions, from poultry, guinea pigs, snakes, goats, cats, budgerigars, right through to all sorts of vegetables, jams, chutneys and fruit. There was the main ring with dressage and show jumping, then the stock yards with bulls, cows, bullocks and weaners competing for 'best of's', all culminating at the end of the three-day show with the Grand Parade. Of course, who could forget that the sideshow area was behind the exhibition pavilions, a big attraction for the young and the young at heart.

Fast and slow merry-go-round rides, a similar merry-go-round ride with little boats instead, on a portable pond. Fairy Floss, Dagwood Dogs and flavoured Icy Slush Puppies for the hungry and brave of heart. Shooting galleries with local larrikins trying to shoot the eyes out of the teddy bears on the top shelf, dodge 'em cars, the big drum beating in front of Jimmy Sharman's boxing tent. Gawking clown heads that swallowed your ping pong balls in the hope of a cheap teddy bear and plenty of other affordable and gaudy attractions, the 'Showies' operated to part us from the meagre allowance that Mum and Dad had given each of us with the instruction, "Spend wisely, there won't be any more".

The third highlight of our year occurred only occasionally but always around Christmas time. This happened only when God had parted the bottoms of the clouds and graced us with a wet season that started with early rain. "If" there was green grass and abundant water lying about by early December, Dad and Mum would consider a seaside holiday just before Christmas; otherwise it was continue on as before, pulling bogged sheep out of the dams, constantly checking on stock and putting out lick blocks, watching the horizons for clouds and ordering Christmas presents out of a catalogue. Twice we holidayed on Magnetic Island, which was a real treat for bush kids, with sand castle building, a daily swim in the ocean, followed by an ice cream on a stick and walks into the nearby hills to try and find koala bears in the wild; or if it had rained overnight a fresh water swim in some of the small cascading streams that drained the hills surrounding the bays.

We stayed at Arcadia's Kooyong Holiday Flats, only a two-minute walk from the beach and McCabe's Corner Store, where there was a never-ending supply of chocolate ByJingoes. There were some real highlights on the island for kids from the bush. Dad used to go to the Arcadia Hotel to have a beer with the locals, one of whom was a chap named Meatball because of the resemblance. Meatball's claim to fame was that he could peel a coconut with his teeth and bare hands, and he made a living from it by challenging southern tourists to see if it could be done — money for jam, he used to say and then spend it all on beer. We loved getting fish and chips from the cafeteria, a huge area edged with verandah rails and a thatched roof. Not to forget the blaring jukebox playing for the lounging Townsville teenagers on the island for their weekends. From my extensive knowledge of Hawaii, just like Hawaii, I thought, only better!

One day, Dad took us all for a trip to Horseshoe Bay to buy a case of pineapples from the pineapple farm that used to operate there in those days. They were the sweetest pineapples we had ever tasted. On the way there, we detoured for a walk up to the World War 2 forts and heavy gun emplacements on the summits of the hills between Florence Bay and Horseshoe Bay. Being only 20 years after the war, at that time they were in much better repair than they are today. I believe one of them is now in a deplorable state and currently closed to the public.

We were always in awe of that famous bikini tree near the Arcadia Cafe, and I will never forget the road to the Arcadia Jetty. The dirt track was built between the bottom of a steep hill and the edge of the waters of Geoffrey Bay, through a jumble of gigantic house-sized boulders that were just everywhere. The one-lane dirt track was a work of art in its construction and at one point went underneath a huge rock that was naturally elevated by two equally huge rocks on either side. Some local wit had inscribed "Don't Knock the Rock" on the uppermost pebble.

Then there was the night of the curlews. We were visiting our O'Brien cousins, who were not very far away from us but were also holidaying on Magnetic Island. The bush and the hills came within yards of their holiday flats. It was the first night on the island for both families. Some of us were going to do a sleepover with our cousins. We were nearly ready for bed. Now, for anyone who has never heard a curlew call before, it is one of the most melancholy, eerie, mournful and haunting sounds.

I will remind the reader here that these seven and eight-year-old kids from the bush had never before had the pleasure of listening to curlews in full chorus. It was to be a brand new listening experience. So when, from out of nowhere, a number of these birds just outside our windows presented their cacophony of sound, these dozen or so kids nearly took the side out of the building. They had considerable trouble nodding off to sleep that night — memories etched forever on impressionable young outback minds.

Once we stayed at a family friend's house in Townsville, two down from Narney Terry's (Dad's mother) house in North Ward. Once again (for bush kids), similarly exciting things were happening like visiting the zoo, going to the pool for swimming lessons, going shopping in air-conditioned stores, going to the movies and watching Christmas carols on television, which then was a relatively new thing in North Queensland. Mum must have organised it, but once with our cousins, we were all guests on a Channel Seven kids' television show. The outing entailed a trip to the top of Townsville's Mount Stuart where the studio was. It was a children's Christmas show with a quiz, a Santa Claus, a clown, and lots of prizes, drinks, and ice cream to go around. We had seen these shows on television but never dreamed that we would ever be on one.

We even got to visit Mt. St. John Zoo, which had originally been owned by the Robinsons, one of Townsville's earliest families, but was then owned by Wirth's Circus. Lions, monkeys, orangutans, crocodiles, snakes and all sorts of exotic bird life were viewed with googly eyes by the kids from the bush. Younger brother Edward got too close to the monkeys' cage and lost his hat to a cunning and quick little monkey. Eddie was not going to lose his brand-new, snappy little straw hat that easily, and he quickly snatched it back, leaving a stunned and irate monkey in the cage to mull over his loss. It was only a year or so later that the zoo closed its doors and cages forever, and Townsville lost one of its own home-grown and developed attractions. But all good things have to come to an end, and it is the same with holidays. So after Christmas and New Year's celebrations and Mum and Dad's shopping for essentials back on the station, we were on the road heading westward and returning to our bush home once again.

If you hadn't had decent rain by the end of February, you were getting very worried; by the end of March, it was action stations to offset an impending drought. During drought years, graziers would try to sell their oldest stock off first to lighten the load on the available feed. As conditions worsened, younger and younger stock would be either sold or put with a drover to walk the stock routes. Invariably, all the other graziers were doing the same, which created a glut on the market with the consequent lower prices.

So, quite often sheep went on the road in the care of a drover, walking the stock routes of western Queensland, or they stayed at home and took their chances. All too often, their chances were very slim, and many of the older sheep and sometimes the younger sheep died under some prickly bush on the hot plains of the western downs. As kids, we often went with Dad in the ute to collect 'dead wool' off the carcasses of the sheep that had died some six months or so before.

A drive-by assessment confirmed the viability of each particular case; if the sheep had died with a fairly long fleece, it was worthwhile collecting the wool. As far as Dad was concerned, any money in the drought years was good money. Even though the animals had been dead for quite some time and were skeletal remains, it was still an unpleasant task. Spiders and crawlies of all types lived inside, and the wool was musty and dusty, but you would grab hold of the wool and shake the bones and the dried-out stomach contents out of the remains and then put the wool into an old wool pack and then into the back of the ute. When we sent wool away next, we often would have a half dozen bales of dead wool to send.

I, along with my siblings, all learnt to drive a vehicle and ride a horse competently by about the age of 10. We were then officially a part of the workforce, often sent solo in a vehicle to do various jobs around the place. We all learnt to ride on an old plodder grey horse, Steel Burn, that had been given to us by Dad's half-brother Alex from not-too-distant 'Killarney Station'. Then, after a while, I graduated to 'Red Charger', a one-eyed pony, as my riding skills improved. His origins are not remembered, but he was a tremendous little horse.

A swarthy, nuggety little gelding, he had a coat of solid rusty red, hence the 'Red'. The 'Charger' part of his title came about because once you got him going and he had that bit in his mouth, he wanted to keep going, but he was not 'an uncontrollable bolter', just keen to go. Somewhere in his travels, he had staked his left eye, but despite that, he was extremely sure-footed in his movements, and I never recall him stumbling or tripping up while I was aboard. Sadly, some time between when I went to Townsville and when I returned, old 'Red Charger' had moved on to that big Horse Paddock in the sky.

Starting the old Lister diesel engine in the laundry to run the 32-volt lights and recharge the battery bank, refilling and maintaining the kerosene refrigerators, feeding and watering dogs, chooks, pigs, and pets were all things that we kids looked after. So the art of thinking for oneself and resilience was instilled at an early age. Whilst we cared as much as we could for our many thousands of paddock animals, the wild fluctuations of drought, flood, fire, and the natural attrition of injury or poor condition amongst our animals hardened us up a little more than the average child in the city. When I was about 10, I was elevated to the status of bore drain delver.

Dad taught me how to drive our brand new, red Ferguson 35 tractor. When he was confident that I knew what I was doing, I used to drive 'Fergie' out to the No. Two Mill about eight kilometres away, to drive down the length of the three kilometre drain with one wheel in the drain to clear any blockages and silt. This happened about once every month, and I was always reminded before departure to be very careful and not to do anything foolish because tractors could be very dangerous, even fatal. A couple of times a year, I was also put in charge of 'dragging' the airstrip. This involved towing two lengths of railway line behind 'Fergie' to clear any grass, emerging prickly bushes and fill in any water gullies from the wet season.

One thing I will always vividly remember from my childhood, and always had an avid fascination with, was Whirly Winds or Willy Willys.

These were usually seen in the last half of the year while it was extra hot and dry. You would quite often see a dozen or so a day at varying distances around you spiralling skywards, taking rolly pollies, dust, leaves and any other lightweight debris to incredible heights before releasing them to float back to earth again. The technical explanation is that an exceptionally hot patch of ground creates a column of hot air above it.

A breeze or gust of wind blowing across it then creates a vortex effect, and away it goes. Some of the bigger ones can be a couple of kilometres in the air and travel on the ground for a couple of kilometres, but usually they are not very large. They can cause significant damage to vehicles, light aircraft, or buildings, and even windmills can be brought down if they are in the path of a decent-sized willy willy. Another fascination with outback travel when we were children was mirages in the distance on a dirt road. We could never quite comprehend that although in all appearances there was water over the road, in actual fact, we were being fooled.

Quite often, we would witness stock having to be put down with injury, incurable diseases such as cancer, or just sheer exhaustion from the prevailing conditions. Vermin such as foxes, pigs, eagles, crows and the very occasional dingo (they much preferred timbered country) were exterminated, usually by shooting but sometimes by trapping or baiting, and we quite often witnessed the damage that these vermin inflicted on the very young or the very old stock as well. So we children knew a little about the vagaries and uncertainties of life beyond the cloistered confines of suburbia's boundaries. Our view of life was not from the comforting feeling of a cotton wool cocoon or through rose-tinted glasses, and so consequently my upbringing was most likely the forming of my realist or pragmatic view of life, so too with my siblings. Little did I know what an attribute this would be for my personal circumstances later in life.

Mum and Dad both had a love of travelling and seeing what was over the horizon, which was, in later years, passed on to all of their children who constantly traversed the globe before settling down. As a younger woman, Mum studied to be a physiotherapist, then travelled Australia, following that up with two years in England and Europe practising her skills. Dad had not travelled the high seas or toured foreign countries, but he had travelled thousands of miles all over Queensland, sitting in a saddle behind a mob of cattle, so I always considered him a well-seasoned traveller, but without the need of a passport.

When we were all youngsters, Mum and Dad made quite a few trips on their own after distributing us kids amongst friends and relatives. They visited Timor, Western Australia, the Ord River Scheme, the Northern Territory, Ayers Rock (Uluru) and New Guinea on various different trips during the early 1960s. Later, in 1976, they travelled to Indonesia, Thailand and Malaysia for a month or so with Lou, my younger sister. For their 25th wedding anniversary, as a combined present, we children (now all adults) bought them a ticket to visit Tasmania, New Zealand and Norfolk Island with airline travel between the destinations and a hire car to see the sights whilst there.

In 1966, Dad and Mum decided to make a trip to NSW to visit many of Mum's relatives, and Dad, who quite enjoyed travelling, had never been to NSW. So we visited, amongst other places, Lightning Ridge opal fields, and our national capital Canberra, including the Australian War Memorial and old Parliament House, which in those years was still in operation. We went to Mount Kosciuszko when you could still drive right to the summit, and it was the year it had pink snow (a dust storm from a couple of years earlier had deposited millions of tons of red dust). We visited Parkes to see the huge, brand new radio telescope that helped in the moon landing a couple of years later, in 1969. In more recent times, it starred in an Australian-produced comedy movie, 'The Dish'.

Mum's relatives, the O'Briens predominantly, could be likened to the hairs on a dog's back around Warren and Dubbo, very much like Terrys around Hughenden. So, consequently, we were always pulling up here, there and everywhere, mostly on farms or properties to visit this Uncle and Aunty or that cousin. Two of the stand-out relations in my highly impressionable young opinion were an uncle who owned a World War 2 Harley Davidson with a side chair and a cousin of Mum's who had an aeroplane in his shed (albeit covered in hay with chooks laying eggs in it), but it was still a plane. We didn't have any other relations with a plane. We were also constantly pulling up so that Dad could administer a little physical parental guidance with his 'pine board' because, as you could imagine, with five children in the back under the age of nine, there was a considerable amount of sibling rivalry and warfare going on.

When we were not fighting, we played a game that we all enjoyed (except for Mum and Dad). It was called "That's Mine", and you played it like this. Imagine five kids in the back seat of the Holden station wagon, all looking over the front seat between Mum and Dad and peering intently down the road, ready to detect the slightest movement on the horizon. The goal of the game was to claim ownership of a vehicle (That's Mine), but you first had to identify it as a qualifying type of vehicle. The three top favourites that were high scoring types were motorbikes, big American cars or semi trailers.

All was silent until the moment of identification, and then all hell broke loose with five juveniles all yelling "That's Mine" at the top of their voices. Early identification could be made when the vehicle was just a distant spot on the horizon, but as the vehicle drew nearer and misidentification became evident, it could cause a major breakdown of cohesive relations in the rear of the vehicle. Looking back on it, I can only imagine that each afternoon Dad and Mum were only too pleased to be pulling into the evening's lodgings to escape the noise, chaos and horrors of the family vehicle.

I do remember we did not get to see three things that we had all read about in Sydney and desperately wanted to see. These were Bondi Beach, Luna Park and the Sydney Harbour Bridge. I don't remember a reason being given, but possibly the thought of the Sydney traffic and concentration problems associated with his unruly passengers caused Dad to skirt around Sydney. We detoured inland for a good way before emerging back onto the coast around Port Macquarie. We overnighted in Grafton and then stayed a couple of days in Ballina in the New South Wales Northern Rivers district. From there it was just a short hop to reach, in those days, the big country town of Brisbane, where Dad felt much more at home and we spent some time visiting a few of Dad's relatives.

One of them was his Aunty Clare Grant, who at that stage was the only remaining member of her family who was still alive. She was quite elderly and we thought quite severe, but she did play her piano for us. She let us have a go on her pianola, and we were amazed that the keys were going up and down in time with the music without touching them. The Grant cousins, who had always lived in Brisbane, were particularly fond of Dad and were visited as well. We had a few days visiting other relatives of Dad's in Brisbane, and Mum and Dad also attended his widowed brother Graham's second marriage to Mary Crawley. After the flurry of visiting, we were once again on the road headed for home on the inland route via Charleville, Longreach and Winton, arriving home to begin another school year on the outback plains with the Primary Correspondence School and School of the Air.

*Christmas holidays at Magnetic Island about 1965.
Mary, Monica and Lachlan standing at table*

Byrne, Mary Lou holding Catriona about 1967 at the Kokoda Pool, Townsville

Christmas holidays in 1965 at Channel 7 studios on Mt.Stuart. Back L-R, Peter, Byrne, Mary Lou, Lachlan, Greg, Ruth Marney Front L-R, Catriona, Marie and Edward

Family photo in 1986

Lachlans tenth birthday. Front L-R, Bernadette Silas, Marie Terry, Lachlan, Catriona Terry, Silas, Standing L-R, Peter Terry, Byrne Terry, Mary Lou Terry Edward Terry and Greg Terry

Lachlan & Byrne Terry controlling Poddy at Elton Downs

Lou and Eddie on their horses at Elton about 1965

Mum and Dads 30th wedding celebrations at Elton in 1986. Daniel in front. L-R, Lachlan, Catriona, Monica, Rupert, Justin, Leona and Mary Lou

Our old horse Steel Burn. Cousin Peter Terry standing, Lachlan, Mary Lou and Byrne on horseback

Ruperts birthday. Monica, Mary Crawley, Leona Terry (Dads mother), Graham Terry. Jackie Walsh, one of our governesses taking the photo

6

EDUCATING THE OFFSPRING IN THE BIG SMOKE

At the end of 1968, as our teenage years and high school approached, Mum and Dad decided to build a house in Townsville so we could all make the most of the opportunities offered in a city atmosphere and within a regular school environment. Well, that was the theory anyway, but at that stage, they didn't know about peer pressure and the changing world of adolescents in the late 1960s and early 1970s. Talk about a steep learning curve for Dad and Mum. Anyhow, a manager with a family was employed on the property, and our family moved to the coast. However, Dad continued to visit the property regularly, especially during busy periods of stock work. Dad was never one to be idle, so whilst living in Townsville, he initially held down a couple of jobs in the construction industry, but this was not the outback of Queensland that he was so well acquainted with, and he soon ran afoul of unions, certifications and regulations.

My brothers, Byrne and Edward, and I were enrolled at St John Fisher's College, which was run by the Christian Brothers. Mary Lou and

Catriona attended St Margaret Mary's College, which was run by nuns and was not far away. Catriona later attended St. Columba School, which was also run by the nuns and was a Primary School at the Catholic Church we attended. Our youngest sister, Leona, was too young to attend school at this stage. Our house was at Cape Pallarenda which was a suburb on its own, located about nine kilometres away from our school. Sometimes Mum would drive us to school, and sometimes we would catch the school buses.

We boys wanted to ride push bikes with all the other kids, but it was deemed too far and not safe enough. In hindsight, that was probably a good call. On the weekends, we were all involved in sports with school, and I was a member of the North Ward Scout Group. Once a week, we used to gather together for a bit of dib-dib-dib, meaning do your best from the Australian Boy Scouts, with the other kids in our scout group. Behind the den was the quite steep rock slope of Melton Hill. We used to construct 'flying foxes' from ropes and poles on the slope, and descend on the suspended cable in a wooden box at an almighty speed from top to bottom. It is a wonder that none of us were killed.

We had the Many Peaks Range to our north, the Three Mile Creek and mangrove swamps to our south, the beach and Cleveland Bay to our east and, behind our suburb to the west, we had the Townsville Common, so there were always plenty of things for us to do. Sometimes, if Dad wasn't using his 'tinnie', we kids would drag it down to the beach and launch it for a day on the high seas of Cleveland Bay. However, we didn't get the outboard motor. We only got what Dad used to call the 'wooden motors'.

My brothers and I, with various mates, used to hike the common, climb the hills, swim in the Three Mile Creek, and explore the World War 2 fortifications on the coastline at the foot of the Many Peaks Range. On weekends, we often rode our bicycles into town, collecting discarded empty soft drink bottles along the way that we cashed in and then spent on milkshakes and ice creams at The Ozone Cafe, which was a shop on the Strand near The Tobruk Swimming Pool.

Dad then bought a taxi cab, which, being his own master and not so much governed by rules and regimentation, was much more suited to him. There were a number of other retired Westerners who also owned taxis. Dad bought Standard White Cabs "Car Eight", which he fondly and humorously referred to as 'Active Eight'. Dad, being a real raconteur, thoroughly enjoyed his time with the cab and loved meeting and talking to all he came in contact with, quite often transporting families and colleagues that he knew from all over western Queensland who were in Townsville for holidays or business. My father never wrote his life story, but from the tales that he told of his life and, in particular, of his time as a cab driver, he could well have written a bestseller.

Dad had many amusing stories of his time driving cabs. One story I remember him telling in particular was when he was one day sitting on the rank outside the David Jones store. He happened to glance in the rear view mirror to see a man strolling down the street, clad only in a T-shirt. He called the taxi base on his two-way radio, telling them, "Base, you had better get onto the police station and get them to send a car down to McKimmon's Rank. They will nab a fellow down here who is only wearing a T-shirt for decent exposure." Base replied, "Will do, Car 8, but don't you mean indecent exposure?" Dad replied, "No base. I said decent exposure because he has got a decent one." The fellow had apparently escaped from the mental ward at the Townsville Hospital, which was not too far away from the city.

Another time at Pallarenda, Dad got home late from working the cab and had gone to bed about 2 am. There had been a group of Aboriginal people having a grog party down on the beach in front of our house since sundown, and we had been privy to all their laughing, shouting and fighting. About 3 am, they all staggered up from the beach, and the first thing they spotted was "Active Eight" parked in the front yard of our house. Since there was no fence around our house, they all started prowling (harmlessly but all gloriously drunk) around our yard, trying to rouse the owner of the cab. A section of our house that included the lounge and dining room was at ground level and protruded towards the street, with the two-storey section, containing kitchen and living room on ground level and all the bedrooms upstairs, at the rear of the house.

At the side of the house, there was a built-in ladder (fire escape) that accessed the roof of the ground-level front section of the house. Anyhow, Dad was awoken about 3 am by a drunken Aboriginal woman that had found her way up the ladder onto the roof and was peering in through the louvres of Dad and Mum's bedroom, all the while in a genuine shrill sing-song gin-style of talking she was telling Dad that "We bin got little bit money to gibbit cabbie if he could take them little bit long way home for these poor drunk fullas. They bin have too much good time on plurry grog and home was too paraway to walk for these poor fullas". It was very unfortunate that they happened to pick this cabbie who, earlier in life, had a lot of experience in handling drunk blackfellas and did not mince matters in getting them to behave.

Roaring at the top of his voice through the louvres (which woke up all the kids and all of our neighbours within about six houses) he ordered the gin to get down off the roof "bloody quick time if you know what's good for you" then he tore downstairs in his pyjama shorts and out into the yard and rounded up all the blackfellas that had become cast in various stages of inebriation around our yard and got them all out into the front yard then told them, "they were all bloody well walking home and to hit the road straight away or he would get the 'bulliman' out to Pallarenda for a trip to the watchhouse". They definitely did not want to see the 'bulliman' so they all very apologetically got going immediately. Dad was the talk of the neighbourhood for months after that episode.

Dad was a great lover of fishing, whether it be a little crabbing in the tidal flats and the mangroves or in his little flat-bottomed 'tinny' in Cleveland Bay. You might have also found him up with his mate Matty Hamilton at their fishing shack at Hencamp Beach near Rollingstone, about forty miles north of Townsville. At other times, you would have to travel about the same distance south of Townsville to a fishing hut they had on the East, West and Middle Barrattas, which was a mud crab haven second to none. In those days, it was accessible only by boat; you can now drive in on a sealed road to a small township.

He also went on many trips out to the Great Barrier Reef on a large launch with his fishing club, who all gathered at the Mansfield Hotel. I went on a couple of reef trips with Dad and his fishing club. Quite often they hired either Frisco or his brother Cocky Watkins on their boat by the name of the "Idle Hour", which was an ex-RAAF crash launch. It was about a six to eight hour journey to get to the outer edges of The Great Barrier Reef. Usually, these were day trips, leaving in the very early hours of the morning and returning late at night. Sometimes they were overnighters with everyone sleeping wherever there was a bit of room, whether above or below decks.

Mum and Dad had also bought a little mango farm of a few acres at the fairly inaccessible spot of Shelly Beach on the northern side of the Many Peaks Range. It was the only farm and leasable block of land at Shelly Beach. Sometimes we all climbed in the back of Dad's old 4WD Willys Jeep, and we would go camping on Shelly Beach for a night of fishing, but because you had to pass through the tidal mangrove swamps on the common, it could only be accessed at low tides. A campfire with swags on the beach watching the stars wasn't all that bad, and a few fish to throw in the fry pan was an added bonus.

After one camping and fishing trip, we called in to pick some mangoes at the farm. Unfortunately, someone inadvertently disturbed a very large paper wasp nest. There were about half a dozen mango collectors altogether who all of a sudden wanted to be anywhere else but the farm and in a hell of a hurry to get there. There was an instant flurry of activity happening in all directions of the compass and I remember quite clearly Dad yelling out as he was motoring along that he definitely did not want anyone following him. After a good wait to let things settle down a bit, Dad went in quietly and brought the 4WD out to collect us, and we went home all sporting quite a few lumps and bumps on us.

On the educational side of things, well, that was another story. While we weren't bad children, we had, however, become a tad more on the rebellious side with our newfound town acquaintances. We were pushing the boundaries more than we did previously in our more solitary, isolated life on the property in the bush. I did Grade 7 and 8 in Townsville, and then, because I was not performing as well as expected in the scholastic department, I did two years at Downlands College, a boarding school in Toowoomba. At the end of Grade 10, I decided that the school environment was not for me and began a plumbing apprenticeship in Townsville. Because I had left school at the Grade 10 level, which was not uncommon in those times, Dad and Mum were very keen for me to get a trade certificate instead of just a labouring job. To this end, Dad, who had many friends in all walks of life, one of them being a foreman at a local plumbing firm, Cathcart & Ritchies, whose name was Matt Hamilton, arranged for me to start an apprenticeship there.

After I started working and earning an income, other things started to feature in my life, such as motorbikes, rock'n'roll music, long hair, girls, bars and, being the 1970s, there was also a little bit of the old 'weird weed' in the equation as well. I believe I was fortunate that I had had a stable, solid upbringing, because for the four years that I was completing my apprenticeship I was running with some fairly wild and unsavoury characters and it could have easily gone quite pear shaped for me if I had continued down that path in the long term.

Some of my acquaintances certainly ran off the rails, ending up in jail and using much harder drugs than the old 'weird weed'. There were needles and pills around in the crowd that I used to knock around with during this period of my life, but using them, and the possibility of addiction, jail or becoming a corpse, frightened the hell out of me, so consequently I made the decision to never go down the needle road. I was quite content with my 'plant-based' addiction, and even that was relatively short-lived. When I married in the not-too-distant future, my family became my priority, and I gave the pot smoking away as well.

It was during my apprenticeship, in 1975, that Mum and Dad decided to return to live on the station as life in the city had not quite turned out as they expected; they much preferred the quiet atmosphere on the property amongst their familiar surroundings. As it turned out, all of their four older children had ended up attending boarding schools anyway, and Dad made the comment in his laconic style that "he and Mum were the only ones who got educated in Townsville". In the end, all of the boys returned to the bush. My sisters, except for Catriona, were trained in nursing and journalism and stayed in the city.

In hindsight, I can see now why Mum and Dad were a little concerned and disillusioned with the attitude of their errant offspring. I have often reflected on what might have been if they had remained living on the station and just sent their children to boarding school like most other kids in the bush, instead of opting to live in the city. However, it is what it is, and the hands of time cannot be rewound. I remained in Townsville and despite all the distractions around me, I still managed to attain my trade certificate in plumbing and gas fitting at the end of 1976.

In those days, Townsville was growing quickly but was still just a big country town with a population of about 60,000 odd people, and one way or another, you just about knew everyone. In mid-1976, through a mate of mine, I met my future wife, who, like most of my friends at that time, had a strong interest in motorbikes. Pam's family had been working on the Greenvale railway line prior to living in Townsville. Her brothers were also friends with people that I knew in the Townsville motorbike circles. After going out together for only a relatively short period of time, Pam fell pregnant. Statistically, it is not the ideal start, but even so, I had been brought up to believe that abortion or abandonment was not an option.

I proposed, Pam said "Yes", and we hooked our futures together and got married at home in early 1977. I continued working in the plumbing industry for a time, and we stayed on in Townsville until after our son

Joseph was born in September of 1977. Dad and Mum asked us if we would like to join the family and help with working the property, which we decided to do. There was a very comfortable two-bedroomed cottage a little bit removed from the main homestead that we could live in that had all modern amenities available, so we left Townsville behind us and moved out to 'Elton Downs' at the end of 1977.

I had often visited the property during school holidays, but it felt good to be home in the bush again. There is an old saying that "you can take the boy out of the bush but not the bush out of the boy", and that felt so true. It was good to be back there on a permanent basis after nine years away. Joseph was followed by our second son, Daniel, who was born the following year in October. When we moved to 'Elton Downs', lighting was by way of a diesel engine that only ran at night time to provide 32 volt power for the lights, with refrigeration courtesy of kerosine fridges. Communication was via the old-fashioned party telephone line system with a local telephone exchange in Stamford and a larger telephone exchange in Hughenden.

This form of modernity, however, was of my parents' era. It came to an end within two or three years of us arriving, with the advent of mains power to lots of rural areas during the 1980s. At the same time Telecom was installing satellite dishes for modern communications with phones that had eight digit key pads instead of the old crank handle of a party line phone, so Pam and I ended up with a new phone in our house as well, instead of just having the old party line phone in the main house. We had electric fridges, freezers, microwaves and washing machines in the two houses. In the workshop, we had electric drills, grinders, welders and a multitude of other electrical gadgets. A satellite television dish was also added to Dad and Mum's house at the later stages of Dad's battle with cancer, as he was in a very weakened condition. It certainly made a huge difference to everyday life for all concerned.

Social life was reasonably good with a local tennis club meeting at Stamford, which was our railway siding, telephone exchange and post office with an accompanying small community of people. Every fortnight, weather permitting, up to 60 or 70 people gathered from about 15 surrounding stations and the small Stamford community for conversation, drinks, food and a hit of tennis. Around the end of the year, if rain had been around, it was sometimes a battle under the floodlights to know if you were hitting balls or bugs, but we batted on. Barbeques were held regularly at 'Elton Downs' and other neighbouring properties, with four of those properties being owned by cousins. Horse racing was a big social event in the outback, and a bi-annual occurrence was the Stamford Races about eleven kilometres distant. Another bi-annual event, about 40 miles away, was the Corfield Races, which served, as you might have guessed, the Corfield district.

Hughenden, nearly 80 kilometres to the north-east, being the main centre for the district with a population of approximately 1,100 residents, hosted many more racing events throughout the year. And of course, we regularly visited Townsville to see Pam's family, and they reciprocated by visiting us at 'Elton Downs' from time to time. They thoroughly enjoyed their stays in the bush with us. Two of Pam's brothers and a cousin worked for us at Elton for considerable lengths of time over the years that Pam and I were together, and they were good bush workers and caught on quickly to stock work. Not everyone does. Unfortunately, the bush was not for Pam as she missed city life, and there were more than a few arguments about this issue. I fully understand the complications of living with the in-laws, but she couldn't/wouldn't live there and I couldn't/wouldn't leave, so after seven years of marriage, Pam and I parted company and we were divorced a year or so later. But with two sons and eight grandchildren, we are still friends to this day. I stayed at the station with our two sons, and Pam lived in Hughenden for a while, but eventually moved on to Townsville with her family and later to the Atherton Tablelands. I always ensured that our two sons, Joseph and Daniel, regularly spent time with her, wherever she was living, during the school holidays.

A mates funeral in 1975

*A toast to each other and the future, Pam and I,
at our wedding at Pallaranda in 1977*

Byrne and his Yamaha 750 in 1976. Wendy McAway on Tony Gordons bike

Byrne, Lou, Dad and Mum in 1974

Lachlan and Catriona in the wading pool of the Kokoda Pool. Townsville, about 1967

LtoR- Eddie, Lou and her friend Annie Crimpston, Catriona, Byrne, in front Leona and Justin looking to the back. Not long after Cyclone Althea, sand debris in the distance and new road being built in middle distance

Me as a second year apprentice plumber in 1974. Curtain out of overturned bus in Cyclone Althea

Me on my first bike in 1974. Dad who went garauntor wouldn't allow me to buy any larger

My lifelong mate, Tracy Forkin at Pallarenda in 1976

Pam and I early in 1977

The Terrys at Pallarenda in 1970. L to R - Edward, Mary Lou, Lachlan holding Justin, Byrne, Catriona and Leona in front

7

LIFE ON THE LAND

In a perfect world, each year would be planned by the farmers and graziers, with predictable outcomes resulting in a lot less stress and worry. But in reality it was planned by the unreliable weather patterns and seasons, combined with the reproductive cycles of our animals. Like all good Australians, we always gambled with the law of averages, and sometimes you had a win. It all hinged on the wet season, which was the key factor for the whole year and usually occurred in January, February, and March. The wet season could be aided and abetted by getting worthwhile early rain spread over a few decent falls, spaced three or four weeks apart in November and December.

In our part of the world, we much preferred to have a Green Christmas to a White Christmas. If you had good early rain, it followed that when your wet season proper started in January, your soil already had a good amount of moisture. The grass would be green and growing, as well as the dams, if not already full, at least having a decent amount of water in them. With an annual average rainfall of about 400 mm or 16 inches in the old measure, our property was on the largest natural black soil grassland in the world. A lot of people mistakenly believe that the trees have been cleared, but not so; apart from coolibah trees along the water courses, it is a naturally treeless environment.

Regarding the wet season and black soil, there is quite a funny, sardonic saying concerning the combination of these two: "If you can stick to the black soil in the dry (read droughts), it will stick to you in the wet". Not a truer word spoken – if you have ever tried to walk cross-country in the black soil of the western downs after any rain. It was during this part of the year, between September/October and February/March, that the Channel-Billed Cuckoo or the Storm Bird did its annual pilgrimage to the Australian continent.

It had a totally different call to the previously mentioned curlews on Magnetic Island, but nonetheless, an eerie and haunting sound during the night. We used to get the odd one out on the Downs country; you would hear them calling, usually in the early hours of the morning before daylight. They were meant to herald rain, but sometimes they were known to get it a bit wrong. Graeme Connors, in his song 'Before The Wet', mentions the Storm Bird, giving the song a hauntingly lonely and forsaken sound that I think conveys the image of this bird very well.

If all these factors fell into place, this would provide an ideal situation for gestating ewes to drop their lambs. Season-wise, on average in a 10-year cycle for our area, you would have three really good years, three reasonable years, and the other four years (or longer) tailing off from very ordinary to absolutely woeful drought conditions. Many city people have the odd notion that people on the land do nothing except sit on their verandahs in a comfortable armchair for 12 months of the year as spectators watching everything happen and then collecting the money from the bank manager at the end of the year. There is so much more to it than that, but there is no certificate that will acknowledge those attributes for the people who spend their lives in the outback.

For the benefit of those who don't know but are interested in and would like to know more, in the next few chapters, I will detail specifically all the different aspects of running a sheep station over a 12-month period in an effort to disprove this misguided fallacy. I do not intend to be boring or claim to be a know-all, but it is my belief that a station owner or a station worker is every bit as good a scientist or specialist as someone that has attended a university for four or five years, the only difference being that they don't have that framed diploma to hang on the wall. Apart from the physical aspect of running the operation, there is also a lot of planning involved, watching the sky for weather signs (not that you can change anything), watching the feed in your paddock, watching the condition of your livestock, watching the livestock sale markets and the wool markets, implementing maintenance programs for station infrastructure and machinery, and finally watching the bank balance.

The ideal factors I mentioned previously don't always fall into place, as with the event that occurred between the 15th and 20th of December 1976. Severe Tropical Cyclone Ted developed in the Gulf of Carpentaria, petering out in central North West Queensland as a heavy rain depression. It was not severe flooding as we have known a couple of times in very recent years, but it was still significant, very heavy rain and for many, it was probably the first rain of the wet season. Most stock, whether cattle or sheep, were in a poor and weakened condition at the end of the year. The KILLER with this cyclone was the intensely and bitterly cold unseasonal westerly winds that blew for the duration of this weather event. Animals, when experiencing cold wind, will seek shelter out of the wind or run before it, seeking shelter.

On the western downs, there is very little in the way of significant tree cover, hence shelter, so they just continued moving westwards until they came to a fence line and they could go no further. There, in poor condition as well as wet and cold, they died. On 'Elton Downs', we lost about 5,000 head of sheep and 1,000 head of mostly agistment cattle, whose skeletal remains against a fence will keep reminding us of the event for years to come. Our experience was repeated right across the north-west grazing communities. Such is life and the hand that you are dealt. When nature is with you, it is great and you can roll with the flow, but when nature is against you, there is absolutely nothing you can do about it apart from pick yourself up afterwards, dust yourself off, count your losses and start again.

Gestation for a ewe is roughly 154 days (five months), so counting back five months from the end of January (just to make sure the wet season hadn't decided to make a late start) takes you back to the beginning of September. So if you want lambs at the end of January, you have to put your rams in with the ewes at the end of August. Everything was based on best practices and probabilities, so if you wanted the best lambing percentages from the joining, you had to have both your rams and ewes bouncing around full of vim, vigour and vulgarity. The best way of achieving that is to first remove 10 to 12 pounds of fleece off them by starting shearing in July. That way, they are lighter and more active, and it helps to ensure those rams don't miss that vital impregnation spot. Every little thing tipped the odds in our favour. We also fed our 250-odd rams on corn and lick-block supplements for a few weeks before joining as well, just to tip the odds a little further in our favour.

Joining the rams and ewes was always done immediately after shearing. The 6,000 ewes were returned to their four paddocks, and the rams were shared equally amongst them. To ensure the lambing occurred in a reasonably concentrated space of time, they were joined for only six weeks. At the end of that time, usually around mid-October, we had to muster the four paddocks, draft the rams off and return them to their own separate paddock near the house, with the ewes remaining in their usual paddocks for their 'confinement'. From September until around Christmas was always the worst time of the year. At the end of September for about three or four weeks you had the very windy weather of the Autumnal Equinox and after that the conditions just got progressively hotter and hotter .... and hotter.

The grass (referred to as feed) became increasingly scarce on the ground as the days progressed. As the feed closest to the dam was naturally the first to be eaten out, the ewes consequently had to walk further and further between the water and the feed as the weather got hotter and hotter, which was not a good combination. We always had supplements out for the ewes to help them make it through to the first rain, but quite a few of the older ewes were just too poor to make it.

This was the time of the year when we were constantly doing water runs, as by now all of the dams would be getting dangerously low and boggy, which would then trap many of the older and weaker ewes as they tried to get a drink. So it was around the dams every day to pull out bogged sheep, knowing you would probably see the same ones day after day. If they were bogged for too long, the struggle weakened them so much that they would never get up again.

Now, as if you didn't have enough to do already with the supplement and water runs and trying to keep as many of the old ewes alive as possible, this was also the time of the year when you tried to attend to the maintenance of buildings, machinery, fences and dams. The biggest maintenance issue was the dams and ensuring that any dams that had been by washed badly in the previous wet season were built up again to try and trap as much water as possible in the anticipated next wet season. We had a Caterpillar D6 with a scoop and ripper to do the earthworks in, on or around our dams, of which we had 14 in total, and they averaged around 25,000 cubic yards when they were first built.

All this time it was getting hotter and hotter, with less and less grass, shrinking water holes or dams, and more and more 'deadies' (bogged sheep), while you were watching the horizon to the north for the big thunderhead clouds. Hopefully, these were going to deliver the early rain that you had been waiting for, which would ease conditions for the end of the year and create a magnificent start to the next year. For a lot of years, the disappointment associated with that period of anticipation could go on right up until Christmas and sometimes even afterwards, well into the New Year. That wait was the killer, the decider of your fate. But then, hang on a bit...... the excitement and the relief that comes with that smell of the first storm rain on dry parched earth followed by the incessant, deafening, croaking of frogs that first night can only be described as the sweetest sensation known to the ears of a family on the land. The first few heavy drops of rain gradually picking up pace until there is a deafening, thundering torrent on the corrugated iron roof that sometimes continues on for hours on end, often accompanied by a full light display, sometimes not. You just wanted to lie there listening and luxuriating in the sound that had taken so long in arriving, but eventually that mesmerising sound took you away to somewhere else as you nodded off to sleep.

In the morning time at 'Elton Downs', when we would awaken, it was to the view of our usually dry Little Warrianna Creek in front of our house, in full flood, swollen to four or five times the width of its normal course and audibly flowing to the unaided ear. This was the miracle that in the space of only a few days turned life's fortunes around, the neglected looking and wizened tufts of black Mitchell grass started turning green, the perrenial Flinders grass started pushing through the damp surface, weeds and herbage springing almost instantly from the ground, little wavelets lapping the banks of our dams and back waters, to indicate another at least twelve months of life-giving liquid, even the oldest and weakest animals transformed into animals of hope that had a new spring in their step.

Within weeks, the grass was knee-high, green, and so thick the sheep and newborn lambs actually had to push through it. And, of an evening, insects like you would not believe, millions and millions and millions of them, all heading towards a light, any light, all lights, it didn't really matter because there were more than enough insects to go around. In fact, you daren't turn on an inside house light for fear of the crawling, flying invasion you would invariably invite into the kitchen and bedrooms. You turned on the external lights around the house and the outbuildings, and lived life on the inside of the house in the half light. Nevertheless, the inconvenience was only a reasonably short-lived affair that we were prepared to work with, for the alternative without rain was unthinkable.

Lambing would start for the ewes towards the end of January (hopefully with a good wet season already started or just about to) and continue through until mid-March. With plentiful water supplies and lush green grass, the ewe could provide plenty of mother's milk, and the lamb would do well until it was also on a diet of grass. If the wet was progressing reasonably, we would leave the ewes to fend for themselves. Animals are not stupid and know what is best to do when they have young offspring using an inborn, natural intuition, so to speak.

If there was heavy rain, the ewes would frequent the higher, harder and drier ground of the shaley ridges to make it as easy as possible for themselves and their newborn lambs. The sight of the strengthening ewes with their butting, nuzzling and tail-wiggling lambs at foot, in the luxuriant green Mitchell and Flinders grasses, gave all a sense of hope and prosperity for another 12-month instalment of life. The lambs grew quickly, and as the grass and boggy flats dried out and the waterholes in the creeks dried up, the ewes and lambs were able to move around the paddocks much more easily.

The lambs were bigger and stronger as well, so consequently travelled further and further from water as the weeks progressed. As the grasses dried out, the roly-poly or tumbleweed was the first to die and start being blown along, ahead of the wind. The roly-poly plant grew like a skeletal ball, if you like, and had no leaves to speak of. Still and all, it was very spiky, and if your legs were unprotected when walking through a thick patch of this plant, it would make your legs very itchy.

Following a heavy wet season, there was a lot of roly-poly. When it died and blew along the ground, anywhere there was an obstruction, it would pile up sometimes feet deep. Along fences, it would be as high as the top wire of the fence and sometimes backed up over the fire plough track two or three feet deep. If there were any willy-willys about, you would see roly-polys flying around in circles hundreds of feet up in the air until eventually they fell back to the ground. You could find roly-poly remains even up in the top of windmill towers in the grease, oil, and dust, having been deposited there by willy-willys.

Something that was still quite prevalent in the outback when I returned to Elton Downs in 1977 was the little Australian bush fly. Or, as Dad so fondly referred to them, "you bloody little black bastards", especially if he was doing some delicate little job and they got in behind his glasses. These were not the blow flies that were such a huge problem amongst our sheep in the wet season. The bush fly was virtually harmless if you could overlook the annoyance factor of having to breathe through your nostrils and never opening your mouth, as well as doing the 'great Australian salute' all day long whilst working.

If you were working outdoors, a man's back when wearing a sweat-soaked shirt would just be totally black with flies, with the sweat attracting the flies. Thousands upon thousands of flies that were simply looking for moisture. Dad told us that he, as a young man in the 1940s and 1950s, had seen the bush fly in far greater numbers than what we were experiencing. That usually temporarily stopped any discussion from us about wanting to have lived in the 'good old days'.

We as kids, and my own two boys when they were youngsters, were particularly prone to the affectionate attention of the bush flies. As kids are not too worried about a fly or two sharing the corner of their eye chasing a bit of moisture, consequently you would get a harmless fly bite, which, as an infection, would swell up for two or three days and was known as a 'bung eye'. When this happened to my boys, I used to call them 'bung-eyed billy boys', which they took great exception to.

To combat this problem, Mum used to make fly veils for us when we were kids and later on for my boys. Now, these fly veils were by no means a fashion statement in anyone's language, and we hated wearing them. They were simply gauze bags just large enough to fit over your head, with elastic at the bottom that would tighten gently on your neck while still preventing the flies from entering. Most kids in the west wore 'fly veils' up until about the age of six or seven years old to prevent the scourge of 'bung eyes' when participating in any sort of outdoor activities.

The introduction of the 'dung beetle' starting in 1965 had reduced the bush fly numbers significantly. Even so, they were still prevalent in the late 1970s but significantly reduced by the end of the 1980s. A Hungarian entomologist by the name of Dr George Bornemissza had arrived as an immigrant to Australia in December of 1950. He could see the problem and knew what the solution was, and he joined the CSIRO in 1955. It was he who instigated the Dung Beetle Project, which virtually meant the end of the line for 'the little black bastards'. Dung beetles roll the fresh dung up into balls and store it below ground in tunnels and hollows for their own use as food later on. As the bush fly lays their eggs in fresh cattle dung, this then means that the bush fly becomes homeless and has a much reduced rate of reproduction, causing their numbers in the ecosystem to plummet. Thank God for the Dung Beetle!

Bogged on the way home from the 1981 Maxy Ball. L to R Dan, Pam, Joe and cousin Mark O Brien

Brother Ed and I getting ready to cut and brand some colts in the Elton cattle yards, 1980

Elton cottage in 1981

Giving the boys a ride on the D6 in 1981

Having a rest at Victoria River Crossing 1981

Joe and Dan off to a fancy dress party at Vuna in 1982

Lambs in to be lamb marked and mulsed at No. 2 yards in 1980

*Little Warriana Creek in flood in the early 1980s.
Shearing shed in the distance*

New quarters being erected at Elton in 1979

Pam and the boys going to Hughenden in 1983

Pam as a model at a fund raising fashion parade held at Eldorado, 1981

The boys and I at Porcupine Gorge in 1982

The flies have been busy here, two Bung Eye Billys, 1982

8

ONE TASK AT A TIME

Crutching is mainly about preventing fly strike. About the middle of April, we would crutch our entire flock of sheep, sometimes earlier if the fly strike was particularly bad. A secondary benefit of crutching was that it helped reduce dung and urine stains to the fleece when we shore about three months later, and also reduced wool blindness. At that time of year, with the wet season just finished, there was still a lot of moisture in the tall grass and damp earth, and with the grass still quite green, the sheep were inclined to scour, which created positive conditions for fly strike, even though we also mulesed.

Some years, for no apparent reason, the fly strike was worse than other years; you could never predict what it would be like. About the middle of April, the lambs, while still young, were sturdy enough to be mustered and walked into the shearing shed about five or six miles away. The wethers (the adult male sheep) were kept in the furthest paddocks, and they had about a 14-mile walk over two days. For them, we had a holding yard about halfway to the shearing shed. After being rested overnight, and with an early start, they walked the remainder easily and quickly.

The act of crutching itself is a process whereby the shearer removes a small amount of wool from the animal. It is mostly a preventative measure rather than a cure for large numbers of already blown sheep. On ewes, they remove the wool from the rear and inside edges of the back legs all the way up to and around the tail. The wethers were crutched, wigged and also had the wool from around their pizzles removed for the same reason of fly strike.

Removing this wool prevents urine and faeces (too much green feed and weeds cause scouring) from staining and moistening the belly wool (pizzles), the wool around the breech and down the back legs, which then attracts blowflies that lay eggs that hatch into maggots. A fly-blown sheep, if not caught and treated with either fly strike dip poison or hand crutching with a pair of hand shears, will be eaten alive. Badly blown sheep can die within as little as two or three days of being struck, and it is an agonising death. The sheep dies from infection and/or blood poisoning as the maggots actually burrow into and eat the flesh of the sheep.

Also, while crutching, the shearers do what is known as 'wigging' or shearing the wool away from around the eyes of the animal. Some sheep that have a lot of wool around their cheeks and forehead can become what is known as 'wool blind'. A sheep that can't see doesn't do as well because they lose their mob, finding it difficult to locate water and feed, and they simply cannot see where they are going. Crutching was the most hectic, chaotic time of the year for us. Because the shearers were removing so little wool from the animals, it was a very speedy operation, and the throughput of sheep was terrific. 20,000 odd sheep, being all the wethers, all the ewes, all the weaners and all the rams, were mustered, crutched and returned to their paddocks all in the space of less than two weeks.

Lamb marking and mulesing were the next major stock handling event, and we did it around mid to late May when the lambs were about two to three months old. Dad used to get a contract muleser from down near Mitchell. Ellsworth Tully came up each year and did a number of people in our district who wanted contract mulesing done. The four ewe paddocks had a common central corner around our No. Two windmill, which were a watering point for all four paddocks, and a set of steel sheep yards handy to each paddock.

Each paddock contained about 1,500 ewes, which averaged a rate of about 70%, meaning each paddock would have a little over 1,000 lambs in it. We mustered each paddock individually, processing those ewes and lambs and returning them to their paddock before moving on to the next paddock. Each day, you would be on your motorbike, horse or in Dad's case, a 4WD utility at the back of the paddock before sunrise. As soon as we could see properly, we would all be mustering ewes and lambs towards the mill, arriving at the sheep yards in about three hours at around 9 AM.

We would boil the billy and have smoko as soon as we yarded the sheep. Then we would draft the lambs off the ewes and start lamb marking. The lamb marking cradles we had and preferred were six steel cradles side by side, set up on a fence with a reasonably small catching pen about two metres square. Each person in the lamb marking team had a specific task to perform and no other. On the catching side of the cradles, there were usually two people in the catching pen: one person catching lambs and loading empty cradles, the other person letting go once the lamb had been processed. On the marking side of the cradles, there were seven different tasks to perform in the lamb marking process.

The tasks in the lamb marking process, in order from first to last were as follows:

1. Ear marking consisted of a registered earmark in the off ear (that is, the sheep's right side ear) for male sheep and in the left-hand or near ear for female sheep. In the opposite ear of either was the age mark, which was about eight different designations decided by each station that differentiated age up to eight years old for purposes of drafting for age.

2. A rubber elastrator ring was put on the testicles of the male sheep.

3. Dehorning any animal that exhibited a preponderance to later grow horns that could possibly do injury to shearers or other stock handlers.

4. Mulesing all lambs regardless of sex. Mulesing was a process of reducing the prevalence of fly strike in the wet season. Mulesing reduced fly strike occurrence by up to 90 or 95 %, which definitely made it worthwhile doing. It involved removing a strip of skin along with the wool starting from the base of the tail of the lamb across the rear of the rump turning at an angle and continuing down the back of the leg towards the hock. When it healed, it would, in lots of cases, be bare of wool, and as the wound healed, it would also tighten up the entire area of the rear end of the animal, ridding the skin of folds and wrinkles. The practice is decried by animal liberationists as cruel and inhuman, but I can tell you it is far preferable to being eaten alive by maggots in later life after being fly blown. Also, it is not a torturously slow operation; anyone who is a good muleser can do each leg in one second. It is a very swift process.

5. Removing the tail, again, is a fly strike prevention process and aids in the ease of shearing. A tail is awkward and time-consuming to shear for very little wool, and it tidies up the appearance of the animal. Once again, there is a correct and incorrect way to remove a tail, and it is all in the way you hold the knife and the tail. Done correctly, you leave a flap of skin that is connected to the underside or inside of the tail, which is naturally smooth and without wool, and this remaining flap of skin is long enough to wrap around and over the end of the tail. The healing that then takes place is around the edges, and it heals much quicker and cleaner. If you just cut straight through the tail, it leaves an unsightly, ugly, bony stump of a tail, which, of course, takes a lot longer to heal.

6. Then you had the man with the powder bottle, fly-strike powder for short-term protection from fly-strike sprinkled all over the raw

wounds and blood to protect the lamb until the wounds scabbed over in four or five days. The order described above is with the least bloody of the operations done first, while the most bloody were performed last for obvious reasons.

7. Lastly, the man that was letting go would try, as he was lifting the cradle to release the lamb, to give it a flick so that the lamb would almost always land on its feet instead of landing on its rear end in the dirt and dust, thereby reducing the chance of infection yet again. All of these tasks had a definite right and wrong way of being done. Lo and behold, if you were caught out doing anything incorrectly, or you were, for some reason, falling behind a little and slowing the whole process up, Dad was not backwards in coming forward to correct your errors and would be more than happy to elaborate about your usefulness in the workforce to you and anyone else within earshot.

Fire ploughing was an annual occurrence and was essential in trying to retain as much grass as possible in the event of bushfire. Essentially, our Caterpillar D6 tractor is towing a V-shaped steel plough to cut fire breaks around the outside perimeters of all our paddocks and cut each paddock into four with two additional diagonal tracks. On our 70,000-acre property, there were nearly 500 kilometres of fire breaks which were done at six kilometres per hour (top speed for the D6). On the prevailing wind side of our entire property, we actually cut two tracks about 400 metres apart and back-burnt the grass between the two tracks.

The reason for this added precaution was that the main road and railway line were not far away on the windward side of our property, presenting a far greater risk. If you had a bushfire early in the year, while you still had a huge body of feed, with a good wind behind it, a fire could travel along at 30 or 40 kilometres per hour, and a single track would not even cause the fire front to hesitate. The fire breaks also doubled as vehicular access for doing water runs, mustering or checking on stock and gave easy and quick access in the event that you had to fight a bushfire.

You don't have to be in the heavily timbered areas of Australia to perish in a bushfire, as my father related to me in this true account below. It is just as easy to do it in a grass fire on the Mitchell grass downs of western Queensland if you are careless or uninformed about bushfire safety. A grass fire can be a very hot, dangerous, and unpredictable animal, and it can travel extremely quickly with the right wind conditions, even more so in the early part of the year, when there is still a huge body of dry grass. In 1954, before my time, but in our district, there were a couple of men who perished on 'Narollah Station' near Corfield. Lance Halloran, the 61-year-old station owner and Ron Batterley, the 17-year-old jackaroo, died because they were in the wrong spot at the wrong time. To make the situation worse, this fire was caused by a lightning strike from a November storm. While on the property there was little to no rain, the same storm system dumped 75 mm of rain on the road between Hughenden and Corfield, making the road impassable for the ambulance trying to reach them with medical help.

Rex Halloran, the station owner's 28-year-old son, tried to come to their aid, but he too became caught up in the inferno. He survived but suffered horrific burns. In a 4WD truck, he valiantly tried to get the two victims to a special train with doctors and nurses that was coming to Corfield, but they passed away beforehand. Fortunately, in my time at Elton Downs, we had to put out only a couple of very mild fires. Dad kept our property well stocked when the wet seasons allowed, and the buildup of 'fuel' was something that rarely occurred on our place.

Of course, during a drought, there was no grass to burn to begin with. Dad never failed to impress upon me the importance of having the fire breaks done as early as possible so that you were able to backburn from the fire break towards the fire, and when attending a fire, the safety of always fighting a fire from the burnt ground. The mistake the 'Narollah Station' men made was that, for some unexplained reason, they ventured out into the middle of the 'fuel', a long way away from the burnt ground. When the wind unexpectedly changed, the fire caught up to them before they managed to make it to the safety of the burnt ground.

The fire ploughing was usually done in April or May, as the grass turned from green and moist to yellow and dry. You needed to have the fire breaks in place before the threat of fire arrived. Before ploughing, you had to hard surface all the cutting edges on the plough. This job entailed removing all the 18-inch segments of the cutting edges on both 20-foot sides of the V-shaped plough frame. It took quite some time to remove the high tensile bolts that were all in fairly difficult-to-get-at positions.

Then was the slow, hot and tricky job of using the electric welder to apply hard surfacing rods to the cutting edge of these segments. Hard surfacing rods were a difficult rod to apply to the metal surface. The fairly time-consuming job, but one that had to be done if you wanted a track swept clean of any grass, was completed after you had reattached all of the cutting segments to the plough with mostly new high tensile bolts. You would not believe it possible, but the constant movement of loose dirt past the heads of the bolts quite often wore the bolt heads away to almost nothing.

Dad's sense of humour came to the fore once again when they had warranty issues with this fire plough, which they had bought from a steel fabrication company in Charters Towers by the name of Lee Engineering. Initially, when the Terry brothers bought the plough from Lee Engineering, they didn't realise the shortcomings in its design. Before the first ploughing season was finished, the superstructure of the plough was literally cracking up and tearing itself to pieces, and it had to be returned to the workshop in Charters Towers.

It is difficult to explain its geometry, but simply put, the V-shaped plough frame itself is the item that should be towed. The tow bar, front wheels and upper superstructure of the plough chassis, whilst attached to the tractor, are only there basically for the raising and lowering of the plough frame either for cutting adjustment or if you wanted to travel from Point A to Point B without actually ploughing. Their design had it so that the towing was transferred via the tow bar, the upper superstructure, and then to the nose of the plough frame. Never in a million years would it be successful; the forces and pressures exerted were simply too much.

Dad travelled down to Charters Towers, not to work on the plough with them, but to try and explain to them how he thought the design should be. Of course, the warranty repairs were going to be an expensive exercise for the firm, and they countered that Dad should not be "towing the plough with that Bloody Great Big D6, of course it would break up being towed by such a big tractor". Dad was not to be deterred, and came back with, "Well, what do you want me to tow the plough with, a bloody bicycle?" Lee Engineering eventually conceded that their design was lacking and made the necessary changes according to Dad's thoughts and ideas on the matter and there were never any further issues with the plough in that regard.

Dam building and repair were also jobs that the Caterpillar D6 was gainfully employed in. For putting down new dams, Dad employed an experienced dozer operator on a contract basis after first pegging out the dam using his theodolite and level staff. I was quite often the person trudging around in the distance, trying to decipher what his pointing or waving arms wanted me to do with the staff. A man that Dad used to employ regularly was Alec Crowley, who lived in Charters Towers and had built quite a few of the dams on Elton Downs. The dams, all of which were about 20,000 cubic metres in capacity, were mostly built when I was a child, about 15 to 20 years previously.

Generally, a dam of around 20,000 to 25,000 cubic metres capacity when new was around 8 to 10 metres deep below the inlet pipe and usually took about a month of long days and non-stop work to build. Dams, as much as they could be, were centrally located in the paddock, as that took the stock pressure off the fences, but that central position was governed by where the gullies and catchment areas were located in the paddock. After I returned home, any dam work was always maintenance work on existing dams, which we did ourselves. We only built one new dam after I returned to Elton, and Dad used a local contractor with his own machines to build that.

After I returned home in 1977, until we bought the property in the Kimberleys, Dad sometimes had at least two of his adult sons at home and sometimes all three of us. My two younger brothers, who were still single, used to come and go as the mood took them, either travelling or working at other enterprises. However, while Dad had the extra hands in his workforce, we accomplished quite a few additional jobs over and above the required stock work. Some internal fencing was refurbished, and some was replaced with a new fence. There were a couple of shared boundary fences, but the workload on those fences was shared with the corresponding neighbours. We also had the opportunity to silt scoop a few of our silted-up dams. It had been about twenty years since a lot of them had been built, and they were half full of silt and consequently a death trap for the weaker, older animals in poor condition at the end of the year.

Another major item that had attention paid to it was what passed for cattle yards at 'Elton Downs'. When it had been built, it was basically just a horse and milk cow yard that had a couple of extra impromptu yards added onto it. The whole construction was far too light, frail and inadequate to handle large numbers of cattle on a regular basis. Dad bought a large amount of surplus railway line, tram line and second-hand steel from Ingham-based Sam Zanghi, a scrap metal merchant who travelled around the west supplying stations with vast tonnages of his metallic goods. We set to work and cut the railway line into three-metre sections to use as posts (half in the ground and half out) and welded the heavy flat steel in between them as rails.

We constructed all our own gates from lengths of 50 millimetre steel pipe, as well as a few safety blinds around the yards in strategic locations that a person could duck behind if being charged by a beast. Over the next few years, we built a set of yards that could easily handle a mob of 600 or 700 head of cattle at the one time with just the one team of workers.

Previously, when using the old yards, we basically had to have two teams working, one actually working the cattle in the yards and the other trying to prevent escape or chasing escapees and re-yarding them for processing.

So the work I've outlined up to this point basically covers all of the easy parts of the year and brings us up to late May / early June. Next, we have the big event of the year, shearing; just as busy but as cold as charity during all of those very early starts over that next six-week period. Then after that was what I considered the hard part of the year, from thereon until about November or sometimes much later, it was extremely hot, dry and quite often windy. I used to find it the most depressing time of the year, whilst you were trying to keep everything alive, anxiously waiting for that life-preserving rain to arrive and remain smiling all at the same time.

Joe and Dan in Cairns on the Kuranda train 1988

A cousin, Dan Mackay lugging a gidyea post out into the open to be loaded onto the truck. Boremba Station, 1989

A visit to Chillagoe with the boys in 1991. Slag heaps beyond the long defunct Chillagoe copper smelting operation

Alan Terry working on the Elton D6 in 1985

Blowing silt out of the Old Dam in 1979. Photo taken early in the explosion, the debris ultimately went much higher than this. When it became evident that we were too close to the dam self preservation took a higher priority than photographs

Byrne and I in 1981 at Elton

Justin, Byrne, myself and John Sharkey. No. 2 yards, Elton, 1983

Pams cousin, Ian Short cutting wood for the donkeys at Elton in 1983

Plug McAway, Elsworth Tully, Byrne, Dad and myself lambmarking at Elton No. 2 in 1980

Post cutting camp at Boremba Station in the basalt country

The bath tub at Boremba Station in the basalt country in 1989

The boys and I on Pallarenda beach in 1988

Yellowbelly fishing trip. Vergemont Creek camp in 1990

9

SPRINGTIME, IT BRINGS ON THE SHEARING

Shearing on Elton started towards the end of July and went for about three to four weeks, depending on the number of sheep we had that particular year. The team that shore at Elton was Jimmy McMillan's team, a local contractor from Hughenden who shore the Elton flock for 25 years. Jimmy originally hailed from Lismore on the NSW north coast and arrived in Hughenden as a teenager in the mid to late 1940s. He worked on stations initially as a ringer but the better money in the shearing game soon had him in the shearing sheds. His wife Dot was the daughter of another old Hughenden shearing contractor Darky Paine who Jimmy had shorn for after first arriving from the north coast.

Over the years, Jimmy McMillan had a fairly steady team of good shearers, mostly local men. Two brothers, Neville and Jacky Carter, Agg Waters, Tommy McGregor, David Waterhouse and Kevie Reid being some of the regulars on the board that I remember. Wayne McConachy was his wool classer for a fair while and before him for a long time was Trevor Hampson. Soda Paine, his brother-in-law, cooked for the team for years. A nephew, Mark McMillan, was pressing for him for a few years. Paul Armstrong, or Cuzz as he was better known, was the presser for a while, then took on the cooking when Soda retired. Vince Griffin was also with Jimmy for a while as a presser.

Wayne McConachy later married Christine Carter, a sister to the Carter brothers that shore for Jimmy McMillan, and they went on to buy Jimmy McMillan's shearing run from him. It was only a couple of years after that the wool industry as a whole suffered Australia-wide when the Wool Reserve Price scheme collapsed. The whole area from Blackall north through Barcaldine and Muttaburra to Hughenden, then west to Cloncurry, back down to Winton and Longreach was a huge area probably about 90% given over to sheep. Relative to the sheep population it had only very small numbers of cattle. It has now reversed to about 90% cattle or possibly more and you are hard pressed to find a station still running a sheep flock.

All the western towns used to have at least two shearing teams in each town; most towns now have no shearing teams. Even if it was only one shearing team, taking 15 families out of a small community has quite an effect on a small town in terms of economies, schools as well as social and sporting activities. Some towns had more than two teams; the township of Muttaburra, with a population of about 600 in the 1980s, had about a dozen shearing teams, which would have been about one third of the town's population. In comparison, Hughenden only had about three or four teams.

An Australian shearing team was no different in size to a New Zealand shearing team, usually 13 or 14 men in total but very unionised with a rigidly enforced set of rules on what you could and couldn't do. You could not shear wet sheep or cancers, cut outs between different mobs of sheep had their own set of rules and starting and finishing times were strictly enforced by the clock. In the late 1970s when the New Zealand or 'Kiwi' teams started shearing in Australia it really upset the apple cart.

The New Zealanders were very fluid in their approach to work rules. It included the totally foreign concept of having women not only in the team but on the 'board' also, who could shear every bit as well and as many as the male shearers. They also used that item of abhorrent and controversial kit known as the 'wide comb', that split the Australian shearing community right down the middle. As well as that, coming from New Zealand, they were not averse to shearing wet sheep and official union rules regarding starts and finishes were not strictly adhered to.

At the end of 1968, when Dad and Mum moved to live in Townsville for our education, Dad had employed a manager by the name of Mick Hazel, who was a native of England. Mick had been in Australia and the outback a long time and was a very thorough and efficient manager, but like a lot of Englishmen, was very officious and did not have a very well-developed sense of humour, which the shearers just 'loved'. Mick had a family with his wife Elsie and two daughters, Margo and Anne. They had previously managed Stamford Downs just to the east of Stamford for Dad's cousin Doug Terry, before starting at 'Elton Downs'.

To set a mental picture of the shed, the shearers started at seven in the morning and did four two-hour runs with a half-hour break between each of them. When shearing in mid-winter, it was always bitterly cold at seven o'clock, and they usually had a fairly stiff, 'lazy' breeze blowing up their backsides from the let-go chute as well, but after the first three or four sheep, the shearers had warmed up. A lazy breeze is one that goes straight through you, rather than around you. There was plenty of noise in and around the shed to reinforce the feeling of business and activity.

There were the sheep bleating as they were being forced up into the catching pens by the incessantly barking dogs. The clattering of the rattles made out of a ring of number eight wire with old empty tobacco tins threaded onto the ring which you would shake and rattle to frighten the sheep up, shouts of 'sheepo' for a catching pen to be refilled with 'woolies', the shearers yakaying as they teased and tormented the passing roustabouts. Shearers pushing a newly brilliantly white, shorn sheep down the let-go chute, having a hurried swig out of their water bag, a quick wipe of their face with their towelling sweat rags, then rushing into the catching pen to drag another wriggling animal out onto the board. Busy, busy, busy.

The buzz of the handpieces, the whirr of the overhead gear, the clunking of handpieces being engaged, and the constant throbbing thump of the water-cooled single-cylinder Lister engine that drove the whirring overhead gear via a flapping 6" flat belt made for a very busy, noisy work scene. The 'rousies' running to keep up, up and down, up and down the board they went to clear it of shorn fleeces and sweep the pieces, bellies and the rest out of the way.

Fleeces are being tossed onto or stacked on the ground around the classing table and thence into the wool bins to keep the presser busy in the wool room with his motorised hydraulic wool press. Shearing was very hard work, but the shearers, as they laboured away, spent a lot of time dreaming up practical jokes that they could play on each other or other unsuspecting people in or around the shed that they thought they could take 'the mickey' out of.

Mick wore a fairly large pair of glasses with the proverbial solid, heavy frames on them, with his favourite style being tortoiseshell colour. When the shearers were on the rams, they would get the sticky black grease off the overhead gear with their fingers and paint a pair of glasses on the last one or two rams of the run so they would initially be very obscure down at the back of the let go pens. All the shearers would be in on the prank and eagerly watching down towards the yards for Mick's much-anticipated reaction.

Sure enough, Mick would be down putting the tar brands on the shorn sheep in the branding race and look down to see a ram peering up at him with a pair of 'glasses' on. He would then tear up to the contractor past all the smiling shearers on the board wanting to know who had done it and suggesting he should be sacked or at least reprimanded, to which our contractor Jimmy McMillan who was quite a character in the humour department himself would have to tell him, "Oh come on, settle down a bit Mick, you are reacting just exactly how they want you to react".

Another send-up they did was one day when Mick was down in the sheep yards drafting up the day's shearing. The shearing shed, the sheep yards and drafting race, the gallows and killing block and a nearby fire pit where you burnt the offal and remains of the previous day's kill were all in fairly close proximity. There was usually a fire going or at least smouldering in the fire pit from the previous day's kill.

So when they played this joke on him, they in fact were much closer to the truth than telling an outright lie. Mick was intently concentrating on trying to do a three-way draft, keeping count on two ways and controlling his sheep dogs all at the same time. In other words, he was reasonably busy and totally occupied when one of the shearers wandered down to the door at the end of the board that overlooked the yards and, at the top of his voice, yelled out, "Fire!".

Mick lost his train of thought completely, as he quickly looked this way and that to see what was going on, a few sheep going the wrong way at the drafting gates as his concentration was interrupted and then cursing as he looked up to the shed as the shearer laughed and pointed over to the fire pit. Mick had been had again. He never learnt to laugh with them or try to think up something equally mischievous to get them at their own game. It just wasn't in his English way of thinking. These and many other madcap antics kept our shearing team and indeed many shearing teams entertained and thinking up other hare-brained schemes to catch out the unwary and the gullible; just for a laugh, mind you, there was never any malice.

Just before each break, the cook would come across to the shed with enough food to feed an army. A 20-litre urn of hot black tea, a huge tin of sugar, a couple of litres of milk, a huge tray of sandwiches, a baking tray full of hot, greasy, freshly cooked chops, a whole fruit cake, little cup cakes and some warmed-up, breakfast leftovers. He would lay it all out on a couple of bales in the wool room and then stand well back out of the way.

All would help themselves generously and drift back out to the board and yarn or joke away as they enjoyed the handiwork of the most important man in the shearing team, the cook. After eating their fill, some might stretch out on the board and have a quick snooze before hearing the chug, ... chug, ... chug, ... chug, ... chug, ... chug, ... chug, chug, chug,chug chugchugchug of the Lister engine being started again to commence the next run, followed by the heavy starting handle being dropped noisily on the engine room floor.

"Alright, back to work you greasy bastards!!" Shearers were quite often referred to as greasy bastards because of all the lanolin on their singlets and dungarees from out of the sheep's wool. Two, sometimes three, rouseabouts picking the fleeces up and throwing them on the classing table as well as sweeping the board and keeping it free of bellies, dags and pieces. On the wool table, you had the wool classer whose only job was to class the fleece for quality.

The skirting of dags, skin pieces, any oddities and rolling the fleece over for the inspection of the classer is the duty of the wool roller. Once the classer has assessed what line of wool he considers the fleece to be he throws it into the correct wool bin behind the table. It is then the presser's duty to load the fleeces into the wool press taking the utmost care to keep the different lines of wool separate.

As each 200 kilogram bale of wool comes out of the press it is the pressers duty to brand each bale accurately with the bale number, the wool line type and the registered station stencil. Then along with the weight of the bale he recorded all the branding information in the Bale Tally Book. The expert who was usually the contractor was a jack-of-all-trades around the shed, helping the penner upperer keep the catching pens full of woolly sheep, counting out shorn sheep and grinding (keeping sharp) the combs and cutters for all the shearers. He was keeping an eye on everything and doing jobs before there was an issue with the flow of work.

Then there was the cook or the 'bait layer' as he would sometimes be called but who was often considered to be the most important member of the shearing team; a good cook ensured a happy team. He started his day at 4 AM, and on a wood fired double oven stove, was busy all day long cooking three meals and preparing two smokos for 14 men.

The shearers were not frightened to speak up if they were not happy with the quantity and quality of the 'tucker'. The Elton domestic pigs, of which there were usually three, were always very happy when we were shearing. It meant two x 20 litre buckets of food scraps every day for three or four weeks and it put them in prime condition for slaughter towards the end of the year for Christmas hams.

The station workforce was also kept very busy during all of this. Once the expert had let the shorn sheep out at the end of each 'run', the station team had to spray all the shorn sheep for lice control and then 'tar brand' each animal for fast visual identification. Usually after lunch we also had to muster enough sheep from the nearby holding paddock for the next day's shearing. They were then drafted to take off any strangers and to ensure that there were no ewes in with the wethers (if we were shearing wethers) or vice versa. The run tally was the bottom line for the shearers, and speed was essential to try to be the 'gun' shearer. Because the shearers were shearing as fast as they could, it was important to have the sheep carefully drafted for sex so that the wethers did not lose their pizzles and the ewes did not lose teats due to an accidental wrong blow from the shearer's handpiece.

During the drafting process, there were other things to be on the lookout for as well that had to be drafted to one side. Even though we had good boundary fences, you had to keep an eye out for 'strangers' from neighbouring properties. There were also 'cancers' to be drafted off for later attention. The shearers would not shear any cancer-affected sheep, no matter how small the cancer.

Even if they had begun shearing the animal and then noticed the cancer, they would then immediately cease shearing that animal. So as we drafted, the 'cancers' were all drafted off. Some, usually only about 20-odd out of our complete flock, were afflicted with eye, nose, jaw and sometimes anal cancers. These were usually fairly advanced and unsightly wounds, often fly-blown and one could not blame the shearers for not wanting to handle these sheep.

These ones we would shear ourselves after the shearing was over, with the aid of a tube of material of some sort pulled over the head of the sheep so the wound would not come in contact with you while shearing. Afterwards, we would put these sheep out of their misery with a bullet. Most of this draft, perhaps 40 or so, were only suffering from a cancer on the ear, which could also be fairly gross to see or smell. However, if we could get a set of Burdizzo Castration pliers over the ear, we could then remove the cancerous appendage with a knife. The Burdizzo Pliers clamped all the veins shut so that when you cut off the end of the ear and removed the pliers, there would be no bleeding, and these sheep would quite happily be shorn by the shearers.

Another abnormality we had to look out for was black wool in the fleece. Sometimes it was an obvious single large patch of black wool in the fleece or a pie-bald sheep, or perhaps blackening in the kemp or even a patch of black wool in the fleece as small as a 50-cent piece. Whilst talking about black spots, it reminds me again of the constant battle that Mick Hazel had with the shearers in the area of humour. One day, Mick was hurrying up the board to attend to something. As he passed by Neville Carter (his main antagonist), Neville yelled out, "Black spot on that sheep in the pen, Mick".

Mick, who was already in a hurry to do something else, rushed into the pen and caught the sheep with the identifying forelock and cheek wool removed. After thoroughly examining it, "Well, I can't see it, Neville". "Have another look then, I saw it there only a minute ago". This happened three times until Neville finally said, "Well, lift his tail up and have a look under there!", whereupon the shearers on the board, who were all waiting for the punchline, burst into laughter. Mick, who should have been awake as to what was going on as soon as Neville opened his mouth, again blew up at having been taken down, once more, by these infernal bloody shearers.

Getting back to the story, however, once drafted, they were then put under cover in case of a shower of rain or an overnight dew, as the shearers did not like shearing wet sheep and had a union rule to cover it. At 'Elton Downs' we had a huge undercover capacity, we had the pens in the shed itself (about a run's worth), there was also a huge lean-to as well as underneath the wool room and classing area in which we could hold about 1,600 sheep, more than a day's shearing for a six-man team. There was also always plenty of watering to be done to keep the dust down in the yards. The less dust content in the wool, the better quality of the product you have.

After the last run for the day was out of the 'let go pens', we quickly tar-branded and treated for lice, then turned out the day's shearing into the shorn sheep holding paddock. While we did that, usually one of the rouseabouts killed a wether for the shearers' meat supply for the next day. A fourteen-man shearing team could eat a whole sheep each day. After we had turned out the day's shorn sheep, we checked in at the shearers' quarters to make sure that everything was in order and all the team were happy, collected the two by twenty litre buckets of kitchen scraps for the pigs, then we could head for home to repeat the process again on the morrow.

This was a normal day, but amongst the normal days, sometimes, when you had a shed full of wool bales, a Reilly's Transport road train might turn up to clear the shed. Time out from the usual duties to load the wool truck, which could easily take a half day. Depending on how things flowed, if you had a cut out in one of the mobs of sheep, you might have to go and bring in the weaners or the wethers or whatever was the next line of sheep to continue on with. We always employed a couple of extra men in the lead up to, the duration of and the tailing off of the shearing.

With wool being our primary source of income, it was sheep work that took up most of our time at 'Elton Downs'; however, we were always busy as there was never any shortage of things to do on a station. After the wet season and before the stock work began, it was an annual and constant battle with two plant pests. Noogoora Burr and Bathurst Burr were both introduced pests whose seeds attached themselves to the fleeces as sheep walked through them. If the plants got thick enough, the seeds on the fleeces would be like a black armour plating. As well as detracting from the value of your wool clip, it was also viewed, and understandably so, in a less-than-favourable light by the shearers.

It was a very time-consuming job, beginning straight after the wet season, and the severity of the growth varied from year to year, but it could keep two men busy seven days per week for at least a month. It usually grew thickest around the dams where the sheep camped each day, but it could also proliferate on the creeks and gullies, so every single creek and gully had to be followed up, no matter how rough it was or how long it took. If you missed a few burr plants (and there were always a few missed) and they went to seed there would be a thicket of burr there the following year. Even though we were always very thorough with spraying the burr, for some unexplained reason, some years it just seemed to explode in comparison to the previous year.

Another introduced pest was the Algaroba tree, or Prickly Acacia, from the Mesquite Tree family, which originated in Mexico. It arrived in Australia sometime in the early 1900s as an ornamental plant and shade tree in a lot of the mining towns. For 50-odd years it remained relatively dormant and then in the 1950s, after some fairly heavy wet seasons, it seemed to literally explode; today it covers hundreds of thousands of hectares all over Australia. In lots of places it is totally impenetrable for mustering purposes. It is very good foraging for any animal that can reach the leaves and seeds. The problem however is that normally only cattle can reach the leaves and seeds, and when they eat them the seeds pass straight through them unchewed and undigested. You then have a seed in a nice warm, moist pile of fertiliser ready to germinate and begin growing even in the driest of conditions.

Consequently the Prickly Acacia gets thicker and thicker, initially around the watering points, but eventually covering entire paddocks. In time it gets so thick you cannot ride through it on a horse or motorbike. As it gets thicker the natural Flinders and Mitchell grasses and herbage which themselves are very good fodder are unable to grow underneath thickets of Prickly Acacia. In every vehicle we always carried a small spray pack of poison to control isolated Prickly Acacia plants that we found in our travels, so we did not have a problem with it. If you saw a Prickly Acacia plant you could spray it right then and there and not have to worry about remembering where it was or come back to it later. We showed no mercy; we sprayed even the smallest of them.

A fully loaded silt scoop coming out of the dam. The scoop gets pulled as far as the outer edge of the bank where it empties and the muck runs down the outside of the dam

A subcontract lorry for Nev Reilly loading wool at Elton in the late 1980s

A yardful of woolies_ in the Elton shearing shed yards. James Halloran in the centre of the yard pushing up for drafting

Air Show at Longreach in 1988 in conjunction with the opening of The Stockmans Hall of Fame

Dad being given a haircut by the Hairy Barber at Elton in the mid 1980s

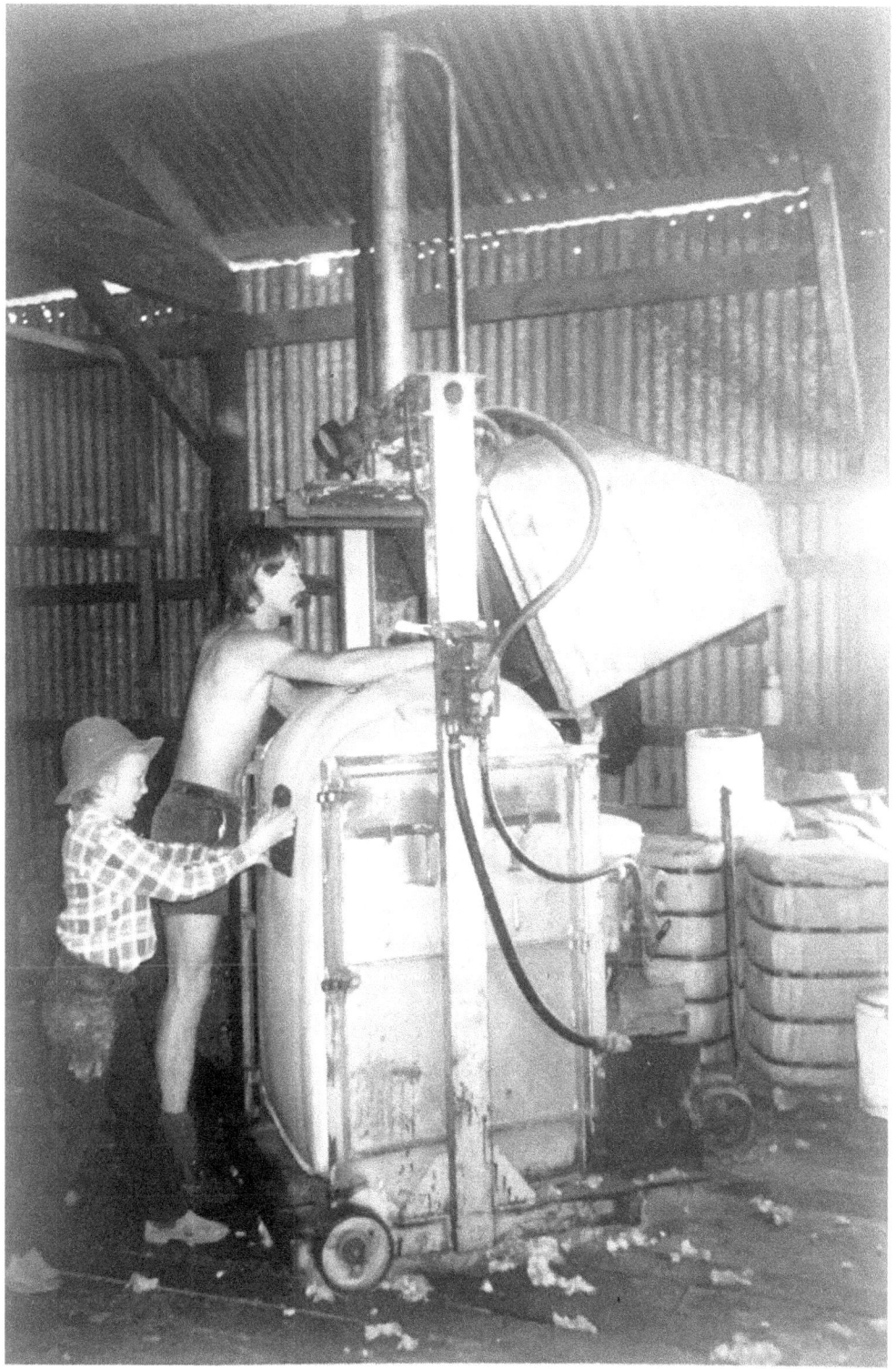

Dan offsiding for the presser with some stencilling

Jimmy McMillan with his team on the board at Elton Downs about 1990

Joe and Dan on the 4 wheeler in 1988

Joe in the leanto squirting some water about to lay the dust

Joe, Kerri (governess) and Dan. Elton woolshed in 1986

Joseph and Daniel at Elton in 1990

On the then controversial Daintree Road between Mossman and Cooktown in 1988

Myself getting ready to run sheep in under cover in the leanto for the next days shearing

The Big Orange at Gayndah, returning from Expo 88

10

NEVER GETTING BORED IN THE BUSH

Most of Dad's dams were put down from the mid-1950s through to the mid-1960s, so they were becoming very silted up. The silting up of a dam is caused by two things. Around the dam for a few hundred metres is all bare dirt, and especially the banks of the dam. During the wet season, there may be a covering of perennial weeds, but later in the year, with a couple of thousand sheep visiting the water each day, it is soon reduced to bare dirt. Then, on windy days, of which there are plenty, a lot of dust is blown over the water, which then settles to the bottom. Year after year, this creates quite a sizable silt bed at the bottom of the dam.

Added to that is when the sheep or cattle come in to have a drink of water. To drink, they actually have to walk into the water a little with their front legs, so every time they drink, they are pushing the banks of the dam into the dam ahead of them, year after year. After 20 to 25 years, you can have five metres of silt in a dam that was originally eight to ten metres deep. The silting problem eventually gets to the stage where all you have is mud. The issue was that it was usually just before the next wet season, and the silt doesn't get to dry out to the stage where you can put a tractor into it to clean the mud out. Between evaporation, soakage, and what is drunk by the stock, a general ready reckoner is that a dam will drop its level by about 30 cm per month. If you have only 3 or 4 metres of water in the dam at the start of the year, you will be in trouble with very little to no water at the end of the year.

One way of rectifying the problem is to do what is known as silt scooping. A silt scoop is an open-mouthed device constructed of heavy sheet steel with no floor. It can be any size you want, but usually they are about two to three metres square. It has two sides and a curved back, all of which is, from bottom to top, approximately waist height. The open-mouthed front is kept apart with strong steel bracing to prevent it from being pulled inwards and out of shape when being pulled out of the dam full of mud. The curved back is made from very heavy steel and has a cutting edge attached to the bottom. Silt scooping can be done as we did it with a single silt scoop, but it simply takes you twice as long to complete the job.

Usually, you have two scoops facing in opposite directions and working in tandem so that when one scoop is on the outer edge of the dam bank and emptying, the other has been pulled in and should be in the muck somewhere near the centre of the dam. The scoops have an arm that is also made out of very heavy steel and is about three metres long. It has about a 45-degree bend in it close to the bottom and pivots from the bottom of the curved back of the scoop.

When the other tractor begins pulling the second scoop out of the dam and the empty one back in, the pull is through this arm. The bend in the arm actually lifts the scoop about 30 cm to 45 cm off the ground, releasing the suction and thereby leaving all the mud behind to run down the outside of the bank. After about a week of long days working at this boring, see-sawing process, you will have a pile of foul-smelling, blue/black mud outside the banks of the dam and the inside of the dam ready for another 20 years of service.

Dad found a much quicker and way more exciting method of removing mud from a dam with the use of about one ton of Nitropril fertiliser. When mixed with diesel, the resultant material is very explosive and then called ANFO. Then the reconstituted, value-added, re-bagged mixture was lowered down the shaft that had been dug into the silt in the bottom of the dam, ready for detonation. To be able to dig the shaft, however, the dam had to have dried out much more than a dam that you were silt scooping. An old friend of his, Alec Crowley, who had originally done some contract dam sinking on Elton in the early sixties and then later worked for Mount Isa Mines, acquired some knowledge about mixing and using ANFO explosives, and he, in turn, then imparted this knowledge to Dad.

"The Old Dam" had been dry for a couple of years when Dad decided to clean out about an estimated 15 feet of silt. Digging the shaft was easy because the silt had well and truly dried out. We were just guessing the amount of ANFO that was required to blow this amount of silt out and put in seven or eight 25kg bags of Prilled Ammonium Nitrate that had been mixed with the required amount of diesel in a hand-operated cement mixer. First, we burnt a measured length of cordite fuse to check the burning rate.

Then we attached a carefully measured length of slow-burning cordite fuse to a piece of gelignite and planted this amongst the bags of ANFO in the bottom of the hole, then carefully backfilled the hole with huge clods of solidified mud that we had dug out of the hole. We then selected a site to observe the resultant explosion which was about 300 metres away, and parked all of our vehicles there. Dad's brother Graham had come over to help as this was a shared watering point, and he was in his new five-tonne Hino truck.

My brother Byrne went in on the 'getaway vehicle', the station bike, lit the fuse and then returned to the spectators at a fair rate of knots. The working party, other family members and a few local sightseers that gathered for the occasion all witnessed the explosion right on time as planned but it soon became very obvious that we were going to be far too close to ground zero. Huge clods of dried mud, dust and plant matter just kept going up and up and up and up. When you are witnessing something a couple of hundred of metres high and moving, from such a close vantage point, it all seems to happen in slow motion.

Then there was an explosion amongst the spectators nearly as large as the explosion we had just witnessed from inside the dam, all looking for somewhere safer to be. The only safe place here was to be under a vehicle and that is where people were going. A few of us dived under the rear overhang of the tray of Uncle Graham's new truck. Unaware that we were under the back of it, Uncle Graham, however, had other plans for his brand-new truck. Unbeknownst to us, he climbed into the cab, putting it in gear and hitting the ignition at the same time. He was gone almost instantaneously, leaving us out in the open again.

Around this time, it was that head-sized clods of half-dried-out mud started hitting the ground around us with great big 'splats' like oversized raindrops, so we started making other arrangements for safety, diving for cover under any other car nearby that had a bit of available space beneath it. When the 'oversized black raindrops' finally stopped descending, we all gingerly crawled out from beneath our protection and breathed a sigh of relief. When we all gathered our wits together, we had a good laugh at the comedic scene that had just occurred, which could have been so much more serious. It was then time to venture into the dam and see the results at our "Alamogordo". There was a significant crater in the solidified silt in the bottom of the dam, but nowhere near enough material had been blown out, so obviously much more ANFO was going to be needed in future operations.

As well as the humorous incident at our observation site there was another comedy show that occurred inside the dam itself. The current floor of the dam, because it had been dry for two years, had a multitude of cracks all over the surface about a foot wide and two feet deep and had weeds and vines growing in and over them. As we crested the bank of the dam for the first time after the explosion, it was to see a fox very groggily making his way over the opposite bank. He must have had a very cool, comfortable and secure den in amongst the cracks somewhere. I am surprised he stayed there with all the noise and commotion that was going on while we were at work digging the hole. I don't know if he survived, but he certainly had a very concussed appearance about him on his very wobbly departure.

If left for a couple of months after "blowing" a dam, it was then dried out enough to safely put a tractor into it to scoop out the rest of the accumulated silt without bogging the tractor. The next year, we "blew" another dam at Elton with much better results than the first. Dad was never one to do things by half measures. He increased the number of bags of ANFO straight from eight to 40, increased the length of cordite fuse adequately and made the observation post about a kilometre from the dam.

We had absolutely excellent results this time around. We had some visitors coming by plane from another property some distance away that wanted to watch but were late arriving; however, they did get to see it as they flew over Stamford, about five miles away. The pilot's estimate of the explosion's height was about 250 metres. Dad enjoyed his notoriety as the explosives expert of the district and did a few dams for other people around the district as well as a few more dams on Elton before he became ill.

Dad and two of his brothers, Graham on "Nottingham" and Frank on "Bernborough", both similar-sized neighbouring properties, had bought a Caterpillar D6 brand new in 1957, together with a hydraulic six-yard scoop and a single tyne ripper. In the early 1950s, the three properties were mainly dependent on sparsely located mills for stock water. There had been the odd small dam that had been put down with antiquated horse-drawn scoops years earlier. The idea of the tractor was to increase the number of decent-sized watering points on the properties as well as doing fire breaks. So, taking into account the wet season of roughly three months duration, each of the three properties had the use of the tractor for about three months, with fire ploughing taking first priority.

In that time, they each did their fire ploughing and in the early years put down one dam of about 20,000 to 25,000 cubic metres capacity, which is an excavation that would hold about nine to ten metres of water. Because they were always fairly busy with stock work and other things a contract driver was usually sitting on the D6, and he would have a caravan for accommodation and a Blitz truck with a bulk water tank, as well as drums of diesel, grease and oils for the tractor. Dad would take fresh meat and supplies out for him every few days. The driver, usually Alec Crowley, would work on his own from when he could see until when he couldn't see for seven days a week, and it would take him about a month to complete a dam of that size.

On our property, as well as 14 dams, we also had four sub-artesian bores for stock water. An artesian bore flows out of the ground under pressure, but a sub-artesian bore does not have the pressure to exit the surface, and the water level in the borehole can be anywhere from 15 metres to 150 metres below ground level. If you have sub-artesian water, you need to have windmills to lift the water to the surface. Windmills needed to be checked and oiled once a month, keeping an eye open for loose bolts on the tower or windmill head or any other untoward irregularity. If the mill was not pumping, the first thing that you did was pull the timber rods to see if a broken rod was the problem. Pulling the rods was a relatively easy and quick job, and with a really early start, you might have it repaired in one day if you put in a long day.

If there were no broken rods, it would be a problem with either the steel casing or the brass pump on the bottom of the casing. You could be there for three or four days, depending on what the problem turned out to be. Usually, it was worn leather buckets in the pump; sometimes, a hole was worn in the steel casing from where a rod coupling had worn through from the constant up and down movement of the rods. It was dirty, dangerous work, and you had to be methodical and know what you were doing. Mill towers are invariably covered in oil leaking from the workings on the mill head over many years, then having a liberal coating of dust and bird droppings mixed in for texture — the overall combination made for a very filthy, greasy and slippery workplace.

Using steel ropes together with double and triple pulley blocks, the column of very heavy six metre lengths of 100mm steel casing (as well as being full of water) would be lifted until the screwed joint was above the level of the 200mm outer casing and then clamped. Each length was then unscrewed from the column of casing and then lowered to a horizontal position on the ground whilst manhandling it clear of the mill tower. All very hard work, and then what you have to look forward to when the problem is rectified is the reverse process of putting it all back down the borehole again. You couldn't ever be too careful on this work because over the years, plenty of men have been badly injured or killed working on windmills or pulling bores, usually from either inexperience or carelessness. However, sometimes men died who should have known better than to do what they were doing. Shortcuts can kill.

We used to use 8,100 hectares of our property for a ready cash income and agisted that country for cattle grazing. This was done generally on a short-term basis, so if the wet season failed or the season turned on us with some light winter rain, we could end the agreement quickly and have more acres on which to spread our own stock out on. We sometimes agisted for cows and calves, but mostly to fatten steers, and we quite often had up to six different owners present. However, when we mustered the cattle, it was all hands on deck with the owners of the cattle attending the muster for three or four days as well. There were many reasons for having a cattle muster; perhaps the fat or store market was really good, and the owners of the cattle decided that if they waited any longer, they might miss out on the good prices.

Sometimes it could be a failed season, either a missed wet season or perhaps there had been a fall of insufficient unseasonal winter rain which could turn the feed from good yellow feed to black and totally lacking in nutrition in the matter of a week. The trick was to know how long to hang on for before you decided to sell and get your cattle to market while the prices were still good. Once everyone decides to sell, the market becomes flooded and the prices collapse. So it was a busy few days with lots of drafting of various mobs of cattle and then the loading of road trains headed for the cattle markets, after which the remaining cattle would be returned to their paddocks.

I will just elaborate here on what I touched on at the start of this chapter. I have noticed over the years that a lot of city folk who don't have rural connections or experience often have a preconceived and biased notion that property owners, whether they are farmers or graziers, are rich and privileged. In the case of company-owned properties, perhaps the owners, if city-based investors, are, but I can assure you the managers and on-the-ground staff on their properties all put in long, hard days, quite often; working "above and beyond" would be the best description.

When working stock, it is usually to a yard, and if things go a little awry and you are not travelling to schedule at 5 pm, you have to continue on as you cannot simply let the stock go mid-journey. The same applies if you have water problems, and regardless of whether you are working with mills or pumps, despite unforeseen problems, the job has to be finished as the stock needs water or they will perish, so you have to ignore both the clock and the sun and push on to completion.

You will often hear the comment, "Oh, look at all those rich cockies, all driving around in big flash 4WD drive Toyotas"; what most don't realise is a number of things. A lot of station people live at least 100 kilometres from their closest major centre, sometimes 200, 300 or even 400 kilometres away. Quite often accessed on dirt roads where a high clearance vehicle is a necessity, not an optional extra and sometimes if it rains, they will need 4WD to get home. Perhaps like a lot of their city brethren, they won't actually own the vehicle.

If their property operates on an overdraft system of credit, they may have bought it by accessing that credit, or it may be on hire purchase, just like a lot of city folk. A property owner in most cases is just like a city business owner or even a nine to five worker, it is just on a different level. It is a delicate balancing act between incomings and outgoings, and whether it is a business ledger book or a household budget each has to be looked after very carefully.

To those that have not lived or worked on properties in the bush, and without wishing to berate or belittle anyone, I hope the contents of the previous couple of chapters have explained a little to the uninitiated that there is a lot more to the daily lives of rural and outback people than perhaps first meets the eye, or what you may have been told. I write from experience. Been there, done that.

Boof McDowall at his reserved spot at the Stamford Races in the mid 1980s

Boys and I at the Brisbane Expo 1988 with our mates from the bush

Byrne doing bearing repairs to the scoop at Wokingham Dam in 1981

Corbett Tritton building the Lane Paddock Dam in 1982

Damion and Lou with Greta in Brisbane in 1989

David Bielenbergs truck unloading a mob of sheep in the Elton shearing shed yards

Daniel Terry Abergowrie College 1991

Digging the shaft down into the solidified silt to lay the anfo in. Barry Boots working at Elton at the time is the face peering out

Ever since a certain movie in 1969 I had wanted one of these. Finally in 1988 it happened, a 1982 Low Rider

Joe and Dan at Blencoe Falls in 1991

Joe, Dan and I flew over the Bungle Bungle Range in W.A. in 1988

Joseph Terry Abergowrie College 1992

Justin and I pulling the rods on the Elton No. 2 mill

Myself, Joe, Jim Glasgow, Ted Gordon and Dan on top. Yellowbelly fishing in Vergemont Creek bound, 1990

The betting ring at the Stamford Races. Jack Close just visible behind the two people conversing in the centre

The boys at the Cooktown lighthouse in 1988

The Terrys and one Brown at Max Wallaces Royal Hotel, Hughenden, New Year s Eve 1987. The night he got too cross threaded to handle the going and left us in charge. Just lock the doors when you leave , he said

11

THE ELLENBRAE EXPERIENCE

In 1983 the family bought another property in Western Australia, in the East Kimberleys on the Gibb River Road, a fairly rugged and remote location compared to where we were in Queensland. We had bought it from a chap by the name of Lorin Bishop who went on to become a rural sales specialist with Elders Rural. He was based in Charters Towers but sold properties all over north west Queensland for the last 25 years. Lorin passed away in 2024 in his hometown of Perth, Western Australia.

My two younger unmarried brothers, Byrne and Edward, went to Western Australia to run this station while I was staying to help Dad run the home property. We bought Ellenbrae Station late in 1983. My two brothers had only just started mustering in early 1984 when Dad was diagnosed with cancer; he was operated on immediately. Dad had always lived life to the fullest, was a solid drinker and smoker all his life and enjoyed a party. In fact, he was the life of the party, always with a twinkle in his eye, a very dry sense of humour and a lightning quick wit.

It was to be a tough 4 years for Dad, before he finally succumbed to the dreaded BIG C. It was at this stage that I stepped into the role of managing Elton for the family because Dad, as much as he wanted to, didn't ever work again at full capacity. For about 6 months he did some vehicle maintenance and repair work in the workshop, but between weakness, exhaustion and pain, eventually even that was too much of an effort for him. He found it extremely frustrating to be hobbled in this fashion, unable to be involved and get out and about on the property participating.

Dad had a number of trips away to the Townsville General Hospital, which he humorously called the 'Palace Of Pain', for operations; but the cancer continued to spread, and in the end there was nothing they could do for him apart from prescribing pain relief in the form of morphine. The problems of running two operations on opposite sides of the continent, with one of them experiencing huge teething problems, combined with its lack of plant and remote situation, caused Dad a lot of needless stress and worry, as he fought the battle that couldn't be won.

It also created some serious problems with the working relationships of other family members over the ensuing years. Hindsight is always a fabulous and valuable commodity when assessing a situation after the fact, but unfortunately, as everyone knows, it is not available before the event. When Dad was initially inspecting Ellenbrae in the latter half of 1983 he was unwell but still unaware of the disease he carried. He was also drinking too much and being influenced by a half-brother, Alec, who due to his past bad track record should never have been admitted to the partnership.

Dad's judgement was clouded, and because Alec had more or less sourced the property, Dad felt obligated. So we ended up with him anyway, thereby creating a lot of friction in the day-to-day operations at Ellenbrae. Some very bad decisions were made in the early days of operations at Ellenbrae. Eventually we had to sideline him out of the partnership by requesting an input of additional operating capital (which was needed) but we knew he could not provide, and so it was goodbye Uncle Alec.

Dad was also probably reliving his youth and focusing on when he and his two brothers, Bernard and Graham, aged respectively 15, 17 and 19 at the time, spent 10 years mustering wild cattle on Westmorelands with horse teams and Aboriginal stockmen, which had been a very successful venture. Times, practices and economies had changed a great deal in the 40-odd years since they had worked Westmorelands. We got together a plant of 30-odd horses that I had helped break in at Elton expressly for mustering Ellenbrae for the first couple of years.

The numbers of cattle on the ground and the area of country that had to be mustered did not make horseback mustering a financially sound proposition. The Ellenbrae pasture was nutritionally very poor, so to get any use out of the horses they had to be kept in feed a lot of the time. Added to that, a poisonous plant called Walkabout Weed was prevalent on Ellenbrae and we lost a lot of our horses to it over the first few years. It was not long before we followed everyone else's practice of using helicopters and portable yards, much to Dad's displeasure. Old work practices and habits die hard.

Ellenbrae Station had a homestead that was only a few kilometres inside the southern boundary, with a very basic set of cattle yards and a basic airstrip close by. Everything at Ellenbrae was basic, including the homestead structure. It was basically just a roof on posts, there were no walls apart from a store room in the centre, and its walls were made from gauze to protect the stores from predatory animals.

The floors were made out of local flagstones that had a concrete slurry poured between them. The house water supply was from a waterhole in Campbell Creek that flowed in the wet season right beside the house. Early in the year when the waterhole was full, it was good water, but it was borderline drinkable water because in a dry year the water level would get extremely low and that was when it did not taste the best.

Ellenbrae was a learning experience for everybody as far as mustering, handling and freighting the cattle was concerned. They were an extremely wily lot of low quality animals, spread out over about one million acres of fairly inaccessible country. For the transportation of any bulls to meatworks or weaner steers back to Queensland to grow out, everything focused on the homestead cattle yards. For the purposes of loading out cattle the homestead cattle yards were as far as any road train could access.

North of the Ellenbrae homestead the landscape was devoid of roads and fences; what wasn't rocky escarpments and hills was a panorama of loose sandy flats with untold numbers of sandy or boggy water soaks scattered about indiscriminately, which made it impossible to use trap yards as a tool to control the herd. To capture the cattle you had to actually muster them into yards and then cart them back to the cattle yards at the homestead.

The 1985 wet season was their second wet season at Ellenbrae when they had an incredibly heavy deluge of rain in the catchment of Campbell Creek, upstream from where the homestead complex was. During the night the creek burst its banks and water was chest deep through the homestead and sheds, causing the boys to climb up into the rafters of the house for the remainder of the night. Anything that was not heavy and solid or fastened into the ground was washed or floated away. All the fuel drums (a full 44 gal drum of fuel can float if there is enough water) floated down the creek, everything in the house was washed away, vehicles were flooded, all the tools and equipment in the shed went underwater. It was complete devastation that took a considerable amount of time to rectify.

There were no roads, and the mustering was all done with bull buggies, helicopters and a couple of motorbikes, into portable steel yards which could be moved from location to location as the mustering proceeded. Byrne and Edward bought a six wheel drive Federal truck (ex-US Army, World War 2 vintage) from Brisbane, which, combined with a dog trailer, was used to cart the portable panels, a load of hay and camp equipment on.

After the muster it was used to cart the captured cattle back to the house yards. Difficulties abounded during the course of the musters, with mechanical breakdowns, many flat tyres from stakes and boggings in the difficult, sandy terrain, together with the occasional total failure of a muster. A failed muster could happen for any number of reasons. The cattle were totally wild and feral and they made a considerable effort to remain that way.

Portable yards are made up of interlocking portable steel panels that would be anchored to some suitably located trees that were sufficiently strong enough to hold some four or five hundred head of wild cattle. Getting the cattle together and moving down a creek as a mob was the reasonably easy part of the operation. However, getting the cattle into the yards was where the challenge lay; it all became a game of total bluff.

The yards were always built on a creekside flat, preferably in a clump of trees that would partially conceal the yards from view prior to yarding, as well as providing some shade while you were working the cattle over the next couple of days. Also, building the yards beside a creek enabled you to pump water from the creek to the yards to cool the cattle and lay dust as it could get incredibly hot in the yards.

Going out from the cattle yard gates like a huge funnel you built two wings to steer the cattle towards and into the yards. Each of these wings would extend about 300 or 400 metres out and they would be built from nothing more than a single barb wire that was anchored to convenient trees as well as six foot high 'steelies'. From this barb wire you suspended two metre wide hessian bagging that created for all intents and purposes a visually solid barrier for the cattle.

If the cattle couldn't see through it, they believed it to be a solid obstacle to their progress in that direction. One of the wings stayed completely on the same side of the creek as the yards, the other was built across the nearby creek at a shallow angle in the direction of travel so that as the cattle, that were intentionally put into the creek for ease of travel, would see the hession and follow it up out of the creek and usually follow it along and straight into the yards.

However, the best laid plans of mice and men can sometimes go awfully wrong. With the hessian adhering to the barbs along with the occasional tie to secure it to the barb, as well as some ties tethering it at a downwards angle, it could be an extremely precarious and unreliable structure. If you had some boisterous and unruly bulls in the mob or some that had escaped from a previous muster just prior to yarding, they were the biggest danger to a successful yarding.

You only had to have the hessian blow up with a gust of wind or be knocked down by some jostling cattle and they would be gone through the gap like the wind. Or if the mob of cattle were strung out too much, the lead would be in the yard waiting, and if the rest of the mob was only just trickling in, the lead could start coming back out of the yard and that would also spell disaster.

A successful yarding was an art form of the highest order that relied on the helicopter, the bull buggies and the horsemen or bike riders working as a team, with all of them being very observant to spot a problem and rectify it to the best of their ability or circumstances allowed before it became a serious problem. Hand-held radio communication between the team members was essential.

Making headway was all torturously slow and hard work but the norm for that part of the Kimberleys. We bought Ellenbrae in 1983 and as far as I could make out, it had really only been lived on and worked in a half-hearted fashion for 35 years beforehand. The only thing I know about Ellenbrae's history is that the leasehold was purchased by Barney Hughes in 1948. Not much had been done since then. We had to contend with three major problems, being the lack of good roads, the quality of the stock and accessibility to reliable cattle markets.

It was in June of 1987 that a terrifying and brutal string of incidents occurred in the Kimberleys that had the local community and our family very worried about the safety and welfare of Byrne, Eddie and other staff members at Ellenbrae. Initially an elderly man and his son were found shot dead at Victoria River Crossing in the Northern Territory, with no clues as to who the killer was.

About one week later three more people were found shot dead at the Pentecost River crossing on the Gibb River Road. From evidence found at both murder sites police now concluded that the murderer was the same person but they had no clue as to this person's whereabouts. However there were extremely serious concerns for the safety of all persons on any station along the length of the Gibb River Road.

There was no phone service at Ellenbrae and the authorities had been trying to contact the station unsuccessfully by two-way radio. A private helicopter had done an aerial reconnaissance of the homestead and saw no sign of people or any movement but did not want to risk landing for fear of their own lives. Unbeknownst to the authorities the entire Ellenbrae contingent were all blissfully unaware and busy conducting a mustering operation.

They were some 40 kilometres to the north of the homestead and were unaware that the authorities had previously been trying to contact them. It was with great relief a couple of days later that we were notified that everyone on Ellenbrae was safe and the danger was over. The shooter had been a German tourist who was shot dead after a shootout with police at Halls Creek, a couple of hundred kilometres to the south a few days after the Pentecost River victims had been discovered.

It was only a few months after this terrifying incident, and on Remembrance Day later that same year, that Dad passed away after his long battle with cancer. He was not old, just 66 years of age, but he had packed a lot into those 66 years. A large and loving family, an adventurous younger life, a lot of travelling, a well improved property and a respected and liked man in his community. Oh, and many fishing tales. Mum was very stoic at his passing but she missed him immensely.

She was fortunate in having a large family, many friends and relations, as well as having a deep rooted faith in her Catholicism. Dad, like his father before him, wanted to be buried in the bush, on his property and a few years before had already picked out his spot about one kilometre distant to the west, on the ridge overlooking the house. Every evening until we sold Elton about 10 years later, Mum would walk up the ridge and spend time with her men.

It was that same year, after four years of sailing into a head wind at Ellenbrae, that Edward decided that he had had enough of the tough, semi-pioneering lifestyle of the Kimberleys, and removed himself to Brisbane to take flying lessons on the Sunshine Coast to further his dreams of becoming a pilot. Whilst taking flying lessons he worked at Expo '88 in the area of security, for the duration of the event's life.

He returned to the Kimberleys as a pilot for a brief period, working for Kerry Slingsby, flying tourists around the area to get his hours up. It was then back to Queensland, where Edward bought an aircraft of his own. He did charter work around North Queensland between Cairns and Torres Strait for a couple of years, before making his way to New Guinea to work for a company called Milne Bay Air.

Byrne remained at Ellenbrae trying to make it a viable operation and building up the numbers and quality of the cattle, but it was tough going with the aforementioned problems. The added concerns of repeated and deliberately lit fires over a number of years in the early 1990s negated his efforts to build and improve the herd.

Byrne was always a resourceful operator with something up his sleeve at all times. So he and his partner Anne turned to the tourism industry in an effort to keep their noses above the waterline. Byrne and Anne were both very creative individuals and turned their hands to providing a very unique style of accomodation together with meals. They also crafted many gift items, also in the unique category that they sold in their gift shop that had been built out of an old cattle crate.

They sold fuel to tourists that had underestimated their requirements on the Gibb River Road. Byrne also charged for his skills as a very practical bush mechanic, getting many a mechanically stranded tourist back on the road with impromptu and slightly unorthodox solutions, often using duct tape, No. 8 fencing wire or the welder. This was not as a permanent repair but simply as a means of getting them to civilisation, where more orthodox repairs could be had. Byrne built a number of detached bedrooms from local stone near the homestead.

Their guests used the famous Boab Tree Bathroom and dined with them and often with other assorted and unique "Kimberly Travellers" in the homestead. Unfortunately the Boab tree collapsed in 2017, possibly due to its root system being continually and unnaturally moist for such a prolonged period of 35 years; consequently the most talked about bathroom in Australia could no longer be used. There was also another alternatively constructed stone building about a kilometre from the homestead that had showers, toilets and cooking facilities, that was used as a community area for people that just wanted to camp on a budget.

In 1992, Byrne had married his partner Anne Thornton in a wedding ceremony at Ellenbrae. There were guests attending from all points of the compass around Australia to celebrate this tying of the knot. It was indeed quite an event, with most guests attending for a few days prior, helping to prepare and organise for the nuptuals and enjoying the company of new-found friends.

Similarly for a few days after as well, helping to tidy up and enjoying the terrific Kimberley atmosphere along with Byrne and Anne's hospitality. There were many campfires, beers, stories told and friendships made in the Kimberley bush around the Ellenbrae homestead over those few days. To cap the trip off, Mum and I had a very interesting journey home via The Tanami Track to Alice Springs then via the Plenty Highway to Boulia, Winton and then home.

We had leased Elton to a cousin after the wool market had collapsed in 1991 and I was just doing casual work and contracting around the district. Byrne and Anne had been doing it tough with a myriad of problems so I elected to go over and give them a hand with their 1995 mustering season. I had heard how tough it was but seeing it on the ground was when it really sunk in. It seemed to be one thing after another that happened to prevent a start to the mustering.

That year was a prolonged wet season which prevented preliminary pre-mustering work from being completed, which meant that it had to be finished before mustering could start. The holding paddock had fences washed down from the wet season rain and we had to build a new loading ramp at the homestead yards which took about three weeks. The old ramp had finally succumbed to the ravages of termites so the new one had been constructed of local flagstones and steel. Checkmate termites.

When we finally started mustering, we had a couple of successful smaller musters that went reasonably well, eventually getting those cattle back to the homestead yards and trucked away. The next muster was mustering country to the south and bringing them down Campbell Creek to where the homestead was situated, intending to use the homestead yards to muster into. We had a large mob of cattle, and it was all going well until the yarding. Some bulls burst through the hessian wing near the yards; the ensuing chaos resulted in the loss of nearly all the cattle. What we managed to get into the yards only just managed to cover the costs of the chopper and the transports.

We had only just recovered from that disaster and were getting ready to do the next muster when, on July 12 1995, we received the devastating news that Edward had been killed in an aircraft crash in New Guinea while employed by Milne Bay Air. Edward died when his Twin Otter aircraft caught on fire during a regular passenger service at Milne Bay. He perished with one cabin attendant and 13 school children on board whilst trying to return to the airstrip that they had only just left.

It was surmised that an electrical spark caused by his radio communications with the company base had ignited some kerosine fumes from bottles of fuel that were being illegally carried in one of the passenger's luggage. The aircraft crashed on the beach about two kilometres short of the runway. Edward's body was brought back to Elton in a Milne Bay aircraft and he was buried beside his father on a ridge overlooking the Elton homestead.

After an interruption of about three weeks for Edward's funeral arrangements, we got back to the Ellenbrae mustering. We did a couple of musters well north of the homestead and then the deliberately lit fires commenced again. The next couple of weeks were spent pushing fire breaks and burning back to try and save as much country as we could, but in that country you would think you had the fire beaten and a whirlwind would get into a smouldering old log a couple of days later and presto you would have a brand new fire all over again. This was now mid-September, and Joanne (nee Stacey) my wife and I had much earlier planned to do a trip around Australia during her annual holidays from the Richmond Shire Council on our Harley Davidson.

Joanne had ridden our bike over from Richmond to Kununurra, with her parents coming along with her in their car to visit the Kimberleys as well. I had planned to take Joanne and her parents out to Ellenbrae to visit, but tensions by this stage were running fairly high there. So we had a few days around Kununurra, Lake Argyle and the irrigation area before setting off down the West Australian coast towards Perth.

We had five weeks to complete our circumnavigation of Australia before Joanne had to resume her duties back in Richmond. A mechanical misadventure beset us with the bike enroute to Perth, but fortunately did not delay us too much. Embarrassingly, Joanne did have to push start our pride and joy for a couple of days. We eventually had to be physically retrieved by the Harley dealership in Karratha, who rectified the problem and got us back on the road.

After that it was a lot easier for Joanne and we went on and visited Kurunji National Park gorges, Mt Tom Price iron ore mining township and the now-abandoned blue asbestos mine at Wittenoom along the way. Joanne had an Uncle and Aunt that we stayed with and I had an old mate in Perth that we visited. In Kalgoorlie there were more relations of Joanne's that we stayed with. From there it was across the Nullabor through Adelaide and onto Melbourne where we stayed with Joanne's sister and brother-in-law for a few days and did a trip out along the Great Ocean Road.

We then travelled up through outback New South Wales via Dubbo and Tamworth to Brisbane. There we stayed with my sisters and Mum for a few days, before making our way home to Richmond via Blackall, visiting Joanne's other sister and husband on their property. We arrived back in Richmond with two days to spare before Joanne had to return to work. It had been a hectic five week long trip, but we enjoyed immensely seeing the length and breadth on our land-based circumnavigation of The Great Southern Land in all its majestic vastness.

Bull catching at Ellenbrae Station in the mid 1980s. Byrne in the photo with one of the Ellenbrae herd improvers

Byrne and Anne at their wedding with the Terry family. Ellenbrae 1992

Byrne and Edward with a muster helicopter at Ellenbrae. Unknown chopper pilot in the check shirt

Byrne at Terry Taylors place in Townsville in the early 1990s

Ellenbrae homestead in 1995. The famous shower Boab tree on the right

THE ELLENBRAE EXPERIENCE

Byrne setting up the hessian blind on the wing of the portable yards for one of the musters

Family relative Kevin Mewing watering the yards after one of the musters. Watering kept the dust down and cooled the cattle off

Hamptons Transport crossing Campbells Creek near the Ellenbrae house with a load of hamburger meat onboard

Preparing for a muster at Ellenbrae mid 1980s. The Federal 6x6 with a load of portable yard panels and a trailer full of hay

The Ellenbrae kitchen with the Queensland wood burning stove. Was good for cold winter nights

World War 2 Federal chassis and Leader COE cab that Byrne built in the Ellenbrae shed in 1988

You were never without a flat tyre at Ellenbrae

12

MARRIAGE, MINING, MOUNT ISA & MEDICAL ISSUES.

It was in 1992 that I met Joanne at a Hughenden B&S Ball, one that some cite as a fail-safe outback matrimonial institution of the Australian bush. In true B&S fashion it was a juggernaut of a night with most people retiring to their swags just before daylight for a couple of hours of sleep, before resuming play at the showground's 'Recovery Party' for a BBQ breakfast and more drinks for another few hours before finally making their way home.

I was very taken with Joanne and followed up very quickly, visiting her family's property near Richmond the next weekend, and as they say, the rest is history. Love quickly blossomed and over the next 18 months or so I either spent weekends at 'Ranmoor' or Joanne spent weekends at 'Elton Downs'. It was nearly always work-related weekends, with her helping me with my work load at 'Elton Downs' or me helping Joanne's family the Staceys with whatever was happening at 'Ranmoor', but at least we were able to spend our time together.

My two boys Joe and Dan were both attending Abergowrie College in the Herbert Valley near Ingham doing their high school years, so there were some trips away attending school functions. Local race meetings, tennis meetings, B&S balls, as well as a camping trip to Lawn Hill Gorge and the Townsville Amateurs Race Meeting were some of the social functions we attended during our courting days. I proposed and Joanne accepted, with a wedding in Townsville in May of 1994 followed by a honeymoon with a difference to Tasmania on a new Harley Davidson Fat Boy that we had bought.

As Joanne had a permanent job with the Richmond Shire Council, and we had leased 'Elton Downs' to a cousin, we decided the best thing we could do was to live in Richmond. We bought what had originally been the Richmond Post Master's residence, right beside the Post Office and directly across the road from Joanne's workplace. One stipulation in the lease agreement for 'Elton Downs' was that Mum remained living in her house there for the duration of the lease. Joanne and I went down regularly and spent time with Mum whilst also attending Stamford area events.

As it was nearly 20 years since I had completed my plumbing apprenticeship and my licence had expired, to re-enter the workforce I needed to acquire a Gold Card. What was required was employment and study to upgrade to that level, so to that end I was going to work in the plumbing gang of the Richmond Shire Council. So I started working in the Council yards, but the plumbing work didn't come to much. In the ensuing 18 months, I mostly did fabricating and machine maintenance in the workshop and ferried equipment and supplies out to roadworks or other council jobs around the shire.

At the end of 1995, my brother-in-law Stephen Stacey had bought a Caterpillar grader and soil compactor after successfully tendering for some contracts at the developing Century zinc mine near Lawn Hill Station in the Gulf Country. He was looking for an operator for his Caterpillar 825 compactor; as not much was happening with the plumbing work, I decided that I would finish up at the council and go work for him. The rosters were abominable (six weeks on and one week off) but the money was exceptional. We spent about five months at Century Mine until the earthworks there came to an end and Stephen found other contracts, we then moved the machines to Ernest Henry mine near Cloncurry where we spent another five or six months on mine site earthworks and three months on forming and sealing the connecting road to Cloncurry.

It was while we were on the mine site road works that a Mack semi-trailer water truck came up for sale that was already contracted to the job. I found the funds to purchase and we were then working for ourselves as contractors. The truck was an old Flintstone Mack with a quad-box gearbox and a bogie axle trailer with a 40,000 litre tank on it. No air con, no music, no carpet, no sleeper box; it was a very basic, no-frills work vehicle. And as I was soon to find out, I would be in it all day and under it or the trailer a lot of the night, but I enjoyed it thoroughly.

During this time, sometimes Joanne came to meet me in Cloncurry and sometimes I went back to Richmond for time off. As we knew they would, the road works unfortunately came to an end a month or so after our purchase, so we then took the truck back to the Richmond / Hughenden area. We sought out council contracts on road maintenance, and managed to get one with the Flinders Shire Council in Hughenden. We had about four months work doing that whilst applying for contracts of our own at various mines in the north west around Mount Isa and Cloncurry.

By this time my boys had both left Abergowrie College after completing Grade 10. Joe got a job working on Glenormiston Station on the Georgina River near Boulia and Dan found a job at Oak Park Station a couple of hundred kilometres north of Hughenden. I was very happy that the boys had both got jobs with good people on big properties. Till my dying days I will firmly believe a young person can't get a better start for their first job than to be working on a station, where quite often you have to get a situation solved with minimal equipment or assistance.

We finally got our break at the end of 1997 and managed to get a start at the Phosphate Hill project 200 kilometres south of Mount Isa, contracted to an earthmoving company on the earthworks project with our water truck. I started working the semi trailer water truck at Phosphate Hill on the earthworks in November of 1997 and bought a second body style Mack water truck a couple of months later. The earthworks included the huge development of the proposed plant site and the mine site fly-in-fly-out township.

There was also the all weather air strip, as well as the connecting fifteen kilometre sealed road. The roster system was four and one, meaning six days a week for four weeks and then one week off. Joanne was not impressed with the fact that she saw so little of me, so she resigned from her position with the Richmond Shire Council and came out to Phosphate Hill and drove the Mack body water truck for the remainder of the earthworks project.

After about eight months the earth works came to an end, and as the construction contractors came on site we started to carry freight daily from Mount Isa, initially in our Toyota tray back. In the beginning, this was just odds and ends like brooms, buckets, shovels, basic office equipment and furniture that was needed as the construction contractors came on site. We approached the few contractors already on site about the construction waste removal and the agreement was simple and verbal, "If you have a hook lift truck and industrial skips here within a week the job is yours".

We flew to Melbourne and bought a hook lift truck with two industrial skips and drove it back up the Birdsville Track with a day to spare. Then as more construction contractors came on site, having the truck and skips on site, as well as word-of-mouth, helped us secure all the waste removal on site. As well as the industrial skips we also had 100 plastic wheelie bins servicing the crib huts (smoko rooms) on site. In the end we had 11 industrial skips and a flat top, ten of which I had built myself at night when I was not driving the truck.

We had three other employees while we were at that mine site and they were with us for a total of about four years. My son Joe had left his 'ringing' career around the Boulia area where he had been for the previous three years. Together with his partner Priscilla Schofield, whose family were from the Boulia district, they had come to Mount Isa in search of the spectacular money in the construction industry. For a brief period Priscilla worked for us in Mount Isa before they both got employed by contractors at Phosphate Hill.

Joanne was coordinating the pick ups and deliveries for both ends of the freight run as well as, with the help of another lady in the office, the mountain of paperwork that was involved. At the start of the construction phase there was a Mount Isa freight company also dropping freight on their way to another already established mine site in the area. However they were very casual; they would unhook their trailer at the camp 15 kilometres away and the contractors had to go and pick it up from there. There were some incredible stuff ups with missing and damaged items that did not do their reputation any good.

Whereas we were moving around amongst the contractors every single day, and we picked up a lot of work simply because we were the "Johnny on the Spot". Every query was answered with "Yes sure, that won't be a problem", and we immediately filled out paperwork for each and every item. Each day started with a plan but because your plans changed by the minute every single day, thinking on the move and flexibility was still a big part of the picture.

The freight business grew very quickly, within a couple of months the amount of freight we were carrying was too much for the Toyota tray back and so in my spare time again, I built an eight metre steel tray for the hook lift truck that worked on the same principle as the skips. The procedure was simple: cart a load of freight down to the mine then drop the tray with the securely strapped on freight in a convenient location to distribute later.

Then it was on to empty the skips and the crib hut food waste wheelie bins, then returning to distribute the items on the flat top and finally put the tray back on to collect the return freight. There was only one problem: it took 24 hours to do all that. So we leased a second truck full time, an eight ton flat top, and hired an extra driver to do the run every second day.

I would then do every second day in the hook lift truck to service our waste removal contracts. In the early days of the freight run it was sometimes necessary to run a second truck, which Joanne quite often drove, coming on site with me delivering freight. The second truck and driver within a short time became a permanent feature. Meanwhile we had a third employee in our Toyota tray back doing the pickups and deliveries between the businesses in Mount Isa and our depot.

When we started the freight business we had bought a small industrial block with a tiny shed and a demountable that we lived in as our town depot. We lived there for about two years, but eventually it became far too small for what we were doing. So we bought 40 acres on the edge of Mount Isa that had a large house with a pool and a much larger shed on it that was suitable for our growing freight business and also with plenty of grass for Joanne's horse and our dogs to run around on. It was also around this time that our daughter Prudence arrived and so we now needed a better domestic space with a lot more room than we had at the industrial block with a donga for living quarters.

There were dozens of different contractors and over one thousand employees on site and we serviced them all, delivering freight from and returning freight to Mount Isa. The downwards freight was usually (but not always) anywhere between five to eight tons with the backloading being not as much but could usually be at least two to three tons and quite often a full load. We were very lucky that Phosphate Hill was accessed via a secondary beef road (one lane bitumen road).

In the four years that we operated the freight business I never saw a 'scalie' on that road, which was very fortunate, as we could quite often be found with a load that was overlength, overwidth, overheight or overweight, or a combination of any or all of these. Leaving Mount Isa so early in the morning and returning so late at night was a weighting in our favour as well. It would have been a very different scenario if we had had to use the main east-west highway as our access road. I never bothered filling out a driver's log book either as I figured it wasn't worth the effort.

The workload remained very busy until mid-2001, when the construction work was coming to an end and demand for our services tapered off very quickly. We supplied a quote to Western Mining who were the operators of the mine to provide our ongoing services but we did not have a hope of competing with the national carriers. We looked around for something else to supplement our income and we bought a small around-town delivery service with a truck and a forklift.

Unbeknownst to us, this business had taken a nose dive in the previous 12 months, which was unfortunately not reflected in the figures that were presented to us, and it was a painful experience for us to learn that as we went. We had been duped with this purchase. There was nothing else on the horizon, a few prospective mining projects in the North West but none had started and as such were of no use to us.

I managed to get our hook lift truck and some skips onto a power station site at Millmerran in southern Queensland which was a long way away, but there was no other work that I could find that was closer. Ultimately we never secured any long term contracts on that site. We took a main roads water truck contract on a fairly large road construction project between Mount Isa and Cloncurry with the hope of more work, but luckily that was very short lived as they were very hard to please and ended up going broke mid-project. So with neither of our water trucks or the skips working and the parcel delivery business not delivering the expected income we had a rather serious income problem.

Here is where the story starts to get interesting. More income was what was needed, so I decided to apply for a job on the Mount Isa Mines lease, as there was good money working there. That was when my problems really started to kick in. I had presented to the MIM medical centre to do the induction health check. All was going reasonably well until the doctor requested that I duck waddle across the room for a distance of about three or four metres.

I was thinking it was a rather odd request, as when I had previously been doing deliveries with our parcel delivery business on the MIM lease I had never seen anyone duck waddling around the mine site, and he had no answer for my query on that. Anyway, the short story was, I had failed the test so there was going to be no well paid MIM job for me and from there it was back to the drawing board.

The doctor added that he wasn't sure but he suggested I should see a specialist because he thought from what he saw that I might have neurological issues. That caused me to think of some things that had been happening to me recently during the deliveries that at the time I didn't pay much heed to. I sometimes had experienced an odd gait, especially when annoyed or stressed. Believe you me, some customers and their unrealistic demands for a $2 delivery used to get right under my skin so I wasn't unfamiliar with stress.

These experiences were hard to describe but I used to sort of trip over the slightest undulations in the pavements or road surfaces, and when up on the back of a truck I couldn't lean over to grab the combing rail and leap down to the ground from the back of the truck without feeling unusually awkward and unbalanced. In the past it had been something I could do with ease but now I had to manually climb down off the truck using hand holds and rungs or rails for my feet.

That was when I began to realise that I could have a serious problem. A well respected lady doctor in Mount Isa was my next visit; while not a neurologist, she worked with people that had issues in these areas referring them on to specialists in the bigger cities. She referred me to a neurologist in Brisbane by the name of Peter Silburn. Shortly after, I was in Brisbane in Peter Silburn's surgery being poked, prodded and asked lots of questions about my family history and my work history. I had MRI scans, CAT scans and a Lumbar Puncture that drained off some spinal fluid for testing. None of those tests came back with any identifiable results.

Going on those results, all that Peter Silburn was able to tell me was that it could be either hereditary or the result of the chemicals used in earlier years on the family property entering my nervous system. However neither of my family branches in a direct line had any history of spastic paraparesis and the chemical use theory could not be proven beyond reasonable doubt either, so there I was in an apparent No Mans' Land. Peter Silburn had diagnosed me with the 'umbrella term' of Spastic Paraparesis as there was obviously an issue but the testing would not conclusively say what it might be. This diagnosis would later prove to be a major hiccup in the bureaucratic jungle of trying to claim the Disability Support Pension.

Bridal group at our wedding reception, 1994. My brother Edward, myself, Joanne and her bridesmaid Becky Overell

Half of Terry Freight Services at Phosphate Hill in 1998

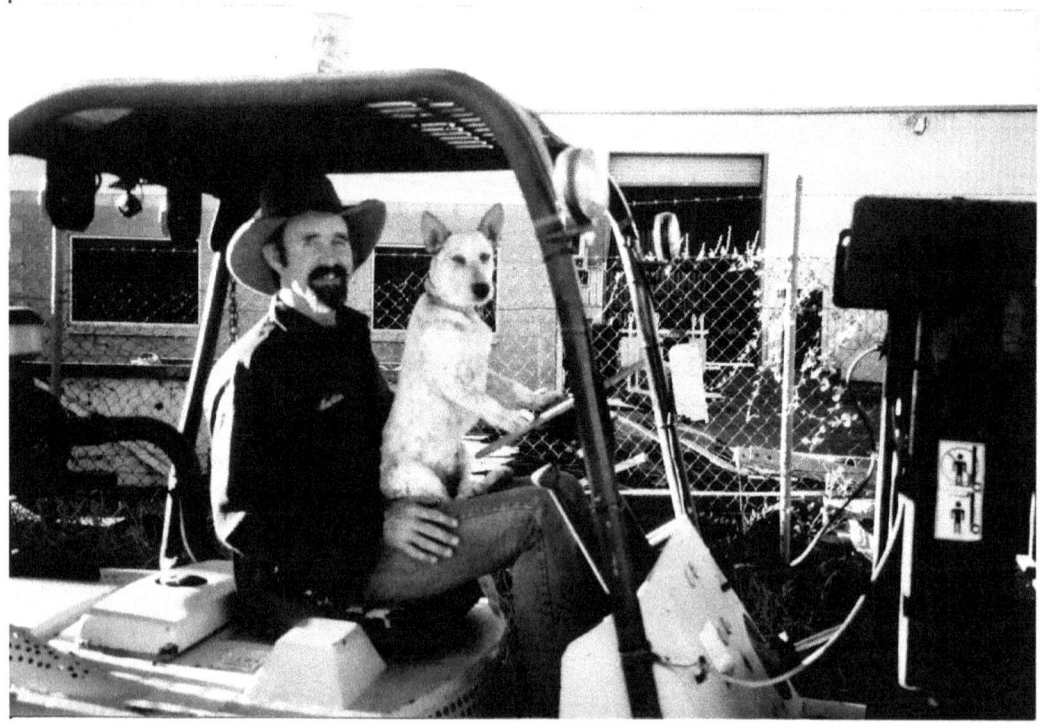

Hector and I on the forklift. 8 Duke St. Mt. Isa 1999

Joanne with her Aunty Hazel in Brisbane, on our honeymoon in 1994 on the new Fat Boy Harley Davidson

Joanne with Stephen and Prudence and Campo. Mount Isa park in 2004

Judith with Prudence and Stephen in 2004. Mt Isa

Prudence and I saying G day to her brand new brother Stephen, Feb, 2002

MARRIAGE, MINING, MOUNTISA & MEDICAL ISSUES.

Mum with Prudence and flower in 2001

The sheds on our rural 40 acre block Hillview, at Mt. Isa in 2000

Three bed bugs of the Terry type. Mount Isa, early 2004

13

TAXIS, TOWNSVILLE, TRIALS & TRIBULATIONS

So on my return from Brisbane to Mount Isa, the big question was, what to do? I had been counting on that fairly healthy projected income from Mount Isa Mines to cover our outgoing expenses which were considerable, and with none of our equipment working we had no choice but to start selling our gear to cut our costs. Eventually, because the overheads were far more than we could afford on our reduced income, we had to sell all the equipment as well as the house on 40 acres and rent a house in town. Around this time commodity prices were very low and Mount Isa Mines was struggling, with the flow-on effect for Mount Isa township being the doldrums with employment and housing prices. It was not good for us trying to sell a house and our equipment.

I had a friend who owned a taxi cab in Mount Isa and was looking for a spare driver. I went to do the driver induction course, did the police character check and fortunately for me they didn't do a medical check that required any duck waddling. Finally after all the paper work was done, I was ready to go, in a sit-down job with the upside of air conditioned comfort. The quality of some of the passengers was less than desirable to say the least. The next two years of taxi driving in Mount Isa was an enlightening experience. The next thing that I did required me to swallow a lot of pride. When we had the local parcel delivery business each week we would get at least 4 pallets of Amway products to deliver around town. In doing this we became friendly with the local Amway Platinum distributors Ron and Joan Croft, who also owned West Leichhardt Station, a cattle station about 30 kilometres out of town, and of course Ron was always spruiking how good this Amway business was.

Basically it was just buying a fairly wide range of household products including cleaning products, a range of kitchenware, a lot of packaged and canned food products, softdrinks, a cosmetics and jewellery range, a range of protein and vitamin supplements as well as lots of other items you could order online and have delivered to your door. The idea was to get other people to sign up and they in turn get others to sign up and you got a commission for the volume of product that the people you signed up used. Sounded so easy, give it a go one day. 10 years prior my cousin and some friends around Hughenden had tried to enlist me into this very same new way of doing business with Amway and I had scoffed at the idea and turned them down, saying that there was no way I was going to be flogging soap suds to the neighbours.

Now here he was, a cattle station owner telling me I could earn $50,000 a year as a starting point just by getting other people to use Amway and here I was (who by this time had visited a neurologist in Brisbane and been given some unpleasant news) staring down the barrel of being (at that stage) in a wheelchair in the next few years so it was, **"Stone the crows, this can't be that bloody hard, here give me the pen, where do I sign".**

By this time we had our son Stephen and another baby on the way so Joanne got in and did the cosmetics and jewellery presentations and I showed the 'Business Plan' to people, looking for customers and potential distributors. As well as trying to build this internet business I was doing

12 hour shifts in the cab 6 days a week. Joanne was working part-time at a clothing store in town and having some success with her area of Amway with the jewellery and cosmetics products, but as far as I was concerned I couldn't sell a box of matches. No matter how hard I tried or how many 'plans' I showed over the ensuing 4 years I couldn't get any takers to join our business. I just didn't have that salesman's gift of the gab and I obviously wasn't 'slippery' enough to persuade anyone to want to become a millionaire.

I began to think that possibly Mount Isa might have been 'outAmwayed', as there were at least 18 want-to-be millionaire distributors in Mount Isa and only about 22,000 people. I later felt somewhat sorry for the residents of Mount Isa as they must have felt totally hammered by people wanting them to join a new, strange way of shopping and listen to this "make a million dollars" spiel while they were doing it. They would have been thinking exactly what I was thinking ten years earlier. So I thought that maybe if we moved to a bigger population centre our chances of making Amway a success would improve. Well, that was my theory anyway. At this time I had never heard about Albert Einstein's famous quote, "In theory, theory and practice are the same. In practice, they are not".

In mid-2004 we made the move to Townsville and set up a home for a fresh start in a new location. I have always been amazed at how much gear you collect in the space of a few years. The sorting and packing of all our belongings and then the organising of a removal truck was a major job, but ruthless won the day, and with a few garage sales we reduced our possessions significantly. Joanne and the children travelled on ahead of me while I packed the car and a trailer with the last remaining items and drove to Townsville on my own. We spent a few days in units on the Strand before finding a house and then unpacking everything.

The stress of the whole event caused me to have what I later found out was a relapse. It was a very distinct feeling of noticeable decline in mobility and balance, usually brought on by a period of stress. I immediately found a job driving taxi cabs in Townsville and continued with that while trying to develop the Amway distributing business in whatever time that I had left over. With regards to the cab driving it was more or less the same overall. I had just exchanged problematic, unruly patrons in Mount Isa for problematic, unruly nightclub patrons in Townsville.

After a further 12 months of pursuing Amway with no success I was totally disillusioned with the concept. We had met all the KPIs, attended every meeting there was to attend over about five years and it had returned us nothing so I decided to let go of my Amway dreams. I felt that my initial thoughts about Amway a decade earlier had been correct. After a further two years of taxi driving I had reached the stage where I was using a walking stick to get around and was of no use to any elderly or disabled passengers.

If they had groceries or luggage that they could not carry or load, because of my walking stick I could not handle their items either. I finished the taxi driving and got a job in the call centre dispatching the taxis to jobs and I persevered with that for about 12 months, but could not build up the necessary speed required on the computer console to enter jobs into the system on busy nights. On the busy nights of Friday and Saturday nights, you had to enter about 120 jobs per hour into the computer system, which equates to a job into the system approximately every 30 seconds.

This did not take into account that on these nights, many of your conversations included talking to drunks who didn't know where they were, where they were going, how many people were travelling or even their own name. Many were belligerent and you would just disconnect them but that still played havoc with your averages. With the aid of the internet, as well as despatching cabs in Townsville, just to make it interesting we also serviced the towns of Innisfail, Proserpine, Airlie Beach, Mackay and Gladstone. When I started in the call centre 12 months previously, I could do about 40 jobs per hour and developed that to about 75 jobs per hour but it became obvious that my speed would not increase beyond that.

To make a long story short I eventually made a mistake dispatching a job in Mackay, where I sent two cabs to the same job about 30 kilometres out of town. That mistake cost me my job. I didn't know what I was going to do after that; I did not have any computer skills, I did not have any admin skills, I did not have any clerical skills. All my skills were in the area of hard work and long hours, and between mobility issues and fatigue I was becoming less and less appealing to prospective employers. I had never been on welfare of any form but decided to consider it as I thought that a better opportunity might not present itself for a good while to come and employment prospects were looking fairly bleak.

So through Centrelink I applied for the Disability Support Pension, but soon found that Spastic Paraparesis (the umbrella diagnosis that I had been given until this stage) was not sufficient to qualify for the Disability Support Pension. I actually had to be diagnosed with a specific condition to qualify. I visited a neurologist at the Mater Hospital and my resulting diagnosis of Multiple Sclerosis came about because of my need of the disability pension, not because he knew what I had - not the best but it was the only solution to our predicament. Even with the diagnosis from the neurologist, Centrelink still knocked my Disability Pension application back for various reasons.

They eventually approved it, but only after we had made three separate applications. Then they made a mess of the approval because after a couple of months they reduced my pension, as Joanne had full time employment and I was only entitled to a half pension. I applied to a couple of Disability Employment Agencies but because I lacked the previously mentioned skills there was not much in any other fields. One agency tried to coerce me into driving for a local bus company but after a trial run I declined that proposal, as it was no better than driving the taxis.

Everything was becoming just too hard. In my life I had always been fairly positive, and being depressed was not a part of my nature. It was at this stage that I started to become very disillusioned with our financial prospects for the future and everything else. So we decided that for the time being I would be the stay-at-home 'Mum', doing school pickups and meetings, after-school activities, the meals, the washing and the cleaning, and Joanne would be the income earner with my meagre pension adding a little to the side. Like everyone else I had seen lots of really simple ideas advertised time and time again on television, that anybody could have thought of, suddenly become a very popular landslide marketing innovation that made someone a multi-millionaire. Still, no matter how much time I devoted to thinking about ways to create an income there were none of those sorts of simple ideas floating my way.

I was also investigating other possibilities of developing some form of reasonable income. I looked at organic worm farming using our backyard as the production area, I looked at a photography course as I had always been a keen photographer. It had to be a self-starting backyard business because we had no equipment and absolutely no capital. However a few negative comments came my way which sowed doubt in my mind and the confidence and self esteem that I previously had took a huge nose dive. I just could not muster the drive to make a start at either of these ventures.

Following our move to Townsville our children had become involved in a local Scouting group. Because they were short of parent helpers I had put my hand up to help and in no time at all I was given the position of Assistant Group Leader, a position I held for a further 2 years. It was also around this time that I became involved with 4TTT Community Radio through a friend that lived a few doors down from our house. He was a volunteer presenter at the radio station and invited me to tag along and sit in on his shows, and I ended up doing On Air training and becoming a DJ myself. However, while both of these activities provided me with social interaction, community involvement and enjoyment they were never going to become an income-earning proposition.

In mid-2008 Joanne decided that she was going to go her own way, so we parted company and 12 months later we were divorced. I had attended marriage counselling previously at her request but thought the whole thing was a bit one-sided and could not quite work out why we were even there. Perhaps I was wrong but I felt that I was no more than snappy, cranky or unhappy with my lot in life. I had never subjected my family to domestic violence, child abuse, drunkenness or drug addiction.

At worst I was not a major breadwinner for the family, but that was something that was beyond my control. When we separated, our children - Prudence 8 years old, Stephen 6 years old and Conroy 5 years old - couldn't understand what was going on and were very concerned that it was all their fault. I assured them that it was absolutely not their fault at all and that sometimes parents just couldn't agree to live together anymore. I told them that I loved them all very much and that I was still going to be a big part of their lives into the future.

I have always held in disregard divorced or separated parents, male or female, that totally disconnected themselves from their children after a family breakdown, Family Law Courts orders notwithstanding. I found myself a tiny flat not too far away and bought a small second hand car, and maintained contact with my children at every possible opportunity. At the start, because I only had a tiny one bedroom flat, it was only on every other weekend to stop over and during the weeks for a couple of hours after school a couple of days per week. I really missed having my kids in my life in a full time sense and sincerely hoped that our divorce would not affect them too much. Even though I tried to act in a positive manner, my self confidence regarding both my family situation and employment opportunities had taken a huge hit, resulting in a few years of not doing anything much apart from the Scouts, the Community Radio station and maintaining a connection with my children.

Having the small Hyundai car that I had bought off my older son Dan gave me a lot of independence, and also allowed me to take the children for school holiday trips that a lot of city kids wouldn't normally get to do. We did a trip to Cairns and the Atherton Tablelands and visited an old friend in Herberton by the name of Harry Skennar. Harry and his wife owned the Herberton Historic Village called 'The Tin Pannikin'. It is a collection of old original pioneering buildings from all over North Queensland but mainly the Atherton Tablelands that Harry Skennar and his wife had painstakingly restored and filled with historic collectibles. I had visited previously, but on this trip the kids and I spent a whole day there exploring.

There was the dentist, the school house, the post office, the newsagent's, the assay office, the blacksmith's shop, the garage, the tin gouger's hut and other buildings too numerous to mention that were all chock full of collectibles and memorabilia from times past. Sadly Harry has passed away now, but before he did he sold his "Village" to an avid fellow collector of history who has gone on to add to and take the "Village" in new directions. It is still open for viewing to this day. A separate business also in Herberton that we visited is the absolutely unique, one-of-a-kind "Spy Camera Museum". This museum features not only spy cameras but a history of cameras in general, all in static displays, also still open to this day.

On another school holiday we travelled north, this time visiting Cooktown and seeing many things of interest like where Captain Cook's "Endeavour" was beached for repairs in 1770, the memorial for Mrs Watson who perished near Lizard Island in 1881 and the Cooktown museum, which is housed in the original Cooktown Catholic Convent building which has survived numerous cyclones. We also saw the Black Mountains, right beside the road just south of Cooktown. These are an imposing, forbidding, mysterious and mountain-sized pile of gigantic, house-sized, granite boulders, that over the last one hundred and fifty years have more than one sinister tale of disappearance attached to them. On our homewards trip we stayed with friends on a sugar cane farm near Aloomba about 40 kilometres south of Cairns. It was an idyllic spot squeezed between the Mulgrave River and a rainforest-clad mountain range behind, down which icy cold streams flowed, supplying their household water.

On yet another school holiday excursion the kids and I visited the west. I showed them some of the places I had worked at or in. We visited Cloncurry, Ernest Henry Mine and Mount Isa. From there we went to Winton and visited the Waltzing Matilda Museum. Onwards to Longreach, visiting their tributes to iconic Australian history, the Stockman's Hall of Fame and the Qantas Museum. From there onto Emerald in the centre of Queensland's coal mining region, then northwards through Clermont to Charters Towers and then a short hop home to Townsville. My fondest hope is that in future years the kids will look back and remember these trips and the sights they saw and treasure the photos that we took, because I feel that the Australia that my generation grew up in is disappearing quickly.

At Hughenden with my cousin Aussie O Neil instructing the kids on the finer points of motorbike riding

Conroy at Central State School, Townsville

Stephen at Central State School, Townsville

Doing the Magnetic Island Forts walk

Kids and Cubby houses. This is where I lived in Pimlico

Kids with Joanne at Juliettes on the Strand, the home of nice ice cream

Returning from Kuranda to Cairns on the Sky Rail

Prudence exploring art at the Railway Estate Pre School in Townsville

Prudence in her Grade 7 year at Central State School, Townsville

Prudence the snake handler at the Kuranda Venom Zoo

Stacey Christmas 2007

Stephens 3rd birthday. Townsville 2004

Stephens_ 3rd birthday. Townsville 2005

The Scooter Kings at the skate park

With the kids taking the tourist train ride to Kuranda

14

ON MY OWN AGAIN

Some time later the Belgian Gardens Scouts Group Leader moved away, so I was automatically elevated to the position of Group Leader, a position I held for a further three years. I quite enjoyed working as the Group Leader of the Belgian Gardens Scouts, but I eventually became very frustrated with the workload, especially with the camps and extra activities away from the den. There was an incredible amount of paperwork to keep us on the good side of all the legal requirements regarding fundraising activities, banking, activity safety audits, Blue Cards and more. Like any organisation we needed parents to run the committee to make all these activities and events happen, but in spite of their kids' involvement, I could rarely get enough hands in the air to run the show.

After our separation and subsequent divorce I immersed myself with 4TTT, the local Community Radio station. I had always had a great love of music and had a fairly extensive collection of LPs and CDs that I had amassed over the years. I had always had a keen interest in the history and connections of different artists and genres of contemporary music, and there was a spot doing a Blues Music Show from 10pm until 12am every Tuesday night. I remained there for five years doing the Blues Show.

The Blues Show with fellow presenter Marko was my main contribution but I also helped out with their promotional live coverages and fundraising at various events around the city. I was on the committee at the radio station and was also involved with cataloguing the music in the library. At the radio station there was an office with a manager, a receptionist and an advertising person so extra paperwork and administration was no longer an issue for me. All I had to look after was my own little area and make sure I played all the sponsors advertisements in the correct time slots on my two hour show.

I remained involved with Scouts Australia picking my children up to attend their respective nights and as one was in Scouts and two were in Cubs this involved two different nights of the week. I also did a lot more photography around the Townsville area after becoming involved with a camera group that used to meet one night per week and also conducted regular photography outings to hone our skills in various aspects of photography. I also began a long and ongoing association with an MS social group that met at a different venue each fortnight for a luncheon with a resultant chin wag that continues to this day, although Covid 19 has seemed to dampen the enthusiasm of some, with our numbers dropping sharply since the end of 2021.

At the end of 2008 the kids and I began a holiday ritual that continued for seven years that we all enjoyed immensely, and that was going to Brisbane for the Christmas holidays on the iconic Queensland Rail 'Sunlander'. We used to get a sleeping compartment and during the night Stephen and Prudence would take the two upper berths, I took the lower berth and Conroy being the smallest and most junior member of the party slept on the floor on a foam mattress that we had brought with us. On one of our earlier trips sometime during the night the brakes were applied quite sharply, and, almost like Superman, Stephen came flying out of his upper most bunk.

He landed in an unceremonious heap on top of Conroy, who was sleeping on the floor, and in the process suffered a greenstick fracture to his wrist. The QR staff were extremely apologetic about the incident and they couldn't do enough for us for the remainder of the journey; if only they had known that I wasn't the suing kind. During the day, the upper berths folded away and the lower berth was wide enough for all four of us to sit side-by-side and read books, play games or simply look out the window at the countryside picture show sliding by.

The children enjoyed sitting in the Dining Car and watching the scenery while we ate our meals, as well as watching movies in the Club Car. Unfortunately, in 2016 the 'Sunlander' was retired after 60 years of service, and was replaced by a train called 'The Spirit of Queensland'. While a few hours faster, it does not have anywhere near the character of that old train that had served Queensland so well, for so many years. While you can still purchase meals, they are prepackaged frozen meals that are heated up and eaten at the seat in your carriage.

Gone for the children, and indeed the adults as well, is the mystique and fascination of the Dining Car. Of ordering a meal from a printed menu with the meals cooked in the galley and delivered to your table by a waiter. Eating at a table with proper cutlery and crockery and with a pot of tea or coffee while enjoying the passing scenery is certainly a pleasant way to enjoy a meal. Despite what they tell you in the travel brochures, progress does come at a cost.

Over the next six years from 2010 onwards I resumed my efforts to develop a source of income in a number of different avenues. I tried my hand at teacher's aide work at Townsville Central State School, where my three children were enrolled. Although the Principal and administration staff had signed off on the paperwork for me to pursue this avenue, I felt that there was never a great amount of enthusiasm or effort from their side of the fence to further my efforts in that area. In the end I felt that I was just a free staff member and had been parked up in the library recovering books. I tried to market my photography at local markets as smaller prints in frames, as well as trying to tap into the family photo shoot market. These excursions were what I would describe as a lot of exercise with very little reward.

At considerable expense I enrolled in a proofreading course, which unfortunately I never had the aptitude to complete, even after getting an extension. It looked easy when I applied but was a lot harder upon receipt of the written material. This was the only effort I made that I regretted attempting. Then I spent a few months developing a second-hand business from home through social media, as well as a home-based barbering business, using community notice boards and social media as my promotional tools. The first was skittled by loud mouthed keyboard warriors announcing to one and all, "I saw that item at a garage sale for $40"; "Hello loudmouth, if you don't want to buy it then shut up, I am trying to make an income". And the barbering venture, well, it simply didn't get off the ground, a handful of customers initially then it just withered on the vine .

Another idea I tried was registering my own home kitchen as a commercial food preparation area to sell homemade foods via a stall at a local community market, along with my artography canvases. Although I still had the aptitude to have a crack at anything, the issues with my condition, such as balance, gait and coordination, meant I no longer had the resilience to go the distance if a venture was not somewhat successful early on. The reception of my ventures from the general public in a financial sense was at best mediocre, so in spite of the old adage of sticking it out for the long term, they usually did not last longer than a few months before I decided to try something else. So I was never caught short for an idea, it was just the application and getting the ideas to a feasible working state with my limited mobility and balance that was the sticking point.

In 2013, a breath of fresh air – and fresh thinking – arrived in Townsville in the form of Dr. Mike Boggild, a neurologist freshly arrived from England with over 20 years' experience in the neurology field in both England and the United States. My previously undiagnosed condition immediately became a diagnosed condition when I walked through his door on my first consultation with him at the Townsville University Hospital. It was a condition more closely related to Motor Neurone Disease (MND) than Multiple Sclerosis (MS) but fortunately a much more slowly progressing condition than full blown MND.

What I had, he told me, was Primary Lateral Sclerosis (PLS), which is a rare neuromuscular disease which slowly but progressively weakens a person's voluntary muscle movement and for which there is no known cure. The destination was the same but it was just going to take me a lot longer to get there. But at last, even though I was aware that there was no cure for this slowly progressing beast, at least I knew what it was that was turning my life upside down.

I also found out a lot of information about my PLS condition and what I could look forward to in the future. The life expectancy of someone with PLS is usually not substantially affected but they can expect the condition to gradually escalate over the course of many years and to experience significant disability in their final years. It is unknown what causes PLS but Dr. Boggild was of a similar opinion as my earlier neurologists, suggesting that it could have been caused by chemical usage on the property when spraying for animal parasites and weed control in the paddocks.

Unlike MS sufferers, who are usually on some form of pain medication 24/7, a person with PLS suffers no pain, just the inability to move freely in normal day-to-day activities and considerable fatigue caused by a busy day. At this stage of my disability journey I had had the condition for about 11 years since the symptoms first became evident, and I had progressed to the stage of needing a walking stick to mobilise as I quite often suffered from tanglefoot or simply lost my balance while attempting to complete the simplest of tasks.

One day whilst free standing and attempting to put a lens onto the front of my camera, from out of absolutely nowhere, I lost my balance and reared over backwards towards the floor. I tossed the camera and the lens in different directions as I went over in an effort to grab hold of something, but to no avail; I ended up in an untidy heap on the floor. I suffered no physical injury, just damaged pride and a huge question in my head as to what the hell just happened.

The camera, however, didn't fare so well; it was damaged to the extent that it was cheaper to purchase a new one rather than repair it. My falls were very random, sometimes only a week apart but more often than not they were months apart. A favourite saying of my Dad's had been, "If you're getting older and not getting smarter then you are wasting your time". I was learning to be a lot more aware of my surroundings and to be much more careful. Another fall that I had quite some time later was absolutely sensational.

One day after I had been shopping and I was at home stacking the groceries into the pantry, I had this sensation of falling backwards. I grabbed for the pantry shelves but missed them. I then went for my four wheel wheelie walker that the groceries were being transported on but alas!, that did not work out as planned either. All I did as I went down was pull it and the remaining groceries over on top of myself as I hit the floor. As I hit the floor my scone hit the corner of the door jamb of an adjoining room which then split my scalp open.

I was yelling out to my landlords who lived next door - but I needn't have bothered, because they had heard the terrible racket and were already on their way. When they arrived in my kitchen I was lying under the wheelie walker in a pile of groceries with blood all through my hair and over the floor. They called an ambulance for me and I was carted off to hospital to get fifteen stitches in my scone. When I returned home two days later, even though it could have been much more serious, we all had a good laugh about the sight that greeted them when they arrived in my kitchen.

Over the next few years, I assisted Dr. Mike Boggild and Queensland Health with my time and my neurological condition in a training exercise set up to test neurologists-in-training about their retention of theory. It was at the opposite end to a research program as this was about diagnostics and recognition of symptoms. It was not a major impost on my time as I had oodles of that, just one morning every now and then where I fronted up at the hospital for a few hours. Then the various neurological students came into the room and with no prior knowledge of my condition or history asked me questions to try and determine what I had. I was quite open to helping anyone that was looking for answers to what caused and what may be able to cure this condition. Not only for myself but for anyone that had a neurological condition similar to this.

In 2014 I had the good fortune to discover an old superannuation policy from my taxi driving days that I had forgotten about. While the cash contents didn't amount to much, it had a Total and Permanent Disability (TPD) clause which I had not claimed and that was worth a considerable amount of money. After about 12 months of back and forth bickering through legal channels, I was able to collect the pay-out figure, which financially put my life in a much better position. The faithful little Hyundai sedan which I bought from my son in 2008 by now had done numerous trips all over North and North West Queensland. It had a huge number of kilometres on the clock and was more or less in a condition where you would not risk taking it on a long, out-of-town journey.

The Hyundai was pushing 20 years old and in an unsaleable condition, so it became a matter of the path of least expense. It was collected by the closest wrecking yard and I bought a much newer Nissan X Trail which had a lot less kilometres on it and consequently was much more reliable. It also had much more ground clearance and was a quasi 4WD, so we could do a little adventuring in it. Following this vehicular transition I did many longer trips with my children to show them things that a lot of city children rarely get to see.

We did quite a few trips visiting my cousins around Hughenden who still owned properties, so they got to see things like sheep shearing and mustering, cattle mustering and cattle work, the Hughenden Agricultural

Show and a country race meeting. A whole range of things that city kids rarely see. I saw it as a broadening of their education. I had already travelled Australia fairly extensively in my previous 50-odd years of living, especially so with my two older sons, but travelling took on a new aspect with my three younger children after I bought the Nissan X Trail.

Another aspect of my life that changed was that I was able to afford to move into new digs that would give my children and myself a much more comfortable and relaxed atmosphere. For the previous six years it had served its purpose, but my tiny flat in Pimlico could now be abandoned. It was a very cramped rabbit warren of a flat, lacking storage space, a carport or air conditioning. It had been created as an afterthought, devoid of any plan whatsoever, simply to utilise a vacant downstairs space and create an income for the owners who lived upstairs. I had taken it at a time of desperate need when my finances had been very limited, knowing full-well its limitations as a dwelling. Its use-by-date arrived when I found a renovated, very comfortable and stylish worker's cottage in the Queenslander-style in Belgian Gardens.

It was much closer to the city, the kids' schools and the beaches. It had two air conditioned bedrooms, two verandahs that were enclosed with Queenslander-style wooden shutters, a large lounge and a modern kitchen with polished wooden floors throughout. There was a carport and a covered outdoor living area at the foot of a half dozen steps, along with a large lockable laundry, giving me plenty of storage space for all my paraphernalia. It was a great place for my kids to come home to when they were with me and I loved living there. It was to be home for the next five years.

At the broadcasting console of 4TTT where I volunteered for about five years

Camping with Tom O Brien on the Flinders River at the Rockies in 2015

Conroy recieving his Grey Wolf award in Cub Scouts

My kids and their schoolmate George Thomas about 2010 at Marionvale with their cousin Olle OBrien

Prudence & Conroy at Camp Barrabadeen, Tinaroo Dam, Atherton Tablelands

Prudence and Conroy at a Scout Camp on Lake Tinaroo, Atherton Tablelands, 2013

Stephen, Conroy and Prudence at Tom Terrys grave on Eldorado in 2010

The kids and I at the Stamford Races in 2009

Toasting marshmellows with the Brown cousins on the Lammermoor verandah in 2009

With Greg and Belinda Terry and their dogs at Lerida in 2009

*ThomasineWith Mum or Nan as my kids used to call her.
In Brisbane in 2010*

15

DELVING INTO THE ARTS

Over the time since I had been back on my own, I had been getting busier and busier with my full time hobby of photography. Since buying an Apple computer, I began experimenting with the photo editing program. The editing or 'manipulating' gave my photos more of an artistic edge and the more I did the more adventurous I became. I was not a big fan of the 'cheap art' from Kmart-style outlets that featured elephants, giraffes or noble savages with their spears, silhouetted against an African sunset. I suppose it catered to a significant segment of the market - it was cheap art and it filled a space on the wall - but that was about where it ended. I felt that they had no soul and no real connection to our part of the world. My Mission Statement became "For an Australian home I can do better". With my photography I was endeavouring to put together a portfolio of images that, whilst contemporary, still had a quintessential 'Australian feel' to them that local art lovers and gift buyers could relate to.

As well as containing the 'spirit of scene' with the capture of the initial image, I was enhancing that 'feel' with editing skills that I was learning on the job. With a lot of the images that I was creating it was a transposition from photography to what I termed 'artography'. I was creating black and white silhouette images from colour photos, creating an artistic or ethereal portrayal of the image. Nothing was too sacred for my lens: fishing, football, kangaroos, meat pies, tinnies and FC Holdens, they were all fair game. My motto was one that appealed to a lot of people, "I will photograph anything that moves, and if it won't move I push it". I walked the streets of South Townsville capturing images of the old worker's cottages from a bygone era. I walked the Strand capturing images of early morning joggers and swimmers in the ocean who were playing "chicken" with the local crocodiles. I walked the CBD streets getting images of shoppers, itinerant hobos, closing nightclubs and anything else that passed in front of my lens. As any dedicated photographer knows, anything to get "that" image. Once you have that "one", then there is the next "one".

I was posting these edited photos to which I had applied the term 'artography' on to my Facebook page and a lot of my friends had made very positive comments as well as suggesting that I look at marketing them, which planted a seed for me. My photography was still just a hobby verging on an obsession, but in about 2016 after giving it much thought and with great trepidation I started a fledgling business called "Art Leasing & Sales". It was basically my photography, much manipulated, printed on to canvas and leased to businesses for display in their reception areas, meeting rooms or offices and rotated quarterly to keep it fresh, vibrant and ever changing. Many of them were edited to the extent that they were simply enhanced and highlighted a local landscape or setting.

There were many others that, in the way I had photographed and then edited them, became a piece of 'artwork' in the more abstract sense. I had literally thousands of images available covering a vast array of Australia, scenes ranging from coastal to outback, animals to machinery, busy cities to quiet rural scenes and all things in between. Initially, I was doing most of my photography in the reasonably local area between Cooktown to Bowen and out to Hughenden, which was an easy reach for my little car. I use the term local in the Australian sense of perhaps anywhere that is within about 500 kilometres of my residence in Townsville.

Initially, I was doing it on my own initiative, just using my own Facebook page and word-of-mouth, as well as a lot of door knocking, to promote my business as the go-to place for office art that reflected the local area that all these businesses were very much a part of and connected to. It was a lot of hard work and the results were sometimes exhilarating, sometimes disappointing, but I kept at it. My Disability Support providers Just Better Care created an NDIS plan for me that utilised my carers to assist me in promoting my business and doing a lot of the footwork for the quarterly rotations of art work as they came due.

Another time-consuming job that my carers were a big help with was the cataloguing of canvases as they came in, as well as a selection of A4 images of said canvases with matching catalogue numbers in a folder for ease of selection for my customers. I was slowly building my leasing customer base, as well as attending weekend markets and any event that would give my business exposure. I also opened an instagram account in addition to my Facebook page, and had a local IT company do a couple of 3 month promotions for me. I went along like that for about 12 or 18 months but it was always a struggle both physically and financially.

In mid-2018, by chance I happened to bump into a friend one day who had purchased the franchise rights to BNI (Business Networking International) for the North Queensland area and he invited me along to their weekly business meeting over breakfast the following week. Bernie Hock had 7 chapters in Townsville and around 20 chapters in the whole of the North Queensland area. I joined the Integrity Chapter and remained a member for the next three years. Within a couple of months, at their twice yearly leadership elections I was nominated for the

Treasurer's position for the next six months, which I accepted. Over the next three years the business networking model that they promoted did work for me to a certain extent but I found that it worked better for some businesses than others.

This is only my own opinion but in the past I have always run hard with my own opinion. I thought that an essential business such as a mechanic, plumber, electrician, tax accountant or a lawyer fared better than a niche business similar to mine, which relied on people having disposable or surplus income. Case in point would be, a person with a leaky roof will probably repair the leaky roof before they buy an artwork to hang on the wall under that roof. Added to that, Covid 19, which began in 2020, had more or less upset the apple cart, or in my case, the art cart, considerably. Lockdowns and social distancing really affected easy access to businesses in relation to promoting my canvas art and also doing the art rotations themselves. The leasing side of my business was a great promotional tool with people viewing my art canvases as they walked in and out of offices and businesses all day long but the real money was in the retailing sector, and I could not crack that market no matter how hard I tried.

During my time with Business Networking International I had an exhibition of about 60 pieces of my artwork at a Townsville art gallery in North Ward. The Drill Hall Studio was a private gallery housed in an historic military building, hence the name. They hosted my exhibition for a fortnight, but it barely covered costs. The gallery staff and the lady who owned the gallery were very good and they had previously displayed some of my images individually but you simply can't force people to purchase an item. Another lady, who was also a BNI member and owned a restaurant, and leased art from me on occasion, made me an offer which I accepted. She hung a dozen of my canvases around her restaurant for two months which I could sell off her walls if there was interest from her customers. There was a lot of pointing and praise going on but no one driving their paws into their pockets to make it real.

With another lady who was a member of my BNI chapter and owned a start-up tea emporium business, we hosted a couple of weekend exhibitions at my home in Belgian Gardens. She had much of her product being all things connected to tea leaves and I added to my already well-clad walls by having extra art at floor level against the walls. Her home-made scones with cream and jam, together with plenty of different flavours of hot tea to sample and a little background music from my stereo, created the ambiance. We had plenty of feet through the door, but once again it was a sign of the times for niche businesses and disposable income with very few buying anything from either of us.

The end for 'Art Leasing & Sales' came about for two main reasons. The first one being the Covid Crisis, which was hitting hard both in terms of available disposable income and the ability of the customer to gather in any public place without feeling restrictions. I tried the people's markets at the weekends, of which there were at least half a dozen in Townsville, I tried to market it to Real Estate agents to include in their thank you hampers to their home purchasers and also to hang in their display homes, I tried to market it to local fundraising organisations as locally flavoured raffle prizes. I tried to market it as a locally produced gift for any occasion from housewarming parties, anniversaries, birthdays, Christmases, long service acknowledgements, a going away present, to a welcome back present and then eventually I just ran out of ideas.

When my car had a major motor malfunction mid-2021, that was the last straw, as I could not afford to either repair or replace the car. The progressive nature of my condition was also a factor that I considered at that stage, as I had gone from mobilising with the aid of a walking stick and being able to carry a couple of the canvases myself in my free hand, to having to use a walking frame in the space of a couple of years. Regardless of the reasons, to offset the disappointments I would like to acknowledge all my carers. A huge thank you goes out to all my carers that worked with me over about four years because I couldn't have physically done it without them. Having my carers helping me represented an input to the Brain's Trust as well, as they quite often thought of a location or an idea about marketing that had not occurred to me.

It was at this stage that I decided to close my business down. It was not despair or depression; it was simply that at the age of 64, and having had my condition for over 20 years, I had simply run out of energy and puff, not to mention marketing ideas. It was time to pull up, have a breather and plan something else that would not require so much in the physical sense or too much in the financial sense. This was when I had my best sales ever, but the half-price tags proclaiming "CLOSING DOWN SALE" on the art probably had a lot to do with that. Of the sixty-odd canvases exhibited I sold about fifty, but taking into consideration the knock-down price, that once again did not leave much in my pocket. After the exhibition I still had about seventy-odd canvases to hand, of which I have sold some since, but on the positive side I won't have to buy any birthday or Christmas gifts for some considerable amount of time to come. Just like on a battery, for every negative there is always a positive.

That something else to do was not long in coming, because one of the businesses that I had leased canvases to previously was also a new start-up business in Townsville. I suppose the closest comparison you could make to 'Life Skills Queensland' was a Men's Shed, but with a very distinctive difference.

Matt and Brittany Hodgson had created this business to provide an outlet for people with a wide range of disabilities within the sphere of the NDIS world that wanted to do something creative. As well as the disabled participants it also provided a range of activities for children, women, pensioners and also for servicemen and servicewomen that suffered from PTSD-related conditions. Activities provided range from wood turning, building all sorts of wood projects, basic small engine maintenance, welding, cooking lessons, macrame, mosaicking projects, 3D printing projects and resin art projects.

Each participant can bring their carer with them if they wish, but there are participants that work on their own as well. All tools and materials are provided, as well as qualified supervisors that rotate around amongst the participants, giving help and ideas where needed. It is a great environment to work in with everyone being interested in and supportive of the other projects on the workbenches around them. I have always been half handy with wood and metal but in my current situation I was short of a shed and the tools to create these masterpieces in my mind so it turned out to be a convenient amalgamation of mind and matter.

I have been working on projects at Life Skills Queensland for just on two years now and completed numerous ideas that I have had. I had always wanted to try my hand at wood-turning and they have a wood-turning lathe, so I started off doing some small wooden bowl ideas. I then moved onto building a shelving unit for my bathroom that had to have a couple of custom-made modifications built into it for it to fit where it had to go, a shelving unit for my laundry, two table-cum-benches for television, computer and books in my lounge room. A couple of very unique clocks were next to come off the production line. Then it was onto cheese platters/serving trays, of which I have done a number of different ideas incorporating different designs in resin. Currently I am working on two coffee tables with resin artwork themes which are destined to become Christmas gifts.

Most of the items that I create have become gifts for different occasions for relatives, or repaying favours from friends, because strangely enough my imagination does have its limits when trying to buy gifts for people. Resin artwork is a medium that is becoming another creative obsession for me and is only limited by a person's imagination, and will perhaps equal my photographic creativity in the future. I feel sometimes that I have become Life Skills Queensland's 'worst nightmare', with my continual stream of ideas for that next project. A lot of their clients are happy to work with projects within their catalogued list.

However I like to create custom items that you would never see again and which they are quite happy to cater for in their workshop. But they do roll their eyes. Everyday I have enough ideas using different materials and products in resin and woodwork with tables, cheese boards, lazy susans, bedside lamps and tables that should take care of any spare time I have for quite some time into the future. The truth, however, being that I will probably never have enough spare time for all my ideas - but keeping busy is the key.

Very rarely is an invention or a creation entirely unique or indeed exclusive. Ever since mankind rubbed two sticks together to create fire there has always been that creative genius to try and make life better or easier. Whether the item is in the field of science, health, mechanics, homewares or in the artistic world, it is more often than not a variation of a pre-existing product. The creator has seen or heard of an item, and then gone off on a tangent to create some variant to cater for an idea that the previous item did not cover. Some go **BOOM!** with success and some go **BOOM!** with disappointment. The world, however, will never run out of inventions or creative minds while mankind is upright and moving around.

PS 004 DUDE ON A HARLEY

PS 014 GUM LEAVES IN SILHOUETTE AT COBBOLD GORGE

PS 05 LERIDA BORE, CORFIELD, QLD. YOU CAN T MISS IT

PS 120 PUNTERS JAM, WOODFORD FOLK FESTIVAL

PS 136 HOLDING AUSTRALIA TOGETHER

DELVING INTO THE ARTS

PS 177 USED CAR YARD WINTON, Q LD

PS 281 WETTING A LINE

PS 346 RAILWAY RELIC MARREE, SOUTH AUSTRALIA

PS 479 SKY BORNE HUNTER

PS 855 WHILE WAITING FOR THE GREEN LIGHT

PS 861 SHARING THE SHADE

A flier for my very first exhibition before Art Leasing & Sales was even a thing, 2013

Danielle Malpas and I ran a few joint home exhibits with my Art business and her Tea House and Florist business

Prudence, Stephen and Conroy helping out at my Art Leasing & Sales clearance sale

Shooting the breeze with Jamie Painter, Support Coordinater from Just Better Care at the Bushland Beach Markets

Talking with two interested ladies at my Drill Hall Studios exhibition

The proprietor of Art Leasing & Sales in a very informal style at the Bushland Beach Markets

When I was a part of Business Networking International with Bernie Hock

With Bernie Hock, BNI and Teresa Hudson at my Art Leasing & Sales clearance sale held in the Community Information Centre

DELVING INTO THE ARTS

With Councillor Mark Molachino at the markets being held at the Carlyle Gardens Retirement Village

16

DOWN THE DUSTY ROAD WE GO

In May of 2015 we undertook the inaugural trip in my new vehicle with a tour of western Queensland and the Gulf Country. We went first to Winton, then Boulia through Middleton, up to Mount Isa through Dajarra. Overnighting in Camooweal near the Queensland border and then onto Cape Crawford, which is the home to 'Heartbreak Hotel' where we camped again. Borrooloola was next in turn then on to visit a family friend Frank Shadforth at Seven Emus Station, camping that night on the banks of the Calvert River. The next morning on to Burketown, Cloncurry and camping that night on the banks of the Flinders River at Richmond.

The next day was an easy day home to Townsville. We towed a trailer which I called "The Compact Caravan" with camping and cooking gear, and on this particular trip we camped and cooked out all the way. The three kids all learned a little basic stuff like how to properly put a load on a trailer and then tie it down without damaging anything, how to safely jack a car or trailer up and change a flat tyre, and how to connect and disconnect a trailer without forgetting anything. All handy stuff to know wherever you may be on your journey in life.

It was in August 2015 that I went to Darwin to visit my son Joseph and his family. Through nobody's fault but my own I overheated my engine in Darwin, preventing my return to Townsville for the school holidays, so instead I flew the three children to Darwin. We had a number of days in Darwin seeing the sights of the once-quirky and quaint outpost of a town that had collected a theatre troupe of odd and outrageous characters. We visited, to mention a few, a number of old historic stone buildings from the first settlement, underground tunnels under the city area built in World War 2 to store bunker oil safe from Japanese bombing, the Fanny Bay gaol, the seaside outdoor movie theatre and the Adelaide crocodile cruise, before we set off for home.

En route we visited the Mataranka Thermal Pools and the nearby grave sites of characters that featured in the book by Jeannie Gunn, 'We of The Never Never'. A little further south we called into Gorrie Airfield, one of the main World War 2 airstrips and truck convoy maintenance depots on "The Track" – which was developed throughout World War 2 to eventually become the Stuart Highway. Then further south still the Overland Telegraph buildings at Tennant Creek. We camped at the Devils Marbles for the night and then onto Queensland, visiting the Camooweal Caves before pushing on to have one last camp on the Flinders River at Richmond before reaching Townsville.

The trips were also a great opportunity to expand my photography database for the business I was developing at that time, Art Leasing & Sales. The scope of subject matter I encountered whilst travelling was wide, including historic, Australiana, landscapes, wildlife, humorous as well as photographic memories for the kids. There were many canvases in reception areas in Townsville city that were the result of photography done on these trips. My preoccupation with photography was the bain of my children's existence, mainly because while we were travelling I would notice something that would jump out at me as a "great image". However, because we were in motion at highway speed and the scene appeared as you came over a rise or around a curve in the road it was quite often a case of having to turn around and return to that exact spot.

The difficulty was increased if there was a lot of traffic or prevailing road conditions didn't allow you to execute a U-turn immediately, and once returned, because you had noticed that "great image" in an instant in time, you did not have time to take in the prevailing conditions at that spot. Quite often, on returning, I would find narrow and steep road shoulders, a culvert, a curve or a crest, or some other dangerous road condition that prevented a photograph being taken at that exact spot. After finding that spot, because I was not mobilising too well, I took most of my photos out of either of the front windows of the car – so that they all had to sit deathly still for the duration which was a bit of an ordeal for them. I can only imagine there were many "Oh, Dad!"s, "Not again"s and "Bloody hell"s muttered under their collective breaths.

In December of 2015, it was time for another school holiday trip. This one was a biggy. Once again our starting point was Winton, which was our first night's camp. Camping just east of Birdsville the next night, and then across the Birdsville Track to Marree, where we 'camped' in a motel because of storms nearby. Then to Port Augusta, over to Broken Hill and Menindee on the Darling River which we then followed, camping a night on the Darling River at Tintinallogy Station. We had travelled on the eastern side of the river, always within sight of the river tree line.

As night drew close, we simply called into Tintinallogy Station, which was only a few hundred metres off the road and built right on the river bank, and enquired as to whether we could camp the night on their river bank. Not only were they agreeable, but actually let us camp at their own personal barbeque area about 200 metres downstream from the homestead. It was indeed right on the edge of the Darling River, and came complete with a barbeque built out of farm equipment, chairs and a table.

We were very touched by their generosity to welcome us to camp right there overlooking the water, knowing that 120-odd years before, paddlesteamers would have been plying their cargos right beneath our noses up and down the length of this great river. Drought had brought boat traffic to a standstill in this river in the past. Our visit was late in the year, but I felt that the river was too narrow and lacked enough water to support the boat traffic spoken of in the historical accounts.

It felt great to be in our swags, beside a campfire and underneath a starlit sky. It was a wonderful location. Then onto Wilcannia, which had been a base camp for Burke and Wills' expedition in 1860, then across the Hay Plain, which at different times and locations had been home to some of my ancestors. It was indeed a strange feeling to be travelling for the first time through the country that my ancestors had lived, worked and breathed in three generations before. We looked briefly around Hay on the Murrumbidgee River before driving upstream to Carrathool located on the same river.

I had heard my father speaking of his great-grandfather in the past, but he, as well as myself, had never visited this area before. We visited my great-great-grandfather's property, 'Rudds Point' on the southern banks of the Murrumbidgee River, which he owned in the last half of the 1800s. As well as the property, he and his son-in-law also operated a local hotel called 'The Wool Pack Inn', which was located somewhere nearby on the property and of which I am sure there would have been many tales of excess from both locals and passing river traffic.

We drove around the machinery sheds and homestead looking for the owners or staff but there was no one about, so unfortunately we missed out on the guided tour and history session. There were some family graves somewhere on the property that we would have liked to visit. We also visited Howlong Station, which was nearby on the opposite side of the river. It had been owned by the Rudd family, who were my great-great-grandfathers-in-law. The current owners of that property did give us a guided tour of the out buildings and their shearing shed, which was also built on the banks of the Murrumbidgee River.

Most buildings that we could see were built right on the river for the very sound reason that goods unloaded off the paddle steamers were there where they were wanted and did not require manhandling any further. Same deal with the shearing sheds, roll the wool bales out of the shed and straight onto the paddle steamers, as well as being very close to the water source for the steam engines. We camped that night on the softer, grassier banks of the Murrumbidgee River. Once again it was a curious sensation to know that a couple of generations previously, in the age of horse-drawn traffic and steam engines, we would have been privy to paddle steamers travelling downstream loaded high with bales of wool. The same vessels travelling upstream would have been loaded with machinery, building materials and workmen of all sorts.

We spent another idyllic night beneath the stars, letting the smoke of the campfire drift over us before floating skywards, listening to all the night sounds as we let sleep coax us towards our next day's adventure. We then motored downstream and overnighted at the town of Wentworth where the Darling River joins the Murray River. One of our early explorers, Charles Sturt, camped at this very same spot on one of his expeditions in 1830. Onto Adelaide, visiting the RM Williams Museum located at an address that with every boot purchase was emblazoned into the mind of every rural person in Australia. I have no idea why but I was always curious about this place – '5 Percy Street, Prospect' – which was printed on the boot lugs of all of RM Williams elastic-sided riding boots, and now here I was. After 50-odd years I had arrived at this iconic mystery place.

On reaching Cape Jervis we took the ferry to Kangaroo Island, where we had two days travelling the length and breadth of that island. Matthew Flinders named Kangaroo Island in honour of the animal that provided the stews and soups that fed his hungry crew whilst on this island on his circumnavigation of Australia in 1802. The lighthouse on the extreme southwestern corner at Cape du Couedic was visited. As was the memorial at Penneshaw, where Matthew Flinders met with the French navigator Nicolas Baudin, who was also mapping the Australian coastline. If you happen to see a cape, island or bay with a very French ring to its name, Nicolas Baudin is the reason.

Then it was onwards, ever onwards around Lake Alexandria, through The Coorong to Portland and Melbourne via the Great Ocean Road. We overnighted in Melbourne with my cousin and her husband in the Dandenongs, before a trip for all on the iconic 'Puffing Billy' train. This was another bucket list dream 50 years in the making. I thoroughly enjoyed our iconic steam train trip through the Dandenong Ranges. Nonetheless, I could not believe in this day and age of cotton wool for everyone in the interests of safety, the passengers of whom most were children were allowed to sit on the window sills of the carriages with arms, legs and body parts dangling outside of the carriages in gay abandon.

But who am I, a fierce opponent to the nanny state of Australia, to be condemning the 'Puffing Billy' people for allowing some freedoms to be expressed on their train. We then continued on down to Wilsons Promontory, the southernmost point of Australia, then back through the Latrobe Valley in the Gippsland area, which is the powerhouse of Victoria, the home of Loy Yang A, Loy Yang B and Yallourn power stations. We continued east to Bairnsdale, then headed north via the Snowy River to see the National War Museum in Canberra. A funny incident occurred as we followed the Snowy River along.

The kids, all engrossed with their devices, were oblivious to their surroundings as we approached a huge number of pale blue bee hives all stacked beside the dirt road. As we drew alongside them, I called to the kids, "Have a look at that", to which they all jerked their heads up briefly. My daughter, not being mentally up to speed with her surroundings, quickly and inadvertently made the comment, "Who the hell would come all the way out here to dump their cupboards beside the road?", which I have never let her live down.

Arriving on the Monaro Plains, we passed through Jindabyne to our overnight stay at Cooma, where we had a cabin for the night. The next morning saw us in Canberra, but we only had enough time there to visit the Australian War Memorial for a couple of hours before needing to keep moving. After lunching on the shores of Lake George and viewing the Big Ram in Goulburn, we arrived in Sydney late in the afternoon. We promptly became lost, inadvertently travelling over the Sydney Harbour Bridge and then having to find our way back as a result. My cousin John Bell and his family were our hosts for the night and our tour guides the next day.

Next morning we were shepherded around the major Sydney sights before we had to get back on the road after lunch. Travelling west this time, we overnighted at the Jenolan Caves then visited family in Dubbo. After Dubbo it was onto the opal mining town of Lightning Ridge and the Black Hand Mine, while visiting O'Brien connections there. Brisbane was beckoning for Christmas, so it was on through Moree, Goondiwindi (the home of that famous grey horse) and down through Cunninghams Gap to the Queensland capital and family. We had a break of a fortnight or so over the Christmas and New Year festive period, with the children staying with their mother's parents and their cousins at Dayboro a short distance to Brisbane's north west.

When it was time to return home, our first stop was at Bundaberg, where we visited (no, not the Bundaberg Rum distillery) the Bert Hinkler museum, with Bundaberg of course being Bert Hinkler's hometown. From there we followed the regional routes northwards to the Town of Seventeen Seventy where we overnighted. In very recent decades the town of Seventeen Seventy has climbed from being a sleepy coastal village of some obscurity to a trendy, thriving little holiday and tourist destination, the place to be. In fact the caravan park was absolutely jam packed and we had some difficulty securing a cabin for our overnight stay. I have it on good authority that Captain James Cook had no such difficulty when he made it one of only three landings on the east coast of Australia to enable Joseph Banks to collect his botanical specimens in 1770. Hmmmm, I wonder where this sleepy little village acquired its name?

After a few more photographs, the next morning we were once again wending our way northwards towards home and our next journey. Our next overnight location was another coastal village that I had often passed but never stayed in. Clairview and its quite large collection of dwellings, ranging from fishing shacks to modern homes verging on mansions, complete with tractors and boat trailers, is reputedly the fishing and crabbing capital of the world – or so the promotional literature claims. Anyhow, we managed to obtain lodgings there for the night. The next morning we breakfasted grandly at the very basic but also very good eating establishment overlooking the beach, mudflats and Pacific Ocean. We completed another bucket list item on the home run by treating the kids to the delights of Jochheim's Pie House in Bowen. That night heralded the completion of another mission as we arrived back in Townsville, ready for another year of education as the kids prepared with school uniforms and books for their school year ahead.

In July 2016 Stephen and I did a 9 day trip to the tip of Cape York Peninsula and Thursday Island. As with most of our school holiday trips the time had to be shared equally with the children's mother so we were on a fairly tight schedule. Our first night saw us in Aloomba staying with friends on a cane farm that bordered on to mountainous rainforest. The next day saw us travel through Mareeba then out bush past the Mount Mulligan coal mine, the site of Australia's worst ever mining disaster in 1921. After rejoining the Cape York Developmental Road we again veered off to investigate Maytown which was part of the Palmer River gold rush of the 1870s.

Back to the highway to camp at the Palmer River Roadhouse, we spent the night sheltering under the verandah roof from the rain during the night. The next evening saw us at another of Cape York's early gold mining settlements which was Coen, so named for one of the Dutch seafarers who explored Australian waters long before Captain Cook. Found ourselves a campsite in the yard behind the pub and settled in for the night. In the days of the Overland Telegraph Coen had been one of the repeater stations and the next morning we went through the Coen Museum which was located in the original Repeater Station.

After that we were back on the Development road and motoring on to the bauxite mining township of Weipa which is also the home of one of Australia's RAAF Strategic Air Defence Bases. Drove around viewing the industrial and mining sites of Weipa before camping at a beachside van park located on the shore of the Gulf of Carpentaria. The next morning saw us on the road again for a reasonably short travel day into Bamaga after riding across the Jardine River by a barge run by a local Aboriginal community. When we arrived at the barge crossing – you wouldn't read about it – it was lunch time.

There were about 40 cars on both sides of the river waiting to cross and we all had to wait while the operators were having their lunch break. We were now operating on Cape York time. Slow down, slow right down. We pulled into Seisia and got a campsite shed to leave our gear in then went to see what we could before sundown. That afternoon we visited the most northerly point of Australia (or should I say Stephen did because it involved about a 2 kilometre long and reasonably rough walk). I waited in the car observing the aerial rescue of an injured hiker which Stephen was actually caught up in the middle of.

After finishing in that area we drove a further few kilometres to Albany Passage which was the site of Somerset, home of Cape York's first settlers the Jardine brothers, after whom the Jardine River was named. First settled in the 1860s, however many difficulties and quite a number of gravesites preceded Somerset's abandonment after 50-odd years. The next morning Stephen and I were on the ferry to Thursday Island and Horn Island. Thursday Island was settled in 1875 and was a major pearling centre up until the 1930s, a defence outpost with a major fort built in the 1890s when fear of the Russians was high. It was also an Overland Telegraph repeater station between England and Australia before the days of radio communication.

It was a major defense and air base during World War 2. Being on a very tight itinerary the next morning after packing our gear in the car we were homewards bound again. Back across the Jardine River by ferry and down the road we went. We made a detour to the east coast about opposite where Weipa was travelling into what is now known as Lockhart River Community but was for a very brief period in World War 2 a heavy bomber base called Iron Range. Not far to the north which we also visited was a bay called Portland Roads, which was a huge American resupply base during World War 2 and home to about 6,000 marines.

Because of very inclement weather conditions, and not wanting to be trapped by the unsealed roads, we had a quick look and high tailed it back out about 100 kilometres to the largely sealed Cape York Developmental Road and continued back down to Coen, where we once again camped behind the hotel, again with intermittent light showers throughout the night. The next morning we were back on the road early travelling south as far as the Musgrave Roadhouse where we took a left turn and travelled east towards Princess Charlotte Bay and then south through Lakefield National Park, that had been created by resuming some huge marginal areas of cattle stations, until we reached Old Laura Station.

After having a look at this old homestead we again took a turn to the east and headed across some really rough country towards Hopevale Community and Cooktown. Staying with an old western friend Johnny Tritton for the night, we revisited some of Cooktown's sights early the next morning before heading south once again. We briefly broke our trip again at Lakeland to visit an old friend Peter Marriot, who has a farm in the cropping area of Lakeland. After retelling a few stories of old times it was back on the road again, and late that night after 9 days on the road we were home again in Townsville.

A section of the Snowy River that we followed along between Lakes Entrance on the Victorian coast and Jindabyne in the Monaro area of NSW

All aboard Puffing Billy in the Dandenong Ranges, Melbourne, Victoria

At the We of the Never Never Elsey grave sites, Northern Territory

Camped on the banks of the Robinson River on Seven Emus Station, Northern Territory

Camped on the Darling River halfway between Menindee and Wilcannia

Conroy, Stephen and Prudence. Following the Diamantina River down between Winton and Birdsville

Cousin John Bell was our tour guide in Sydney, here overlooking Bondi Beach

L to R Bill O_Brien, Conroy, myself and Stephen at Mums grandfathers house Hatton near Warren, NSW

Looking as Happy as Larry with Gunsynd at Goondiwindi

My gate opener on our Cape York trip was Stephen.
He was my only passenger on this trip and there were only a few gates on the Mount Mulligan detour

My pit crew changing a flat tyre about 100 kms east of Birdsville. We camped the night at a roadside rest shed not far from here

On the most south westerly point of Kangaroo Island is Cape du Couedic. This is the Admirals Arch which the kids hiked to while I waited in the car

My three kids at the Adelaide River War Cemetary

Our campsite on a river flat on the southern outskirts of Winton

Possibly not so well known because it is on the Old Stuart Highway but this natural rock formation with a decent sort of log stu

Stephen and I did a side trip into Maytown, an historic gold mining town on our way up Cape York

Stephen and I on our Cape York trip visited the site of Australia's worst coal mining disaster, Mount Mulligan. An explosion in 1921 took 75 lives

The Australian ancestral home of the Terrys on the Murrumbidgee River between Carathool and Hay, NSW

The northern most point of Australia is at this spot on Cape York Peninsula. Stephen walked to this spot, a little too rugged for me

There are no windmills in mainland Australia north of this one. Located at Seisia, Cape York Peninsula

17

LOOKING FORWARD, LOOKING BACK

December 2016, with Prudence behind the steering wheel making use of her L plates and with Cloncurry as our starting point, we visited the old, long abandoned mining town of Kuridala, before travelling on to Dajarra, once the biggest cattle loading railhead in the world. We stayed the night at an old mate's roadhouse. We travelled on to Boulia before heading west towards Alice Springs and, depending on your opinion, on the famous or infamous Plenty Highway. We fueled up at Tobermorey Station on the Queensland-Northern Territory border, then pushed on to camp the night on the Plenty River. The next day we inspected the historic Alice Springs Overland Telegraph Station, which has been restored faithfully to original condition. With very threatening storm clouds hanging over Alice Springs, we went upmarket and moteled it that night. The next day we drove around The Alice seeing sights such as the Todd River, a heavy transport museum and The Ghan Train museum.

We booked for a camel ride but a torrential, flash thunderstorm stole that one from us. As we left Alice Springs heading for Ayers Rock via Kings Canyon, a few kilometres out of town we viewed the graves of John Flynn and his wife, pioneers of pedal wireless sets and the Royal Flying Doctor Service. After viewing a few spots such as Standley Chasm and the Ochre Cliffs we camped near Kings Canyon. Before travelling on to Ayers Rock (Uluru) and the Olgas (Kata Tjuta) the kids did the walk into and up onto Kings Canyon. I left it to the kids with instructions to take lots of photos of the hike while I rested in the car. We arrived at Ayers Rock about midday and went straight to the attraction, because I was keen for the kids to climb it before it was closed to climbers forever.

Because it had also showered at 'The Rock' the previous evening, the Rangers had the climb closed for "safety reasons" because it was "too wet", telling us it would definitely be open the next morning. So we contented ourselves with cruising and hiking the tracks at the base and drove to The Olgas to have a look there. We camped the night at the Uluru Campgrounds and were down at The Rock waiting at the appointed time that the Rangers had indicated it would be open. Alas, we were dudded again because it was now "too windy". I was very disappointed to have to leave without the kids having climbed it. Back to the Stuart Highway then to travel towards southern destinations. Originally intending to stay with friends on Lambina Station in northern South Australia, we found their road blocked by muddy conditions and flowing creeks, as they had also had rain, so we then had to backtrack to the Stuart Highway and continue southwards.

So it was back to the highway again and southwards to camp at the next roadhouse on the highway. The next day we arrived at Coober Pedy, the opal mining capital of Australia. The highlight of our stay there was a night in an underground motel and an evening at the Coober Pedy Drive-In Theatre, which was indeed a very primitive affair, but "when in Rome", as they say. I went a few kilometres out of town to the longest barrier in the world, the Dog Fence, while the kids took in the underground accommodation. It was onto Woomera Rocket Range next which, although closed now, was famous during the 50s, 60s and 70s as the location of Australia's involvement in the space and arms race. On reaching Port Augusta the following day we found my friends from Lambina Station, who were, unknown to us as we had been unable to contact them, there for emergency medical reasons.

We moteled for one night in Port Augusta because of inclement weather, travelling the next day onto a lonely beach just south of Port Lincoln that had once been a whaling station, where we spent the night. The next day it was onto Coffin Bay, famous Australia-over for their delicious oysters, and then from there onto Streaky Bay. Once again spending a night there in a cabin because it was unseasonably cold and windy. The next day saw the X Trail heading back to Port Augusta to head north for home on the Strzelecki Track through the Moomba Gas Fields to Innamincka and the Dig Tree.

I had the initially sound idea that as well as being our most direct route home, the kids would also get to see one of Australia's perhaps most iconic locations. However wet weather once again played a foul hand in altering our travel plans. Near the Innamincka turn off the dirt road had been closed by police because of a drenching from an unexpected rain event and we had to return to Port Augusta, and then detour via Broken Hill, Wilcannia on the Darling River, Cobar, Bourke, once again on the Darling River and then to Charleville. It turned out to be a long short cut on our way home and the Dig Tree had to wait for another school holiday trip.

July 2017 saw me with only Conroy for a passenger. On this trip we visited the area we had missed because of rain on our last trip, known as the Corner Country, where the states of New South Wales, South Australia and Queensland meet. As mentioned previously the area is known as the iconic camp place of the ill-fated Burke and Wills expedition of 1860. We began by travelling west to Charters Towers then south through Clermont, Emerald and Springsure, to arrive and camp at Carnarvon Gorge for the night. The next morning Conroy did some hiking and photography for me before we travelled on to Roma. There we investigated the history of the first drilling for oil and gas in Queensland about 100 years ago, right in the township of Roma.

As it was very late in the day, we overnighted in Roma and headed further south the next morning. Our first stop was at the township of Surat. Surat's claim to fame is that it was the destination of the very last Cobb & Co coach run in 1924. It also has a Cobb & Co coach museum, in a building that was owned by Cobb & Co and used for a store, as well as the coach depot. We then travelled south again, and on reaching St George, we turned towards sunset and kept motoring through Cunnamulla before pulling up for the night at the Eulo Queen Hotel in the township of Eulo.

Eulo was settled about 1870. It was primarily a service centre for nearby cattle stations and a small opal field. It was also the home of Isobel Gray, or the legendary 'Eulo Queen' as she was known. She and her husband owned the local hotel which is now named in her 'honour' and they were usually only one short hop ahead of the law. It once held the world famous annual lizard racing event which was eventually stopped by conservationists. Nearby mud springs are also a tourist attraction that helps the local economy along. That night we dined in the pub and camped in their backyard. The next morning we were on the move early travelling westwards towards Thargomindah, which also had much interesting history, being settled in the late 1860s to service nearby stations. In 1898 it was the second town in Queensland after Brisbane to have electric street lighting. It was the first town in Australia to have hydroelectric power, which was provided by a turbine running off pressure from the town's flowing artesian bore.

A couple of hours looking at the town and a bite to eat before moving on again, this time past the famous Nockatunga Station to the also famous nearby Noccundra Hotel, which was built from hand hewn sandstone blocks in the early 1860s. From here we were on a southerly course to the NSW town of Tibooburra, passing through the NSW/Qld border at the

'Warri Gate'. Tibooburra saw a number of the early outback explorers, including Burke and Wills, pass through the immediate vicinity on their way to other places. A short lived nearby gold rush put Tibooburra, or The Granites as it was originally named, on the map in the 1880s and it has been there ever since. Conroy and I dined at the hotel and swagged it at the caravan park. The highlight of our overnight stay was seeing a couple of restored T model Ford cars on a circumnavigation of Australia, especially the hand crank cold start (it was a very cold night) early the next morning as they set off.

The next morning we set off again, first passing through Camerons Gate at Camerons Corner where the three states all intersect. Located there is a roadhouse and campground that hosts the Tri State Golf Competition each year, a novelty event designed to attract the more adventurous golfers to this remote 'brown'. After lunch and photos at Camerons Corner it was on through the Moomba Gas Fields to Innamincka on Coopers Creek. We dined at the Innamincka Hotel that night. This area was settled immediately after Burke and Wills' untimely demise on the banks of Coopers Creek in 1861. The Innamincka Hotel laid claim to the largest bottle heap in the southern hemisphere at their back door until the empty bottles floated off down Coopers Creek in one of its legendary epic floods.

Conroy and I camped on the banks of Coopers Creek for one night listening to the dingoes howling in the cool desert night air. We watched a brace of pelicans silently paddling upstream in the cold water next morning as we had breakfast and a pannikin of tea, before setting off for the Dig Tree after breakfast. There was much history to be absorbed at the Dig Tree, which was located on Nappa Merrie Station. I felt we absorbed too much information during our short, hour-long stay. The atmosphere of the area where Burke and Wills spent their last days over 160 years ago but push on we had to, for we were very quickly running out of available time.

We followed the Queensland and South Australian border northwards to enable us to visit another state boundary corner, namely Haddon Corner, which we briefly visited for posterity's sake. Then we pushed on for an after-dark arrival into the small western township of Windorah, which was also located on the banks of Coopers Creek, but much further north than our previous night's camping site at Innamincka. We had a meal at the local hotel and then retired to swag it for the night in the camping area of Windorah's caravan park. Early in the morning, to the chorusing of a contingent of pink and grey galahs, we rose to be on our way to Charleville, passing through Quilpie mid-journey.

This is the area of Australia that was first settled by the Duracks of 'Kings In Grass Castles' fame, which was a book written by a descendant, Dame Mary Durack. On arriving in Charleville after a week of camping on the ground, we sought accommodation at a legendary hotel in this area, the Hotel Corones. This grand old hotel, which was built and run by an Italian family in the 1930s, was a nod to the accommodation that you would normally find in a much larger city. From here we went to Blackall, where I dropped Conroy with his country cousins on his mother's side to spend the remainder of his school holidays, and I continued on home to Townsville. Another educational trip done and dusted.

July 2018 saw another Gulf Country trip. As passengers on this trip I had my youngest son Conroy and my grandson Dacey. We travelled to a one million acre working ecotourism cattle station called Lorella Springs and met up with my eldest son Joe and his family, who had travelled down from Darwin. They had travelled down with two other families that were friends of theirs. This trip was different to all our other trips in that we were not moving on each day and did not cover many kilometres. Instead we camped at the Lorella Springs homestead and did day trips to places of interest around the property.

The campground was situated on a spring-fed running stream, which our kids all had an interest in as they were catching cherabin in their dilly pots, which then led to the cooking pots. There were many sandy tracks to different waterholes and attractions around the property, all sign posted to reduce the possibility of getting lost. The rule was that you could travel wherever you liked on the property and camp wherever you liked as long as you did no damage, did not leave rubbish anywhere, notified the management of the area you were travelling in and of course of your intended return date.

Our biggest excursion on the station was an overnighter down to the coast of the Gulf of Carpentaria. We camped overnight on a creek that we couldn't swim in and could only admire because of the 'large lizards' that you could not see but knew without a doubt were in there looking back at us, waiting for their next meal. All too soon it came to an end and everyone had to return from whence they came. We returned home by a different route via Cape Crawford, or to use its colloquial name, the Heartbreak Hotel, then to the Barkly Roadhouse, then onto Camooweal, camping for the night just outside town on the Georgina River.

The next morning when we refueled in town the boys had a look at Freckleton's Stores, which in days gone by had supplied hundreds if not thousands of droving teams with the basic supplies. Freckletons Stores were among a select few stores in the outback where it was said you were able to purchase anything, from a ship's anchor to a thimble, and just about anything in between. Moving on from Camooweal we were on a quick home run journey staying with cousins overnight in Hughenden, before arriving back in Townsville the next day.

Even though they still had their 'screens' with them, I saw our trips as a mind expanding exercise for my children to highlight to them that there was a whole lot more to Australia and their lives than the Townsville city limits and their ever present 'screens'. Besides doing the regular checks under the bonnet at our fuel stops, they attended to the hooking on and unhooking of the trailer, checking tail lights and indicators, checking tyre pressures and making sure the safety chain and tow ball was all secured. They all became very adept at working as a team to unload and reload the trailer, at pitching in and doing chores to set up camp for the night.

They experienced cooking up a meal in an impromptu setting, usually in a low light situation and with limited cooking utensils. If they finished their allocated chore, they helped someone else that had not finished, and did not climb onto the bleachers and become a spectator. I tried to impress upon them when travelling and camping together, or indeed doing anything, that it was important to be a cohesive unit and work as a team, all pulling together to realise a goal, or else social cohesion could unravel fairly quickly. The learning also extended to the changing of flat tyres on the car or the trailer should that occur, regardless of time, location or temperature.

I really enjoyed the trips observing the country and learning the history of the places that we stayed in and passed through, but it was not such a hit with the kids. However I am sure they will look back in appreciation later in life and on reflection will regard the time spent with Dad as not a complete waste. It was not long however before I noticed that as soon as I mentioned a holiday trip, they all suddenly had other things on whereby they could not possibly go on the trip with Dad. It was quite amusing to see them thinking of excuses as quickly as possible, to be the first or second one with a valid reason to get an exemption and not have to go. And what happened to the unlucky slow third one? Well, they became the default passenger who went on to be Dad's gate opener and gopher on yet another trip exploring the wondrous vast expanse of our great Australian landscapes.

On one of our trips we were on the Plenty Highway travelling from Boulia to Alice Springs and we came upon a couple of young British tourists in trouble. They had experienced a flat tyre and for some unfathomable reason they did not have a car jack with them, so had travelled about 40-odd kilometres on the flat tyre, consequently destroying both the rim and the tyre. We pulled up to help but with me being on my walking stick it was more or less up to the three kids to effect the tyre change using our jack, which they did quickly and efficiently, to the astonishment of the travellers.

Of course coming from a totally different environment to the harsh outback with its unfathomable distances and sparse scattering of human life, they were absolutely amazed that three young kids, all under the age of 17, could change a flat tyre in the absolutely sweltering conditions all by themselves. All useful skills in the journey of life and attributes that not many city kids or foreign tourists possess. They also saw and learnt many things about the history of Australia; there were not too many monuments or information signs that we went past without pulling up to find out what it was about. A sign was a sign to the kids that a stop was imminent.

Interspersed between travelling with my children I also began doing trips visiting my elderly mother and three sisters in Brisbane on a more regular basis. On these trips between Townsville and Brisbane, because I was never on a tight schedule, I also had the opportunity to detour off the beaten track to visit friends of mine, and out-of-the-way places of interest that I had not had the chance to visit previously. That ever elusive photographic scene still continued to lure me on and on. On a number of occasions I had my mother's 'little baby brother' with me, who was 92 and still very keen to travel and take in the sights. Uncle Mike was a wealth of information on Australian history and locations and still keen to add to his database of information. He was a great conversationalist with a terrific sense of humour and he was great to have for a travelling companion to break the boredom of conversing with myself.

I did a couple of trips with my mother and Uncle Mike to visit relatives in New South Wales, returning to their old stamping grounds where they had both spent their younger years. These trips gave them much enjoyment, with a personal chauffeur to go here, there and everywhere. They revisited the highlights of their younger years on properties around the Warren and Dubbo areas where, as the old saying goes, "there were more O'Briens than hairs on a dog's back". We also gave the relatives and friends in Sydney and coastal areas a good going over, just so no one could say they had been missed out.

My two youngest sons Stephen and Conroy, along with Prudence for a short while, were still involved with Scouts Australia at the time, so having a more reliable vehicle meant we could attend some of the bigger regional Scout camps in North Queensland. We attended a four day camp at Lake Tinaroo on the Atherton Tablelands, along with Scouts from all over North Queensland. We attended quite a number of group camps in the Townsville area, travelling to Ayr, Ingham and Charters Towers. Although we travelled by bus to this one, we also attended a Cuboree in Maryborough that was one week in length, and there were Cub Scouts from all over Queensland attending with a wide variety of activities to keep the Cubs active and interested. It included a whale watching excursion out in the waters off Fraser Island, which turned out to be quite a windy and chilly day, but for kids that had never seen a whale it was a highlight of the trip.

A feature at Ayres Rock known as the Kangaroos Tail

At the Corner Store where the three states come together and they hold the novelty Tri State Golf Championships

Coffin Bay the home of the famous Australian oysters was visited on the Eyre Peninsula of South Australia

Conroy and I at the Eulo Queen Hotel, Eulo on our way to the Dig Tree

Conroy and I camped on Coopers Creek not far from Innamincka and in the vicinity of where Burke & Wills perished in 1860

Conroy and I visited the first hydro electric lighting plant in Australia at Thargomindah

Conroy and Stephen in the back and Prudence at the helm of the Holiday Express in SA

Conroy on Coopers Creek at Burke & Wills Dig Tree

Conroy opening the Warri Gate on the NSW border between Nocundra and Tibooburra

Doing a whale watching excursion while attending the Maryborough Cuboree

On our Ayers Rock trip we visited the 1960s and 1970s Rocket Research and Development town of Woomera

On our Dig Tree trip, Conroy at Haddons Corner

On the replica Endeavour when it visited Townsville

Once again having their photo taken with another of those bloody signs

Prudence getting up the hours on her Learners Licence during our Ayers Rock trip

Stephen, Conroy and Prudence at Cloncurry before we head to the Red Centre

The last operating Cobb & Co coach run in 1924 terminated in this building in Surat. It is now a museum

The site where Rev. John Flynn and his wife are buried just west of Alice Springs

18

MOVING ON WITH MND

In the early days, when my symptoms were first becoming apparent, no one seemed to know what I was suffering from, even though it was painfully obvious that there was a major issue manifesting in my limbs. I first noticed awkwardness, unexplained tripping and, when relaxing on our lounge of an evening, repeated bouts of mild but very noticeable foot tremors that I could not control. I was referred to Dr. Peter Silburn, a neurologist in Wickham Terrace, Brisbane, but after blood tests, CAT scans, MRI scans and a lumbar puncture test, nothing. The best he could come up with, even though there was no history in my family, was a very general diagnosis of hereditary spastic paraparesis, which could have been any one of quite a few different conditions.

In 2006 after the move to Townsville, and no longer able to hold a job that required physical input, I was attempting to claim the Total & Partial Disability Pension. Nearly every Australian would have had the frustrating experience of dealing with the little paper shuffling tin gods of a government department. Even though I could provide evidence of every letter of referral and every visit to a doctor or neurologist since 2002 and the fact that I could no longer hold a job because of my physical impairment, I didn't have a diagnosis for a specific condition. In their highly esteemed opinion it was simple; I didn't qualify. Although the wording from one application to the next didn't vary all that much, my fourth application was eventually successful.

The fourth application had two extra words added after I visited an understanding Townsville neurologist by the name of Dr. Jon Reimers . After explaining my situation to him and the number of applications I had submitted, he added Multiple Sclerosis to my application form. Problem solved. That opened the door to MS Qld and occupational therapists who assessed me for all sorts of aid devices to make life easier in the house. Rails for my shower cubicle, walking sticks, wheelie walkers, lift chairs, special shoes and all sorts of items that you would not have imagined. Not that I needed them all immediately, but it was good to know the sort of items available. I also became involved with a social group, 'Townsville MSers', who met once a fortnight to shoot the breeze, about not only the latest MS updates, but just to talk and swap notes of our difficulties and give each other support in a positive fashion.

While there have been negative aspects to my journey, they have been far outweighed on the scales of life by the positive things. I am very fortunate to live in the times that I do, as compared to even fifty years ago there have been huge advances in research, treatment and aids to make life easier for people living with disabilities. Daily living is much more accessible, with nearly all businesses these days being extremely 'disability friendly', from entrance ramps, to aisle access and toilet facilities. I still go for my Driver License renewal each year, even though my financial situation has made owning a vehicle these past four years an impossibility, because on occasion I can still hire a car when I want to, to do a special trip that Queensland Rail and my scooter can't accommodate.

The last few decades have seen huge improvements in the disability sector, with a big item being electric mobility scooters. Over the last four years I have clocked up 12,000 kilometres on my electric mobility scooter, but it is now in an end-of-life crisis. I am definitely not a convert to the 'green' renewable energy push, but Chris Bowen (Federal Minister for Climate Change and Energy) would be proud of me. It is possible to do 45 kilometres on one battery charge, so I can still do all of my social engagements, shopping and health appointments with ease. My new scooter, that I picked up at the beginning of 2025, has got some custom modifications made to it making it better than the last. It will be able to do about 90-odd kilometres on the one battery recharge, and has much bigger storage lockers on it for purchases made on my shopping forays.

In 2023 through 'Townsville MSers', who quite often have a guest speaker at their functions, I had the good fortune to be listening to one Justine Martin. This lady was nothing but positive. She also suffered from a rare form of MS, had twice been diagnosed with differing types of cancer, and had had a number of other negative experiences in her trips around the sun. She is at the top of her game running seven businesses that saw her working as a book publisher, an in-demand public speaker and a mentor for aspiring authors. As she spoke she told us that she was planning a book about the resilience of people with disabilities and was looking for contributors to this book. Why wouldn't you put your hand up for someone that could make you the next James A Michener? Together with a few other people my hand rose towards the ceiling of the Dalrymple Hotel function room.

I had never had any serious aspirations to write a book, but because I had always been an avid reader I had wondered offhand how to become an author. Thoughts like, 'Where do you start?', 'Where do you end?' and 'What do you put in the middle?'. Anyway, Justine returned to her home state of Victoria and we began meeting on Zoom to start work on this proposed book, and all my curiosity was satisfied. I discovered that the main key to writing a book was not to worry or overthink it, just start writing – which I did. 23 contributors were given a chapter each to write with a limit of 3,000 words. The joy of writing is that it just seems to keep coming – sometimes you get a mind block – but with a few thoughts and suggestions from your mentor, off you go again. Anyhow when I got to

6,000 words I had to bring it to an end, and do some serious editing to trim it back to the required number. It was all a very interesting exercise both in the composition and the editing. "Whispers of Resilience" was published and launched in mid-2023.

Now that I had had a taste of the power of writing and 'telling a story', I wanted to continue this addictive pastime. I had always been a fan of biographies and real life stories and was not much into fantasy or novels, apart from those written by James A Michener, in the genre of historical fiction. So that was the starting point for this book, my memoirs and recollections of stories passed down about my family and other locals in the Hughenden district. Through talking to friends about what I am doing, I am fairly confident that there could well be another book in me yet. A friend of mine who is a fair bit older than me has had a very interesting life working in the bush, but does not have the drive to get it down on paper. He has agreed to talk with me and let me record our conversation, which I will put down on paper for him, with him having control of the final output. We shall see where this leads.

Continuing to mention positives I must make mention of the MND and Me Foundation, which is a Brisbane organisation that I have become involved with. I first became involved with MND & Me whilst one of their research team members was visiting Townsville to deliver an information seminar to MS & MND people, long before Covid 19 hit our shores. I joined their organisation online initially, just to be a part of the group and benefit from any information that was flowing through. After a while, as I became aware of the scope of work that they were doing, in both the areas of research and support, I decided to be a part of the regular observations to assist in the collection of data to aid the research. This was not just for Queensland or Australia but is being added to an international database. As time went on, I became more and more involved with them because of their regular visits to North Queensland to assist and support MND sufferers.

There are about five variants of MND, which, although rare, are paralysing and wasting diseases that are usually very aggressive. Life expectancy can range from 1 to 5 years after diagnosis, with 27 months – or in everyday English, a little over two years (not very bloody long) – being the average, and in the final stages is more or less a complete paralysis of the body. I consider myself very fortunate that the variant that I have been afflicted with is PLS, or to address it by its full title, Primary Lateral Sclerosis. PLS is even rarer again.

The end result of PLS is the same as the other variants of MND, but as it is a very slowly progressing form of MND it will just take me a lot longer to arrive. I have had gradually worsening symptoms at this stage for 25 years, and while my functioning is fairly limited compared to what it once was, I can still mobilise independently, and dress and bathe myself. None of the neurologists have given me any indication that my time on this rock, even after 25 years, is becoming limited.

I don't wish to sound morbid or self-centred, however as time goes by my ability to move, to converse and to think and process information will become increasingly limited and my cognitive processes will also be affected. In the past as a younger man I always had an awkwardness conversing with disabled people, because aside from the physical difficulties I just didn't know what to talk about with them. Because their lives were so limited physically I felt that it was rubbing their faces in their lot in life by talking as if nothing had happened or was wrong.

I now know, looking from the other side of the fence, that it is exactly the same as talking to everybody else. They want to talk about everyday stuff. In this day and age it is becoming much easier for disabled people to converse because there is technology like text to speech apps for iPads and laptop computers, and Eyegaze apps where you can use your eyes to activate the keypad on a laptop to write a message. The Information Technology Age has created so many useful tools, not only for the general public, but to assist people that are physically and mentally disadvantaged.

In early 2020, when the Covid epidemic began to take hold, everyone was becoming very concerned with the unknown quantities and consequences of the disease. My sisters became very concerned that they could pass it on to our elderly mother by way of the shopping, as well as the cooking and cleaning that they were doing for her on a weekly basis. They asked me if I would go down and live in isolation with her and assume those duties, thereby bypassing the risk of their coming and going from the wider community. So, together with my mother, we were confined to her unit in Brisbane for about three months and did not venture outdoors for anything. My sisters were doing our grocery shopping for us and then leave the groceries on our doorstep for us. I would then retrieve the groceries before wiping every single item down with disinfectant to remove any Covid germs before bringing them in.

It's quite ridiculous when you pause to think about it now, but such was the paranoia in the early days of the Covid 19 epidemic. We spent our time listening to music, examining old photos, watching a lot of television and reading or rereading lots of books. Because Mum's unit overlooked quite a large area of bushland, we also spent a lot of time on her verandah observing the native wildlife, as well as some cattle and horses that ran in this area, and had many conversations and recounted tales of the days spent in the bush on the property.

Initially, in the early days of the Covid 19 emergency, when we were being treated to images of people dropping in convulsing heaps and dying in the streets of China, it was a terrifying scenario to think about. In addition to this, they were promoting the theory that the elderly were far more vulnerable if they caught Covid 19 than the rest of the population. However, my doubts and scepticism about the impending global catastrophe were being more and more fueled by our political and bureaucratic minders as they shuffled through media conferences with their denials and double speak on the issue.

Over the course of a few months, they moved from the position of no mandated vaccines and lockdowns, to not allowing movement outside your garden, facing unemployment if unvaccinated, and a myriad of other restrictions and enforcements. All increasingly enforced by a thuggish, brutal overbearing police force, the likes of which Australian people had never before seen. We all know now that it was a colossal hoax perpetrated on the world by an as yet unproven number of international players, both political, bureaucratic and corporate, with most of our politicians taking sides with them. Still, at the time, it was all very scary stuff. Still is.

After about three months, when the initial scare of Covid 19 had passed, I returned home to Townsville; but after that event, I spent a lot more time visiting my mother in Brisbane, travelling down there roughly every three months. It was then that I became more involved with the MND and Me Foundation, after I attended some of their Support Group meetings at their head office. Because I was going to be down in Brisbane on a fairly regular basis I then signed up to become a study and source of data for their research program.

As an organisation, they are very involved in every aspect of the MND cause, from client support and disability equipment supply to fundraising in many different activities, including marathons, raffling hot rod vehicles, gala dinners, quiz nights and bicycle rides to different locations. Their fundraising, along with government funding, is mainly channelled to their research programs that are conducted at the University of Queensland at St Lucia in Brisbane. The data that is collected and analysed is added to data on an international level in the search for either the relief of, or a cure for, Motor Neurone Disease.

In 2010, following Scott Sullivan's MND Diagnosis at the young age of 38, he founded MND and Me to support people with MND. A husband and father of two young children, he did the first fundraising ride for the Foundation himself by riding a specially built tandem bicycle from Brisbane to Sydney. I never ever met Scott but he ran the Foundation in the early stages after he was first diagnosed and he had the foresight to purchase the building it is now housed in, The Queensland MND Centre in Coorparoo. In 2014 sadly Scott passed away two months before the building renovation was officially opened but it is now the home of the Foundation, housing the offices, a meeting room and a large equipment resources centre, as well as hosting events and monthly support groups. Following Scott's passing, Paul Olds was appointed as CEO and built the Foundation up to service the whole state of Queensland, as well as grow the research funding available, including the first ever Scott Sullivan Fellowship, a three year grant for an MND researcher involved in patient-focused MND Research. In February 2020, Jane Milne took over as CEO from Paul and still holds the position today.

To Care and To Cure - that's the mission of the MND and Me Foundation. In 2024, the Research funding has grown to include 4 x one year Impact grants per year, a three year early career research fellowship and the Scott Sullivan Research Fellowship. In the 23/24 financial year they funded $720,000 worth of projects in Queensland. Their Care services aim to provide equitable access to targeted support services for people living with MND, as well as their carers and families. The service offering includes: MND Concierge Service, Equipment Rental, Information Sessions, Support Groups, Allied Health Support, Carer and Past Carer Support, Equitable Support Coordination, Communication Assistance, Child Psychology and an app that assists with the administrative burden of living with MND.

In recent times the MND and Me Foundation have been running a regular two day event that they call The MND Roadshow in major regional centres of Queensland. The idea is to network all of the following: researchers, neurologists, allied health professionals, occupational therapists, support workers and people living with the condition. One day is devoted to the medical side of things, but if sufferers wish to attend on that day they may. The second day is focused on people living with the condition and enabling them to tell their story, so that everyone with MND knows that they are not on their own. The aim is to have a Roadshow in all of Queensland's major regional centres and return regularly as time goes by.

Early in 2023, because I had seen so many other fundraising initiatives, I had the idea to help with their fundraising by riding a mobility scooter around Australia. I had plenty of time at my disposal, I had a mobility scooter, I liked travelling and it would be, I thought, a lot of fun. However, during a recent visit to Brisbane, I had a meeting with a chap who had previously done fundraising for the MND and Me Foundation by doing a solo ride around Australia on his bicycle. My purpose was primarily to pick his brains on what to look out for and expect on this mammoth task and I was very thankful for his revelations.

The resulting conversation revealed a number of things, the first being there were many unseen pitfalls to fundraising on this scale that I had not considered. Firstly he had taken 12 months off from his job and he had also used a huge amount of his own finances to run his campaign. My initial thoughts were to use Highway One as much as possible to promote awareness and to enhance the fundraising aspect of the endeavour. The main obstacle to this idea however was that it is actually illegal to travel around the continent on a bicycle or a mobility scooter using Highway One to get from Point A to Point B.

With backup escort vehicles behind and ahead of the mobility scooter I imagined that to be legal and compliant but it is actually illegal. Other aspects that I had not considered were the intricacies of the promotional campaign and the vagaries of fundraising. From Cairns to Adelaide along the eastern and southern coastlines, where most of Australia's population is based, would be where the fundraising and promotional efforts would be most effective. There are a huge number of fundraisers travelling the Australian continent, and to get support from national suppliers like fuel or food outlets you have to plan five years out from your event, which is another thing I had not anticipated.

It soon became evident that, albeit in ignorance, I had been far, far too optimistic in my expectations of what was achievable. I still plan to do some form of Awareness / Fundraising Campaign for the Foundation, but it will not be in my first chosen activity.

At Life Skills Queensland with Charlie the shop dog looking at some drink coasters I made

During a photo shoot for Big Mikes Mobility For Life. With Linda, one of my support workers from Just Better Care, Townsville

My campaign vehicle during the Referendum

My main form of transport these days. A little slower than I would like but still better than walking

Self Portrait

Where would you be without a sense of humour

Writing talking or talking writing With my writing mentor and publisher Justine Martin

*With Jamie and Mary Painter from Just Better Care
at their inaugural Disability Ball*

19

REMEMBERING THE MAN THAT WAS DAD

Dad's life was a rich tapestry of experiences and characters. He was an incredible people-person and he had a knack for holding a conversation with just about anyone he ran into, and it was not hard work for him – he enjoyed the art of banter. He had an incredible talent for telling a story and could hold people enthralled for hours at a party or gathering, whether it be reminiscing about his early years, telling jokes or just general knowledge about any bush subject matter. It lost nothing in the telling when Dad was telling it. Mum might have been annoyed with him about something, quite possibly an irreverent comment about the Pope or the local priest, but a half hour later everything was usually back on an even keel, with a few smooth words and a grin or two he would be forgiven.

He knew people far and wide around Queensland. It didn't seem to matter where you went with Dad, he could always manage to run into someone he knew or had met in his travels. I never knew his father, as he died when I was only about three years old, but from what I was told Dad probably inherited that trait from him. However from what I was told about my grandfather Tom, he was also more abrupt, and would make his point in no uncertain terms. Tom Terry traded a lot of stock over the years and bought and sold many properties throughout his lifetime. Dad and his brothers got along tremendously well together for a lifetime, especially Dad, Graham and Bernard, who had soldiered along together at Westmorelands for the best part of a decade.

Tom had them as part of his workforce from about the age of seven or eight, so they must have worked out early in the piece that it was better if they all got along well. Dad's next youngest brother Edward died at 13 years of age, and as is their want, being consecutive siblings, he and Dad were the best of mates. He slipped and fell over at Eldorado in the shower room and went to the Hughenden hospital with a broken arm. He contracted pneumonia and died a week later. It must have really affected Dad because he never spoke of Edward to me, or to my knowledge, any of his children. My younger brother Edward was named in his memory.

As a child Dad had what might be considered a limited education. On Saranac and Eldorado, his father employed tutors to give his brood of offspring basics in the three R's, and then later on he and younger brother Graham spent two years at Abergowrie College in the Upper Herbert valley near Ingham. Dad's brothers Bernard and Frank, with their half brothers Stuart and Alec, went to Riverview College in Sydney for a couple of years. Thomasine went to Loreto Convent in Kirribilli on the north shore of Sydney for a few years. Through interschool sports, Mum actually knew Thomasine in Sydney, having no idea that she would later marry her brother. Mum, attending a Hughenden race meeting when in Queensland for the first time, saw this girl that looked familiar to her. Upon chatting they worked out that it had been through interschool netball during their recent boarding school years.

I still have one of Dad's exercise books from his final year at Abergowrie College in 1937. Together with a cursive, copperplate handwriting style it contains all manner of his own very neat, hand drawn diagrams of basic mechanical knowledge from hydraulic jacks to windmills to road building design. In later years Dad could turn his hand to almost anything in our workshop shed: arc welding, oxy welding, timing an engine, steering alignment or replacing a head gasket. It didn't seem to phase him at all and it was all self taught through reading, working with others that knew, as well as good old fashioned trial and error. He also had his own theodolite and staff and pegged out all the levels on the dams that he employed contract dam builders to construct on Elton.

It wasn't until later in life, when he returned to civilisation from Westmorelands, that he acquired a lot of these skills. His father, understandably, having been born in 1877, was very much a man of the horse-drawn era. He may have had a few woodworking tools to make or repair a gate and suchlike, but that would have been the extent of it. He still used horse-drawn earth scoops and fire ploughs up until about the 1940s. He was a lover of Clydesdale draught horses, and over the years bought a number of champion Clydesdale stallions to breed his own Clydesdales. He became converted when his sons convinced him of the benefits of moving with the times and he bought an FDE crawler tractor, scoop and ripper in 1952.

All through the 1940s, Dad and his brothers were operating Westmorelands Station in the Gulf country on the Northern Territory border, which featured minimal mechanisation as well. Dad, at the age of seventeen, with a little tuition from a seasoned station saddler on adjoining Wollogorang Station, became the station saddler on Westmoreland for the duration of their 9 year tenure in the gulf. He was responsible for probably a dozen pack saddles, a dozen riding saddles and bridles as well as greenhide hobbles and ropes. Graham was the cook, with the staple being fairly simple fare of corned beef, potatoes and onions, and damper with a little jam or tinned fruit and custard to break the monotony. Bernard was the bookkeeper/organiser. They all took it in turns to be boss of the show as well as taking it in turns to go to Burketown in the wagon for supplies.

Mention of going to Burketown with the wagon reminds me of another story that Dad told me. It concerns an unbroken colt that Dad had taken out to Westmorelands in the first mob of 100 plant horses that he had taken out in 1940 and had been turned into the 80,000 hectare valley that they used as a bullock paddock, where they also kept about 200 head of plant horses. Apparently his father had taken a shine to this particular horse as being a very fine type.

It was a thoroughbred with a hint of Clydesdale showing through, a big, strong fine style of horse, and every year when Tom went out he asked about this horse and as to whether or not it had been broken in yet. When the reply was in the negative he was not shy in voicing his displeasure about what a useless mob of stockmen they were; the fact that there were only about 200 horses in an 80,000 hectare horse paddock and you weren't going to see every horse every year didn't even rate a mention.

One year they were going to Burketown for supplies and Uncle Bernard sent the indigenous ringers out to bring in a mob of horses so that they could select a team to pull the wagon. Who should turn up in the mob but the 'apple of Tom's eye'. The horse by this time was about six or seven years old and the boys sensed that this was the ideal time to curry favour with their father over this issue. They threw a rope on him and tied him to a huge post in the middle of the yard and left an indigenous ringer there with him to chase him backwards and forwards with a hessian bag for the rest of the day to teach him to 'bend his neck' as they say. They left him tied up to the post for the night so he wouldn't forget about who was now in control - this was the sum total of his 'breaking in'.

The next morning at daylight they harnessed the rest of the team to the wagon first. When they were ready to go, they 'choked' this horse down to the ground, put a blindfold over his eyes and a set of 'spiders' on his feet. Then they dragged him over to his future lead place in the team with another horse and harnessed him up on the ground. Removing the spiders and then the blindfold, he was now ready to go. Dad reckoned it was a pretty wild trip that first day while this horse got used to the new program. They travelled about 25 kilometres compared to the normal 15 kilometres with him doing most of the pulling. The first night he was left in harness and tied to a tree with a good stout greenhide rope. Each succeeding day he displayed considerable improvement as a member of the team.

When Dad arrived back at Westmorelands with the supplies about 10 days later, he had become a very tractable and educated horse. Being a little on the heavy side for a saddle horse, he became part of the pack horse plant. Of course the next time that Tom visited Westmorelands, the boys took great pride in showing Dad the new horse. Tom was justly proud that the job he had been pushing for was completed. The boys thought it best not go into too much detail about methods used or how the process had been undertaken. People will say it was brutal or harsh, but they were not there doing the job. Dad and his brothers didn't have the time, equipment or manpower to do a job where you got accolades or awards for your achievements, they were there to produce results the quickest and most convenient way possible.

It was not until they returned to civilisation at the end of 1947 that Dad and his brothers started to turn towards mechanisation, dragging their reluctant father with them. A motorbike, a truck and a new shearing shed, amongst other things, were added to the station equipment inventory. Dad and his brother Frank were the two most mechanically minded of the brothers I believe. As Tom Terry's sons kept bringing large mobs of cattle in from Westmorelands for the next 9 years he had to find somewhere to park all these 'hides', so he started buying up local properties close to Eldorado.

Elton Downs was the first one and then the neighbouring property, which was Nottingham Downs. Stamford Downs neighbouring Eldorado was already owned and they had never sold Saranac since they had lived there in the 1920s. Later on Tom bought Fermoy Station south of Winton for a few years when they had too many cattle for their own country around Stamford. Dad and his brothers did quite a few droving trips with cattle between the Stamford district and Fermoy Station during the 1950s. In total the Stamford aggregation was about 125,000 hectares, which they used to fatten their Westmorelands cattle on, as well as other cattle that they bought and sold. He quite often bought properties as "drought-proofing". In dry times he would buy additional properties simply for the grass so he would not have to pay for agistment, selling them again when good seasons returned.

Dad always enjoyed a joke, and with his brothers liked to 'take the mickey out' of anyone that they thought would take the bait. Dad once told me that one day they were mustering cattle on Stamford Downs, and Tom had told all of his boys as they mustered to keep an eye out for some sheep that had been missed in that paddock previously, and also to count them. When they all arrived back at the mill with their mobs of cattle about lunchtime, Tom was waiting at the bore with the billy boiling and some lunch for them. Tom was a bit agitated, hopping from one foot to the other, as he wanted some information about the sheep he had asked them to keep an eye out for. They were all in on the joke and gave some head nodding and "ahh"s and "umm"s but were not forthcoming with any details.

Finally Tom could contain himself no longer and wanted some answers; "Well what the bloody hell did you all see, you have been out there all bloody morning, you must have seen something". Graham, who was always a bit on the droll side, answered, " Well, up on the ridge there I saw 21 and a few lambs with them and up the gully there on the far side there was 43 that I didn't see". Well Tom almost had a fit and erupted, "How the bloody hell do you know how many there were if you didn't get to see the bastards". "Oh, Frank saw them and told me about them", Graham answered. All Tom could do was some huffing and puffing when he realised that his smart alec sons had taken a rise out of him, at which they were masters, apparently.

Another day they were working around the homestead and were all having lunch at the house. Tom always sat at one end of the table and carved the meat; Leonie, his wife, sat at the other end and served the vegetables. The rest of the family sat around the huge dining table waiting for their plate to be passed down. As he carved, Tom was going off about the morning and everyone's shortcomings, what they could have done that would have been better. Eventually everyone was served, Tom's harangue ended and the meal started.

Tom thought he better turn the conversation to a lighter note and made a comment on the weather and how hot the day was. Frank sitting at the other end of the table said, "Hey Dad", and then waited. Tom impatiently replied, "Yes?". Frank continued,"If you think it is hot outside, you should try sitting out here in front of you", meaning he was full of hot air. Well, you could have heard a pin drop as Tom glared at him and the others tried to contain their mirth.

Dad loved to take photos and 8mm home movies of the family and his travels with Mum. When we were kids there was nothing we loved more than slide or movie night, and it did not matter how often we saw them, we never ever got sick of watching a rerun. I still have some of the slides and movies in a digitalised format but we lost a lot of them when the roof of our house blew off in Cyclone Althea in 1971.

The love of photography was also something that Dad had obviously inherited from his father. After Dad passed away in 1987, I was helping Mum go through his cupboard sorting all of his stuff out, and I dragged out this old canvas-covered box from the floor at the back. Covered in dust and cobwebs, it had obviously not been out of the cupboard for a long, long time. It contained a very old, bellows-style, dry plate camera of wooden construction, with a chest height wooden tripod.

It was not in operating condition, but it was all intact, and, as I discovered, was his father's camera that Dad had never said anything about. I believe this camera, which I still have, would date back to the very early 1900s, and sheds a whole new light on all of the old family photos taken in the Burdekin area and the Hughenden and Winton area as well when they first moved out there. I have collected a lot of old family photos in recent years, some dating back to 1910. I now believe that my grandfather would have taken all of them with this very camera and I never ever knew. So to be totally truthful, my love of photography probably originated from my grandfather with my father as the conduit.

Dad was an extremely generous person, both with his time and finances, and on a number of occasions got caught out big time by people who failed to honour their commitment to repay him. Without mentioning any names, he helped a person that he had known for quite a few years by financing him into a taxi cab in Townsville, to the tune of probably around $25,000 at the time. Dad was old school – if he knew you reasonably well, a handshake on a deal was good enough, there would have been no paperwork attached to the deal.

Not too long after they had embarked on this arrangement, Black & White Cabs became aware of the business arrangement and made it known to them that they had contravened their rules by not advising them of their financial partnership. I am not aware of all the technical issues of the dispute but on becoming aware of the legalities, this other person reneged on the deal and did not make another repayment to Dad after that time. That person still owed Dad most of that loan when he passed away about 25 years later.

He got caught out a few other times on stock deals in one way or another. One such deal was when a person who was a relation by marriage had a large mob of 'in lamb' ewes for sale. Dad took the offer through the agents when he found out about them. On the day of the inspection, Dad arrived a little bit earlier than the stipulated time and found the mob of ewes only just being yarded.

They should have been yarded a couple of hours previously to let them settle down and cool off a bit before inspection. Now one of the older tricks in the book, when selling ewes 'in lamb' that are not 'in lamb', is to put them in the yard for a couple of days without water. Then just before the inspection time, let them onto water, and being very thirsty they will gorge on water, swell their bellies up and they look as though they are 'in lamb'.

Dad would have known of a few of these types of shonky practices but had not deliberately turned up early suspecting that this person would pull this sort of a stunt on him and so gave him the benefit of the doubt. However a few months later when there should have been a few thousand lambs on the ground and there were none, Dad took it on the chin, and had to admit that his brother-in-law put one over on him.

It was only much later that I realised why, when that person visited, things were always a little bit strained. Dad had politely told him that in the future it was going to be his 'shout' – everytime. Dad became much more wary in later years, but still people were all too aware of his generosity, and you would quite often see people sidle up to 'shout' him a few drinks for a while, to soften him up for 'the bite' to invest in a 'sure thing' race horse or a flash new motor car or some similar thing.

Dad always liked a cold drink on a hot day – and on a cold day as well. It was only later on in life that I realised and accepted the fact that Dad would have been classed as an extremely well functioning alcoholic. I certainly have never held that against him, as a lot of people share that problem and I could have quite easily been there myself. We, as kids and teenagers growing up, not being part of an abusive, dysfunctional family, didn't really notice the alcohol because it was just a part of our life. He was a hard worker, never lazy, not abusive, never a fighter nor a wife beater. He consumed a lot of alcohol throughout each day, but still did his work, did it well and worked long days with everyone else.

He was also very generous with his grog. If there were a team of workers at Elton, no matter how many, there was always a couple of beers each at the end of every day. There would be a couple of cartons of beer for the shearers when the shed cut out. No visitors to Elton could ever claim to have gone thirsty. He did not buy his beer by the carton but did it in style and bought it by the 80 carton pallet from Toowoomba, which arrived on Reilly's Transport, usually when they came to load wool at crutching and shearing time.

I remember it well because I was part of the human chain that passed the cartons from hand to hand between the semi trailer and the old boundary riders' hut where it was stored. His drinking caused some tension between him and Mum because it was a problem that I believe developed after they married. Unfortunately, as statistics tell us all, it was ultimately his undoing, in that it caused the cancer that ended his life at the relatively young age of 66.

Dad enjoyed going to the local horse races, but was never a race horse man as such. He left that up to his brother Graham at Nottingham. Uncle Graham always had a race horse or two on the go and used to race all over the west and in Townsville as well. I don't know how Uncle Graham did it but once he managed to convince Dad to partner him in a race horse that won a few races in Townsville. Dad was not in the partnership for long however; although he loved good horse flesh, he just was not interested in race horses.

It may have been the time involved, the training and the going to a race meeting somewhere every weekend. Dad had a mate John Harris from 'Violet Vale' on Cape York Peninsula who had cattle on agistment at Uncle Bernard's place, 'Star Downs'. He owned a very successful southern racehorse by the name of Colonel Blimp. This stallion had won a lot of starts in south east Queensland and John Harris left him at 'Elton Downs' for about 3 years covering our mares. We ended up with about 20-odd very good styles of horses, large frames, good confirmation and very nice quiet temperaments.

REMEMBERING THE MAN THAT WAS DAD

Accident in the Dodge on the Toowoomba range, mid 30s Leona Terry in foreground, Rupert looking at camera, Frank Devine with hand on car, and gateman tollkeeper obscured in background. Tom Terry photographer

Dad and Mum with all but two of their family present at the Dubbo reunion of the O Briens in 1982

Dad with his two youngest Justin and Leona in Townsville about 1983

Eldorado schoolhouse early 1930s. Standing, Mr. McDermott, Frank, Bernard. Seated, Thomasine, Edward, Graham, seated @ rear, Rupert

Fording the Robinson River on Seven Emus Station. One of Dads annual fishing expeditions with his mates to where ever there were fish

John O_Brien, Catriona Terry, Monica Terry, Leona Terry, Raquel Johnson and Rupert Terry. Central Australian trip in the mid sixties

L to R Sinbad Johnson, Mat Hamilton, Trevor Hall, Rupert Terry. Undoubtedly on a fishing trip some where but location unknown

Monica and Rupert Terry. Pallarenda, Townsville, 1984

Mum and Dad, Peter and Wendy Terrys wedding in Cairns, 1983

Wedding breakfast reception at Queens Hotel Townsville. L-R, Tom & Leona Terry, Rupert and Monica Terry, Irene and John O Brien

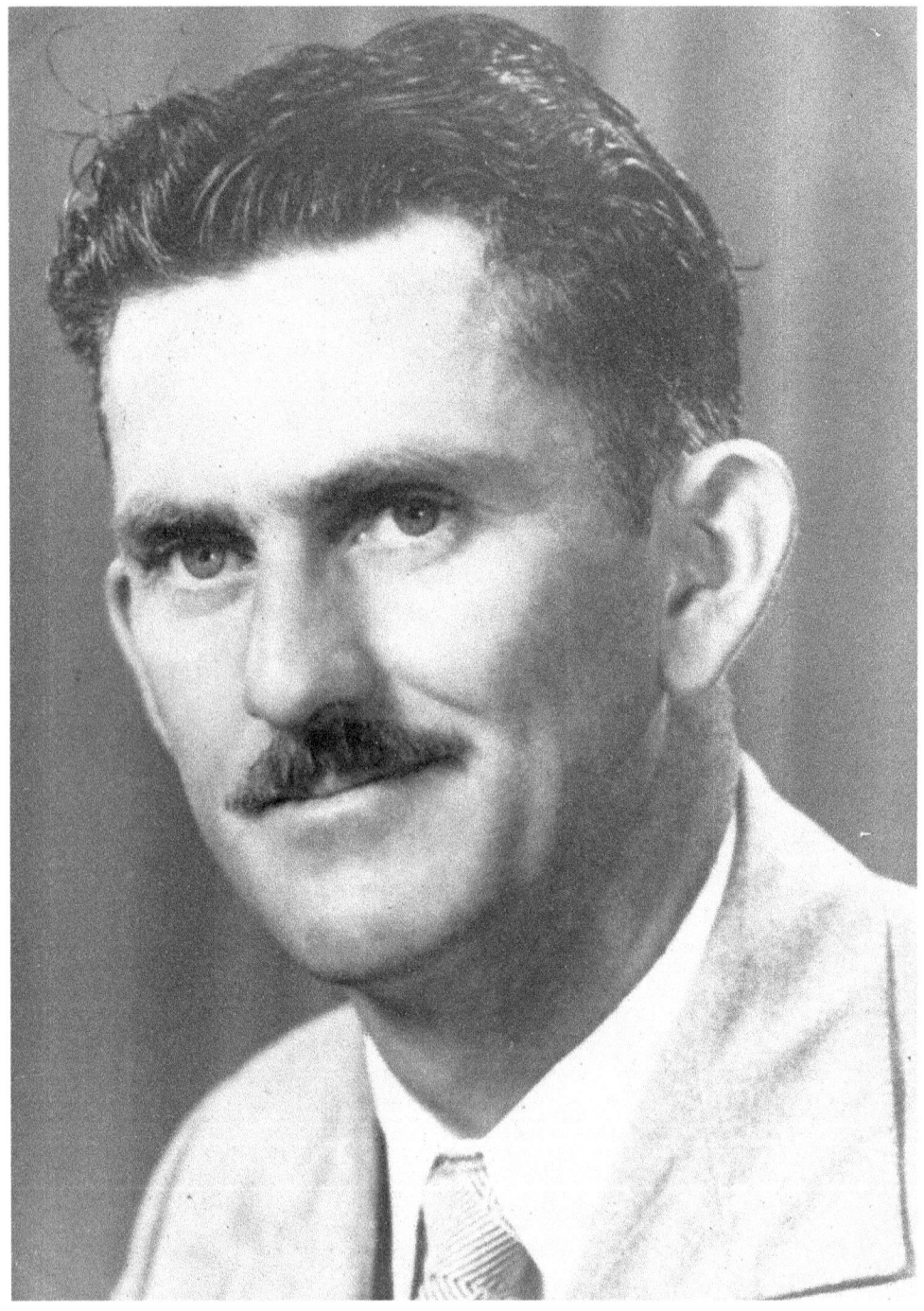

Rupert Terry - 1956

Rupert s 10th birthday at Eldorado, 1931

Watercolor of Saranac homestead where Dad lived until he was 10. Painted by a travelling artist photographer that travelled by horse back around the stations - circa 1920 s

The bride and groom, May 1956

20

DAD, THE ENTERTAINER

Dad was also a self-taught musician, playing piano accordion, harmonica or the old Australian instrument, the good old gum leaf. He could knock out a very decent rendition of a tune on nothing more than a gum leaf. This had come about when at Westmorelands and on the stock routes droving cattle, with nothing more to do of an evening, he turned his hand and ear to mastering the harmonica and the leaf. A treasured memory was that as kids we loved sitting around before going to bed as he played tunes and told stories. I remember he used to sit up tapping his feet in time to his playing and he either used an old tin pannikin over the harmonica or he would cup one hand over it to modulate and change the sound of the harmonica. While he played, his blue eyes would deliver a unique, intense stare of concentration to his rapt youthful audience that was unforgettable. Unfortunately, I never acquired Dad's natural talent, and whilst I love music I could not play a tune to save my life.

He used to play quite a few of the old traditional Irish folk songs and ballads, like 'The Pride of Erin', which he used to call 'Come Back with Hair On', the 'Wearing of the Green' and 'Black Velvet Band', and a few old Australian classics like 'Waltzing Matilda', 'Springtime, It Brings on the Shearing' and 'Eumerella Shore', as well as others. He was also quite handy with a piano accordion, which used to make an appearance from out of the depths of his wardrobe on the odd occasion. The Stamford Races that were held twice a year sometimes had a dance at our shearers' quarters, which the locals and some Hughenden folk attended. There was a piano permanently left in our shearers quarters which I think the race club might have owned, and Dad would add his harmonica or piano accordion to the mix. A lot of fun was had by all. I think the piano accordion might have also been a victim of Cyclone Althea because I don't remember seeing it after Townsville in the latter years of Dad's life.

Some people are quite happy to remain stationary in their own spot in life for their entire lifetime, but not so with Dad. As I have mentioned earlier he had numerous overseas travel trips with Mum, sometimes accompanied by their daughter Marylou to places like Timor, New Guinea, Indonesia, Philippines and Thailand, as well as to Tasmania, New Zealand and Norfolk Island. International jet set travel to tourist destinations was not a prerequisite for Dad's travels. The other end of the travel spectrum, where nothing much more than a swag, a camp oven and plenty of beer were needed, also featured in his many trips, as he also loved going on fishing trips each year with his mates Trevor Hall, Matty Hamilton, Boof McDowall, 'Sinbad' Johnson, Donny Ross and numerous others that were also lovers of drinking trips of the fishing kind.

Sometimes to visit an old mate Willy Shadforth, who owned Seven Emus Station in the Northern Territory, or more familiar ground like their old Westmorelands Station in the gulf country, which was now owned by the Gould family. Always to a property of someone he knew; one year they went to Marina Plains on Princess Charlotte Bay north of Cooktown, which belonged to a friend of Boof McDowall's. For a couple of years he organised marlin fishing trips off the coast of Cairns, and whilst rubbing shoulders with Hollywood stars such as Lee Marvin, bagged a catch only 100 lbs below the Australian record weight at the time. On another occasion he got a group of friends together, including Trevor Hall from Townsville, and they flew to New Guinea by private charter to Bensbach Hunting Lodge, a deer hunting and barramundi fishing operation. This trip had some hair-raising events regarding the flight attached to it that could have ended in disaster, but fortunately all turned out well in the end.

In the early 1960s, many of Dad's colleagues in the Hughenden area were either already pilots or learning to fly and acquiring a light aircraft of their own. John Hanrick from 'Peronne', Pat Delahunty from 'Glennreigh', Max Stoneman, who owned Hughenden's 'Grand Hotel', Frank Davis from 'Wairungha', Tommy Spence from 'Culloden', Allan Logan from 'Arjuna' and his cousin Allan Terry from 'Illalong' and a few others, were all ones that were counted as friends of Dad's. The dentist in Hughenden at the time was a fellow by the name of Tim Gaffney, who also owned a plane and was known as the Flying Tooth.

Dad decided to join the flying fraternity of the bush and began taking flying lessons with plans to purchase his own light aircraft. I don't know what it was, perhaps a couple of fatal local plane crashes around that time, perhaps a drought and the subsequent shortage of money, but something caused Dad's ambitions of soaring with his arch enemies, the eagles, to never come to fruition. Although Dad had a very well kept airstrip at Elton, we never owned a light aircraft.

Dad loved to tell a joke or play a prank on someone. One particular incident I will never forget was a time that we had all been invited over to 'Bernborough Station', which was his brother Frank's property. On our arrival, our cousin Michael, whose birthday it was, came tearing excitedly out to meet us. "Uncle Rupert, Uncle Rupert, I want to show you my new pet lizard". "OK, Mikey, I would love to have a look at him". So Michael very carefully and laboriously extricated his little Tommy Roundhead lizard from his matchbox and passed him over for inspection. Dad then holding the five cm long lizard up by the end of his tail, rotated him this way and that and then back again, then made the comment, "He is very fat Mikey, looks quite tasty".

And then quick as a flash tilted his head back and put Michael's pet lizard into his mouth, then some very over emphasised chewing motions followed by a few deliberate and large swallowing actions. Well, poor Michael could just not believe what his now saucer sized and shaped eyes were telling him. This couldn't be happening, surely not, …… his idol, Uncle Rupert, had just eaten his pet lizard, ……… right there in front of him. Just before Michael burst into tears about the fate of his pet lizard, Dad reached into his mouth, and from under his tongue, with forefinger and thumb, dragged the little lizard out again. Dad, all the time, had just held the lizard trapped beneath his tongue. Michael was elated to be reunited with his pet and that was a joke that we have laughed about for years. The look on Michael's face.

Dad also loved reciting poetry and knew quite a few that he could recite from memory for us. A couple that I got him to write down for me I have never heard before or since, with authors unknown. For lovers of bush poetry I have included the following three poems that Dad had painstakingly transcribed onto paper for me over the years. I say painstakingly because he never had a written version of any of these poems, they were all in his head and he was always remembering another verse, especially with 'My Flinders River Maiden'. When we had the version of 'My Flinders River Maiden' you see on these pages down on paper, Dad said that there were even more verses but he could not remember the others in their entirety. The other two poems he said were the complete versions with nothing more to be added.

I hope you enjoy these absolutely unique versions of Australian bush verse and I would be glad to hear if anyone has ever heard any of these poems recited before. Dad had a lot of poems either cut or torn out of "The North Queensland Register" newspaper that had been sent in from many different contributors over the years, including the renowned

North Queensland poets, 'Bob Bloodwood' or R.C. Pearce and 'Bill Bowyang' or Alexander Vindex Vennard, who was born on Vindex Station near Winton. They were all in the proverbial old shoe box but once again I believe they fell victim to Cyclone Althea. As with so many other things, they were to be never seen again when we lost the roof off our house at Cape Pallarenda that morning.

As well as collecting poetry, Dad was also a collector of anything interesting, always picking up and on the lookout for Morella stones, fossils, bottles, coins, in fact old artefacts of any sort. Dad had quite a collection of interesting old memorabilia that he had collected over the years. On the rare occasion that he bought out the jars that contained his treasured coin and note collection, I was always goggle eyed at the spectacle. He had one coin that he had found along where the old Cobb & Co coach road used to go through Elton. It was a round coin with a square piece from the centre removed and the raised lettering was almost obliterated, but on appraisal from a coin collector it was revealed that the coin was of Chinese origin and about 400 years old.

I remember one fossil that he had found near the No. 2 mill; when it was alive millions of years ago, it would have been somewhat like a modern day crab. What Dad had found would have been the actual body of the creature because you could see where three legs obviously attached on either side. It was about 30 cm across the back and about 10 cm thick. The amazing part of what Dad had found was that it separated into three different parts like a puzzle. You had to jiggle it about a little to get it apart or put it back together again but it was an amazing find. Whenever Dad was walking about anywhere, he always had his eyes on the ground for his next big find.

Perhaps someone reading this book may be able to shed some light on the history of these poems or perhaps even knows who the author of these three poems was. As with a lot of bush verse they are written with a sardonic sense of humor attached even when espousing the most serious of issues like the human condition of love, such as in the following "My

Flinders River Girl", which is one of my favourite poems. I have no idea who or where Dad got these poems from but they are definitely treasures.

My Flinders River Girl.
Author unknown. (related by Rupert Terry)

Once I loved a shearer's daughter on a station in the west,
She was just a common waitress, but a cut above the rest,
She was young and she was pretty, and her rosy lips were full,
This was on the Flinders River, where the jumbucks grew the wool.

So I took the old Rum bottle, and I broke it on a gum,
For the Flinders River maidens never liked the smell of rum,
Then I heard I had a rival and I asked her was it true,
And she hung her head and answered, "Yes, his nibs the jackaroo."

Well, I'd often seen him hanging around her through the day,
When he should have been attending to his duties miles away,
Such a cheeky little beggar, but as any fool could see,
He'd be just a dainty morsel in a knuckle up with me.

So I said to him next morning," You audacious little cow,
Let the girl come out and watch us, and I'll fight you for her now."
I was certain that would bluff him, for I'd always held the view,
That the softest snap of any was the new chum jackaroo.

Well it didn't, for he answered as he blinked his beady eyes
"If she's willing it's a bargain and the winner takes the prize",
So we put the case before her and she clapped her hands with glee,
"You can fight it out between you boys and I'll be referee."

So we didn't waste no time in talking but straight away agreed to go,
To a spot the girl had chosen on the river flat below,
I disliked the situation for in any case I knew,
That I'd have to bring the doctor to attend the jackaroo.

Then we cleared a space around us on the battle ground to be,
While we took our instructions from our handsome referee,
Now make it willing boys but you must pay due regard,
To the straight out rules of boxing and the rabbit punch is barred.

Well I thought I had a melon as he faced me by the creek,
He was barely eight stone seven and his arms looked thin and weak,
He looked so small and weedy and he seemed frightened too,
That I thought "It's just a smack or two then goodbye jackaroo."

But very soon he showed me how a jackaroo could fight,
He was handy with the left and he was handy with the right,
He'd dance away so lightly every time I'd try to close,
And he nearly always caught me such a stinger on the nose.

Well he gave me such a lesson in the art of self defence,
That I wondered if the girl was worth all the bother and expense,
For my face was all cut and bleeding, my eyes all black and blue,
There's no doubt that he was clever was that cheeky bloody jackaroo.

But he turned his eyes a moment to avoid a patch of mud,
And I picked him up and flung him in the Flinders River flood,
Well, we rescued and revived him and he said "You've won the bride."
"You can take her now and keep her and I hope you're satisfied."

So I put my arms around her but she pulled back with a scowl,
"Don't you be in such a hurry, he's the winner on a foul."
When I told her that I thought that all was fair in love and war,
She said she'd never witnessed such a dirty trick before.

T'was in vain I coaxed and pleaded for she stoutly held the view,
That I lost the fight completely when I fouled the jackaroo,
Were they married, yes, of course and lived as happy as could be,
And I heard he got promoted, but I didn't wait about to see.

Well I hope that they are happy but I wonder after all,
When they link their arms together and the past events recall,

Do they ask each other was the verdict just and true,
When I fought that losing battle against the new chum jackaroo.

'Gates', to my way of thinking, is quite a humorous poem about a person that would have obviously had a fair bit to do with gates and the time to observe and describe their little quirks and oddities. As with a lot of bush verse, and similar to 'The Hobo From Hughenden Town', the scribe is a little preoccupied with the end of life situation and writes as though the character may have paid for all his sins by what he has experienced from his time here on earth.

GATES.
Author unknown. (related by Rupert Terry)

St. Peter put his yo-yo down and rubbed his saintly eyes,
As through a cloud, a figure bowed, pursued by swarms of flies,
Came tramping up to heaven's gate and stood there in amaze,
Then dropped his swag and tucker bag and said, " Well spare me days"

"I've humped this here Matilda from the age of seventeen,
and there ain't a track in all the outback that us two haven't seen,
and when I rolled my final swag, I'd thought I'd cleaned the slate,
but now, 'Stone the crows, before me nose I see another flamin' gate."

"In fifty years of hoofin' it and covering all the while,
Twelve miles a day at least, and two gates to the mile,
I ain't much good at figures, but by the way I calculates,
In my career I've opened near on fifty thousand gates."

"These gates they fairly haunt me, there were gates of every sort,
Rusted gates, busted gates, high, low, long and short,
Gates that seemed to challenge you and gates that seemed to cringe,
Lazy gates, crazy gates and gates that hung on half a hinge."

"Gates all tinkered up with fencin' wire, and gates all pretty scroll,
With patent catches and homemade latches and gates made out of poles,

Wide gates and narrow gates, big barriers and small,
Saggin' gates and draggin' gates, I've wrestled with them all."

"I've opened 'em and shut 'em till the sight of all I hate,
I'd rather miss your heavenly bliss than open that there gate,
What's that? 'You'll open 'er for me', now that's what I call nice,
And shut her too, when I get through? Well, this must be Paradise."

I get the impression from the way it is written that 'The Hobo From Hughenden Town' relates to a much earlier period of Hughenden's history. It was known as a bit of a rip roaring town in the early days as it was the railhead for stations and settlements further out. Stock movement with both sheep and cattle were done by droving teams. Mail and passenger conveyance beyond Hughenden in any direction was done by Cobb & Co. coaches. Camel trains also collected and delivered loading from the railhead in Hughenden, as well as many teamsters with wagons transporting goods both away from and to Hughenden. Everything was much more labor intensive than it is in the modern day and age. So consequently in the early days of Hughenden, right up to about the 1930s, as well as the businesses in the main street it boasted of ten hotels, five of which were in the main street. Owning a hotel was quite a profitable business both for accommodation as well as food and beverages. And hobos were obviously tolerated.

The Hobo From Hughenden Town
Author unknown. (related by Rupert Terry)

Oh I dreamt that I died and to Heaven I went,
And stood by the gates where eternity is spent,
Accosting St. Peter I said, bowing down,
"I'm a recent arrival from Hughenden town."

"Will you grant me admittance St. Peter?" I said,
But his only reply was a shake of his head,

Then near him I noticed a friend from the coast,
With a smile more inviting than St. Peter could boast.

So I said to St. Peter "Excuse me old hoss,
Will you stand aside please while I speak to the Boss",
But he locked the Pearly Gates with his Ivory key,
And wheeling around, he spoke sternly to me.

"I've a good mind" said he, "to dispatch you to hell,
And it won't be in the bar of the corner hotel,
Before I admit you," said he with a frown,
"I must read up on the record of Hughenden town."

Then he beckoned two angels, (such sweet little things),
With number plates stamped on the tips of their wings,
Some parting injunction St. Peter bestowed,
And they disappeared into their starry abode.

The angels he said, always flew in a pair,
For sheiks, he explained, were a problem even there,
When the angels flew back with a huge printed card,
St. Peter perused it and then looked at me hard.

"It states," he observed, "that your town, so to speak,
Is just a collection of pubs on the creek."
"It's a model of beauty," I quickly replied,
"So perfect that people stopped there 'til they died."

"And it states you're a poet of doubtful renown,
A beer drinking hobo from Hughenden town,
You climb on the counter and stamp with your feet,
And kick up the devil's own row in the street."

"A libel!" I cried, "for the beer quota's small,
And sometimes I never get any at all."
"I'll allow you to enter." St. Peter replied,
Then unlocked the Pearly Gates and opened them wide.

"I've decided," said he "an exception to make,
In your case, though only for novelty's sake,
But it's not on account of the record you bear,
But merely because you are the first one from there."

A bogged Toyota on one of Dads many Gulf fishing trips

Anne McClelland, Rupert Terry, Joan Douglas at a Stamford Racecourse working bee in the 1950s

At a Brisbane night spot with Ron & Neta Grant, Rupert Terry and Carmel Ryan in the late 1940s or early 1950s

Christmas Day at Eldorado 1955. L to R, Graham, Cath Delahunty, Allan & Di Terry, Rupert, Monica O_Brien, unknown, Leona Terry, Bernard, unknown, Stewart Terry, Tom Terry, Thomasine Terry, unknown, unknown, unknown. In front, Robert, unknown, unknown

DAD, THE ENTERTAINER

Dad always enjoyed new adventures like blowing the silt out of the Old Dam in 1979 using explosives

Dad sighting in his .222 rifle at the Saranac mill. Dad used to take great pride in doing most everything he could himself and that included reloading his own ammunition

Keith Grant, Thomasine Terry, Ron & Neta Grant, Rupert Terry, Carmel Ryan in the early 1950s

Monica O Brien at Eldorado in about 1949

Dad, Mum and my sister Lou did an Asian trip in 1976. Here is Dad and Lou handling some snakes in Thailand. Mum declined the offer

Rupert Terry and John Harris from Violet Vale Station discussing the worlds problems over a beer. Fishing at Princess Charlotte Bay in 1978

Terrys about 1928. Taken at Saranac. L to R - Alec holding the horse, Thomasine, Graham, Edward, Rupert, Frank and Bernard. Stewart leaning on the horse at rear

Tom Terry moving into the mechanised age. Rupert and Mr. McKay (who delivered the machine) operating the FDE Cleatrac, 1951

21

REMEMBERING THE WOMAN THAT WAS MUM

Mothers are loving, compassionate, endearing, kind, strong, tough, and protective. As well as extraordinary, intuitive, patient, gentle, inspirational, caring and mindful. All these words describe a mother as it is the core part of their genetic makeup.

They are resourceful in caring for and protecting their offspring. They are the primary reason that the young survive their early years, and having provided by example the above traits, for them to hopefully go on to successfully find a mate and continue the existence of their kind. For some reason humans, with the most advanced brain of all life forms in matters of reasoning and calculating, take the longest of all to attain maturity and the skills necessary to survive on their own.

It does not matter whether they are of the animal world or the human world; the females of the species all share this same attribute of nurturing. Of going above and beyond in terms of unconditional love, time, effort and patience to look after and educate their young. In some cases, such as war, famine or other natural disasters, even giving of their own life itself.

Mum invariably burnt all of her candles at both ends to try and accomplish this, always being by far the first out of bed and the last into bed even on the coldest nights of winter. I was Mum's firstborn, and naturally as such, over the years, I always felt a special empathy with Mum, but have never ever tried to position myself to be treated as a favoured child and nor would she have countenanced that parlaying of favours either. I have always considered all of my siblings as equals in the family.

I would like to relate the story of my mother, who exhibited the above traits for her entire life until she passed away recently at the age of 100 years, 2 months and 10 days. Her whole life revolved around what she could do for her family or for someone else, while her own comfort or needs were always put on the back burner. My sisters who visited her daily at the nursing home in the last 12 months of her life told me this story.

Every day one of my sisters visited her each morning and evening, and on most days, if the weather permitted, they would also take her for a walk for ten or fifteen minutes around the extensive gardens in her wheelchair. Mum would say, "You must be tired pushing me around the garden, here pull up for a minute and you get in the wheelchair and I will push you for a while". 99 years old mind you and still wanting to hop in the harness.

Mum was born in outback NSW in 1924, which was five years prior to the Great Depression era. I believe this instilled a number of strong traits into her later character. Anyone who lived through those depression years developed very resourceful habits, possibly more so if you lived in outback Australia. If nothing else, Mum was very resourceful; she also had a very tenacious nature, persevering with a task long after anyone else would have given it up as a lost cause.

Mum's father was a second-generation, Australian-born O'Brien, and her mother was a second-generation, Australian-born Byrne. They were both of strong Irish stock with a very staunch Catholic faith, strong family links and a tenacity to stick to a given course or task to the absolute end. So, Mum and her four younger siblings all had a strong physical, mental and moral code instilled in them at a young age. Even their extended family were very close-knit and worked together closely, both physically and financially.

Her early years on the property were in the fading days of carts, wagons, and horse teams, and in the very early motor age, when life was lived and travelled at a much slower pace. Her grandfather's enormous house at 'Hatton' was built in the 1920s, but only when they were able to afford it, and even then they dug the clay on their own property, constructed a kiln and made all their own red-fired bricks to erect the walls. They had their own extensive vegetable gardens and orchards to supply their household needs. It was a very different way of living than families in the modern age and it is not hard to surmise that these surroundings formed Mum's later strong and resilient character traits.

When Mum was about ten years of age, her father balloted for and won a much larger block of country in western Queensland, which necessitated him leaving his family for extended periods to work the property. This was when Mum began her education at boarding school in Randwick, Sydney and her lifelong association and attachment to the Brigidine Order of nuns. Eventually, her mother lived nearby with her siblings, who were also attending school in Sydney. Mum excelled at school in all subjects, and her final day of school was one she said she would never forget, the day of the Japanese attack on Pearl Harbour.

On leaving school, Mum spent about six months as an unqualified fill-in teacher with the convent school of her old hometown, Warren, in western NSW. Because of the war effort, her father's staff on the Queensland property enlisted in the defence services, leaving him on his own. Mum took it upon herself at the tender age of 18 to go up and help him run the station for the next two years. Compared to the relatively closely settled Warren district, the Hughenden district of western Queensland would have felt primitive and isolated and had a distinctly harsher environment.

Mum, as always, made do, fitting into the environment she was in and learning what she had to. So early in 1942 Mum headed north from Sydney by train. From Brisbane she found herself as one of very few civilians on a troop train, which she found a very interesting trip. There were many troop trains heading north at that time (just after the Japanese attack on Darwin); consequently it was only the first couple of trains that got anything to eat. The railway station canteens simply could not keep the food up to the number of people passing through.

At the end of 1943, her aspirations found her wanting to attend university to train as a foreign diplomat, but in that era in Australia, that was a male-dominated field, and would have ruffled too many feathers. So she decided to study physiotherapy instead, which was also male-dominated, but she was admitted, and after 4 years of hard study at the Sydney University, matriculated at the end of 1947.

She worked in Sydney for a while, then set off to travel around Australia. With her good friend, fellow physiotherapist Audrey Hardy, she later went on to travel through England, Ireland, Scotland and the continent, using their physiotherapy skills to fund their travels. This was in the early 1950s, with things still being very raw and war-damaged just after the Second World War. Food and fuel rationing were still in place in England while Mum was over there.

Discomfort and inconvenience did not worry Mum, in fact they made her keener and she just continued on unaffected. She loved people and learning about their way of life, and she could fit in and adjust to whatever was going on. She was no princess who needed to have à la carte dining or be waited on in any way whatsoever. So the rough and tumble of post-war Britain and Europe, with its limited amenities and services, didn't deter Mum's adventurous spirit and quest for learning about foreign lands and customs.

On returning to Australia, she left the physiotherapy profession and returned to help her family on the western Queensland grazing properties, ultimately meeting our father. They must have been both very smitten with each other, for after a six-week courtship, he proposed to her and she accepted. I only became aware of this snippet of information after Mum had passed away in 2024 via one of my sisters. Apparently Mum was still wanting to travel and had accepted a physiotherapist's position at a hospital in Canada and was planning to leave the Hughenden district in the very near future. Dad must have had his eye on her and decided he had best leap into action. The rest, as they say, is history.

Their marriage produced seven children over 12 years, all whilst developing a large grazing property in the Hughenden district. We were loved, nurtured and cherished, but we certainly did not live a flamboyant lifestyle. The home was originally a boundary rider's one-room hut that had been added to and added to and added to over the years as their family grew. It was quite a ramshackle affair that was as hot as hades in summer and as cold as charity in winter, but it was home. Mum was involved in the local church in Hughenden which was 40 miles distant, community events and local branch politics, while looking after seven children and cooking for many who were engaged in work revolving around the station.

In times of grief, stress and turmoil, Mum was very stoic. I think I have only ever seen her cry in times of very close personal bereavement. The first time was in 1965 when I was about seven, as she received a phone call to say that her mother had died in Brisbane from a heart attack. I think Dad was away and it was only us kids at home with her. I can remember she sat at our office desk, just sobbing on the phone, and being only seven I didn't know what to say to her to ease her pain, perhaps because I barely knew her mother. Grandma had a bad heart and the western Queensland weather was simply too hot and rugged for her to endure.

She used to visit Terranburby for three or four months during the winter, spending most of the year living in their house in Brisbane. Grandpa used to regularly visit and spend time with her before she passed away due to heart attack at the relatively young age of 65 in 1965. She and Grandpa were readying themselves to go to Mass on a Sunday morning and were just waiting for their taxi to arrive. Thirty-odd years later her father passed away in 1996 at her brother's nearby property in the Hughenden district. Our father predeceased Mum by 37 years, and she lost two of her sons to accidents in 1995 and 2001.

My first wife Pam fell pregnant to me after we had only been going out for a relatively short period, hence the marriage and then, seven years later, a divorce. One of my sisters married under the same circumstances and ended with the same result. Another brother lived with his girlfriend for a number of years before getting married, and they too separated after a number of years. Like a lot of Australians my siblings and I were not regular church goers when we became adults, we were more just the 'weddings and funerals' contingent. Mum was aware that we had all smoked marijuana from the end of our high school years and enjoyed more than a moderate amount of grog at social events.

Her youngest son, as a young man, started acting oddly, engaging in self-harm and assuming an aggressive attitude towards family members and others for no apparent reason. Then assuming another name, he became estranged from the family, which evolved into ongoing difficulties and litigation with the family, including our mother in later years. In spite of all this, while Mum was certainly concerned about her offspring's life choices, she was never condemning or belittling of her children for their lack of moral fibre or their problems in life. Instead she held her tongue in check and tried in her own way to understand issues and help in whatever way she could.

Mum never suffered chronic health issues but, in her final years, suffered from slow-developing dementia, which worried her greatly. She was acutely aware of and very embarrassed about her failing memory that always seemed to leave her in the lurch with names of people she knew well, along with everyday items of general use. Mum's great love was general knowledge and as her dementia progressed, this one aspect of her new and changing life caused her much worry. Not being able to think of the right word to use in the context of a conversation or remembering commonly known basic places and countries caused her great irritation.

Even so, right up until her passing, she knew all her immediate family that she saw on a regular basis, even if she did get our names a bit muddled up from time to time. She knew that she had it wrong, and eventually, after going through a few names and a good sound self-scolding, she would get it correct and then have a laugh about it. I believe that what carried her was her strong Catholic faith that she had from a child, as well as the fact that she also possessed an incredible sense of humour even when the joke or misfortune was on her.

Her faith was something she had that none of her children possessed in adult life. I don't know just what it was, perhaps the generation that she grew up in helped her in some way to remain so staunch. It is not that her children did not believe in a Greater Being, but I believe that her children's generation had more distractions that caused them to lose focus on their own mortality. Also the many scandals of the Catholic Church that were being exposed in those years caused a lot of questions and doubt in the minds of the young.

She had many serious disagreements with the progressive priests, nuns and parishioners in her church. The 60s and 70s era in which we spent our formative years would certainly not have helped, with many of our peers and influencers pushing boundaries vocally, morally and intellectually. She would often sit in a quiet spot and pray or read the bible or religious material and spend time with her God, but while convinced and strong in her faith she was by no means what a lot of Australians would refer to as a 'bible basher'.

Even when her church in general was rocked by scandals, she had the ability to continue on regardless, which I suppose was what she held as the big picture, the belief and not the building. I believe that the seven years she spent at the Brigidine Convent in Randwick, Sydney, played a huge part in Mum always holding her own counsel and not letting her peers or doubtful and persuasive others influence her decisions. Invariably, once Mum had made her mind up about a matter, you had to be a good talker and have some extremely good points to argue to sway her course. She returned to her old school for reunions and loved the sense of family with her old school friends, her mentors and teachers, the nuns of the Brigidine Order. She remained in contact with many of them by correspondence.

My relationship with my mother was always a good one and was probably influenced by the fact that I was her firstborn child and presented her with her first grandchildren. But in saying that, I also presented Mum with many of her headaches and worries in my youth. In spite of my sisters jokingly referring to me in later years as Little Lord Fauntleroy or The Golden One, as her children we were always treated and loved equally by Mum. My two eldest sons arrived over a decade earlier than any of her other grandchildren and after my divorce the boys stayed with me on the property. So consequently they developed a closer and stronger relationship with their grandmother than my younger children did.

We ate in the 'Big House' with Mum, and she helped with their raising in more ways than I could count during their formative school years, which they didn't always enjoy at the time. In their adult years as they raised their own families they came to appreciate her efforts much more. It is amazing how a few years and change of circumstances can alter someone's perspective of a situation. By the time my younger children arrived on the scene, Mum had moved to live in Brisbane and they only got to see each other a couple of times a year at most. Hence they did not share that same relationship my older boys did.

Being a grandmother, she loved all her grandchildren, but Mum did not take any nonsense. If you were out of line or not performing to your best and her steely gaze settled upon you as the miscreant, you were definitely becoming wishful of being somewhere else. Apparently Mum as a child was fairly forthright and outspoken, according to her grandmother, and she had, as she told it, a somewhat turbulent relationship with her own grandmother. When my daughter Prudence reached the age of about 10 those same interactions seemed to be repeating themselves.

An amusing incident occurred after a bit of a Mexican standoff over some issue one day when I heard, "Dad?". I replied, "Yes Prue, what is it darling?". Her next question had me stumped and it was, "When is Gran going to die?". I had not expected such a forthright and to the point question and had to think about that for a bit but all I could come back with was, "Well I suppose she will get around to it when she is ready". What else could one say?

It has been said by some that my nature and Mum's were very similar, while others said that I had Dad's characteristics. I have always held, along with many others, the belief that two people can both look at a third person and they will both see different traits and neither can see, or will have difficulties seeing, the traits that the other person can see. I always marvel at the genetic makeup of men and women and the results when the cross pollination of reproducing occurs.

The similarities between uncles, aunties, cousins, brothers and sisters from both sides of Mum and Dad is sometimes so remarkable as to be almost unbelievable. It is never confined to just looks either; build, height, weight, gait, speech, laughter, hair - in some fashion or other they all get a look in. I see it in my brothers and sisters and children all the time, sometimes only fleetingly but it is always there. It is amazing that

DNA, something that you need a microscope to view, can produce such visible resemblances.

After Dad passed away in 1987 we buried him on the ridge of his choosing about a kilometre west of the house. Before we sold Elton, my younger brother Edward in 1995 would join him in the long yard on the ridge. Just before sundown each afternoon, Mum would take her old three-legged dog Spock and walk up and spend a little time with her men. Later on in the long yard a memoriam was added for Byrne, who was buried in the Kununurra Cemetery in Western Australia. Even though Mum was quite social and enjoyed entertaining visitors, she was always quite happy with her own company and of course there were always people about with station-related activities, as well as community activities occurring on a regular basis.

She never mentioned, entertained or looked for male companionship with a prospect of remarrying and remained on her own for 37 years before she herself passed away September 14, 2024 in Brisbane. At Elton we regularly had visits from family and friends, so Mum still led a fairly full and active life. Mum travelled often to Brisbane, to visit her daughters and grandchildren, and used to regularly visit Ellenbrae for up to three months in the winter months to see her son there.

Her own father, after her mother passed away in 1965, remained a widower for nearly the same number of years until he passed in 1996. She was never ever the boasting type but I think she was quite proud of the fact that she was the first one of the O'Brien clan in Australia to attain the age of 100 years. Some came close, very close, but she was the one who took the line honours. As though making sure everyone was looked after, the eldest was the last to leave us.

Kath Ray, Monica O_Brien, Jean Allison and Sue McAdam in Perth. 1948 Western Australia

Audrey Harvey and Monica at Yaralla Hospital. 1946

Ballroom at Hotel Darwin in 1949

Brigidine Convent Centenary in 1983. L to R - Margret Donnelan, Zelma Hardie, Mother Lawrence, Monica O Brien (partly obscured) and unknown

Irene O Brien with Monica circa 1926

Lara Waterhole on Cabanda in Oct. 1956. L to R-Anthony O Brien, Ebb Hayden, Eileen O Brien, Marion O Doherty and Lenny Fitzgerald

Monica Terry – 1956

Monica O Brien, Joan Knapp, Mary Murray and Eileen O Brien at Brigidine Convent at Randwick, Sydney. February 1938

O Brien siblings photo May 1940. Back row l to r - Bernard, Rene, Mike. Front row l to r - Monica and Eileen

Cutting the cake, May 1956

Last day of school for Monica. 7 12 1941

Monica Terry (nee O Brien) & Sue Pemble-Smith (nee Moore) at Sues home in Toowoomba in 2016. Seven decades after training together as physiotherapists

Manjimup fire tower. W.Australia 1948

*Rupert and Monica Terrys 30th wedding anniversary.
May 1986 at Elton Downs*

22

MUM, THE KNOWLEDGE GATHERER AND GLOBE TROTTER

From the early age of about five or six years old, when she was old enough to read, Mum's quest for knowledge began. She wanted to read her father's encyclopedias and was very put out when told she was not old enough for 'those' books. Mum was always a great lover of knowledge, whether academic or lived experience. She always had an avid interest in botany, science, history, ancient civilisations, geography and theology. She excelled at all of her subjects during her school years.

They included Geography, History, English, Mathematics, Latin and Religion. She set great store in her children also to be well informed. So to that end, in about 1965, Mum and Dad – probably at Mum's behest – bought a set of Encyclopedia Britannica, of which I think there were about 22 volumes, from a travelling salesman who was in the Hughenden district. They were with us for seven decades; they went to Townsville in 1969, survived Cyclone Althea in 1971, and returned to Elton in 1975 to continue imparting wisdom.

As school children, we did use them a lot, but as young adults moving away from home, it was left to Mum to wear them out – and wear them out she did. Her ever-inquisitive nature had the volumes always opened up, with bits of paper sticking out everywhere, earmarking some item or other for future reference. When we sold 'Elton Downs' in 1997, we presumptuously thought that Mum would not want to take the bulky and heavy Encyclopedia set all the way down to Brisbane, so we included them in the list of lot items in the auction.

We were so wrong. Mum was absolutely aghast that we would divest her of her treasured Encyclopedias. So they came off the sale list and found their way to her apartment in Durack, Brisbane, where they saw even more use than before. When Mum passed away in 2024, after 70 years of service, they were not in the best of condition. As everyone now carries a set of encyclopedias on their mobile phone, no one in the family wanted them, so they were then given away.

She was always eager to take on anything offered in the way of employment or further education. The only two exceptions I ever heard her mention were early in her life. One of them was a job at the Import Procurement Department of the NSW Government, when she returned to Sydney to commence her university course around 1944. She was only there for about six months and hated every minute of it, mainly because you never did anything except, as she said, "You just sat at your desk and tried to look busy or filed your fingernails". Another very short job was a stint in a bandage factory around the same time, which did not do much for her self-esteem.

As children, we all listened avidly to the stories of her youth, the tales of 'Murrimbong', her boarding school days, and working with her father for two years at 'Terranburby' during the war years. The stories of working briefly in Sydney before starting study for her physiotherapy certificate. Then the stories of her travels in Australia as she practised her craft, followed by her tales of travelling in England, Scotland, Ireland and the Continent when she was a young woman.

Her stories were all just random mentions, so we didn't have much idea of the continuity, breadth or scope of her interactions on the overseas jaunt. After Mum passed, I found a diary of her European adventures as well as a cache of letters that she had written home to her parents, which eventually, after both of her parents had passed, found their way back to the original scribe.

Mum used to write very hurriedly, and you had to be almost a hieroglyphics expert to decipher her scrawl. However, eventually, I managed to read all her letters and transcribe them to a much briefer version while still retaining the original natural flavour of her letters, containing the sense of awe and wonder she found in all that she saw and people that she met in her travels. From that transcription, I am writing this chapter.

Recently, not long before her 100th birthday, my sisters found her Physiotherapy Certificate of Training in surprisingly good condition amongst a pile of old papers and documents. They cleaned it up and had it framed for her to take pride of place on the wall for everyone to admire and comment on when she celebrated her 100th birthday. At the time of completing her Physiotherapist Training at Sydney University, there was a Polio epidemic sweeping Australia. Consequently, physiotherapists were in big demand, and there was no shortage of work anywhere in Australia. Mum worked in Sydney for a while at the Yaralla Army Repatriation Hospital, but soon, the far horizons were beckoning her to investigate them.

She successfully applied for a job in Perth, Western Australia and spent twelve months there. She enjoyed her work within the polio epidemic parameters and working with many afflicted children that were being treated with the "Iron Lung". She made many lifelong friends during her time there with the Durack family, a well-known Australian grazing dynasty. She also met the Guilfoyle family on the train when she travelled to Western Australia, who happened to own the 'Australia Hotel', a leading establishment in Perth. There were numerous wildflower excursions as well as trips to the Kauri forests and also Albany township in the southwest corner of Western Australia. She also travelled to Rottnest Island and other beach spots with her new friends.

After her time in Perth, she did a short stint in the Northern Territory in what passed, in those days, for its capital city, Darwin. She did this as a favour for a friend of a friend who had not had any time off in three years. She was in Darwin for about two months during the 'troppo' time of the year for them. Darwin has always had the reputation of possessing somewhat different social habits with a decidedly frontier atmosphere, even in modern times, which she found very interesting and entertaining. She had the opportunity to meet the 'famous' Dr Clyde Fenton, a pioneering Flying Doctor of the Northern Territory. Mum's impression of him was that, despite his legendary daredevil flying status in the Northern Territory, being slightly built as well as quietly spoken, a more unimposing person you could not imagine.

However, his exploits were notable, including flying at night without certification, taking off and landing in impossible locations that resulted in more than one aircraft crash, and disqualification by the Department of Civil Aviation for flouting their regulations, as well as insurance companies not wishing to view his applications. One of Dr Fenton's claims to fame was that in 1936, in his tiny single-engine aircraft, he had flown from Darwin to China after his sister died in childbirth. With nothing more than a simple compass, a ruler, a pencil and a child's atlas as his navigational aids, he went to bring his mother back to Australia. As well as a few hair-raising frights whilst flying, they also experienced a number of geopolitical and diplomatic issues.

In 1949, Mum finally returned to the family property, 'Cabanda', 70 km north of Julia Creek, Queensland, after working in her profession around Australia for approximately 18 months. She worked with her family on the various family properties for about a year before the travel bug once again bit. This time, she had planned an international trip to the mother country, and would be away for about two years. Apart from her marriage and raising her family, this trip would be the outstanding highlight of her life, and she often spoke of it. She decided to visit Europe in early 1950 because of the stories she had heard from her paternal Aunt Margaret, who had lived in Europe between 1937 and 1939 while her niece, Alice Bolger, was training in opera. Another reason for Mum of course, was her familial connections to Ireland, which weighed her decision to visit Europe.

Originally, she was going to travel to South Africa for an employment opportunity there, but civil unrest put paid to that adventure. Instead, she decided to travel via Sri Lanka and the Suez Canal to England, departing Australia by ship in April. The sea-borne choice of travel was a no brainer for Mum as airline travel in the early 1950s was in its infancy and quite expensive. The first leg of Mum's international trip was not 'jet set' by anyone's standards.

Her brother drove her in a 4WD war surplus Blitz Wagon in March of 1950 from 'Cabanda' to Julia Creek. Because of the wet season, boggy conditions and a distance of some 70 kilometres, that journey took about 12 hours. Then, by train for the next 270 kilometres to Hughenden, which took some 24 hours, water lapping at the base of the tracks most of the way. Eventually arriving in Townsville, she continued to Sydney by air with her neighbour and friend from Julia Creek, Noreen Paine.

Boarding the ship, the SS Ormonde, in Sydney on May 2 1950, she sailed down the east coast of Australia to Melbourne, where her best friend and physio colleague Audrey Harvey from Hobart joined her, and they continued to Perth. Docking for a day or two in Fremantle, Mum briefly visited some of her old colleagues at the West Australian hospital where she had previously worked. The ship then left Australia, with its first port of call being Colombo in Ceylon, now Sri Lanka.

They both enjoyed the exotic sights, sounds and food of their first foreign country for a couple of days before continuing their westward journey towards Great Britain. They also docked briefly in Aden and did a bus tour of the city and surrounding area. They docked at Suez and Port

Said but did not go ashore. After a voyage of about five weeks, they sighted the White Cliffs of Dover and, not long afterwards, were sailing up the Thames River to dock in London and disembark on June 10.

Her father's bank, the Bank of New South Wales, had arranged for their London office to book them hotel accommodation for their arrival. The London office had booked them a room for a fortnight in Berners Hotel, one of the leading hotels in the city. Eager to explore and do what they had come to do, they only stayed in London for a week before setting off on a hitchhiking adventure to Cornwell and Devon in the 'Toe of England'. Hitchhiking was a little 'out there' back in the 1950s, especially for two females on their own.

However, not to be deterred, they set off, getting lifts with many fascinating characters of many nationalities. Oft times, such was the novelty of two Australian girls hitchhiking, if their driver was a local, they were invited to share lunch or dinner at the home of their driver's family. Each evening, putting their Youth Hostel cards to good use, they swapped tales with other kindred spirits who were also enjoying the English experience. Especially for Mum, it was as far removed from the Australian outback that she had departed only six weeks previous as you could possibly get.

Their first stop of note was at Windsor Castle to watch the 'Changing of the Guard', where they also sighted the Queen Mother and the young Princesses. In her letters home, she was often in awe of the countryside, the beauty, the opposing quaintness and grandeur of the assorted structures, the antiquity of the ruins, and evidence of civilisations past. And so, with Windsor Castle as their starting point, their tour of southwest England began. Bracknell, Winchester, Southampton, Salisbury and Bath were towns they passed through as they soaked in the scenery, hospitality and history.

Bristol, Wellington, Lawnton, Exeter, South Brent, Kennack Sands, Plymouth, all quaint, quiet, country towns and villages, some of the smaller ones, little changed mostly for possibly a couple of hundred years.

Falmouth, Penzance, St. Anthony Head, Lands End, St. Ivy, Bodmin Moor, Jamaica Inn, some large towns, some sleepy little villages, some by the sea, some a little way inland, but all steeped in history going back to the Roman occupation and before. Honiton, Wells, Frome, Overton, Sandhurst were all observed and experienced then almost before they realised it, their first fortnight in England was over, and they were back in London.

They had both been accepted for physiotherapist positions beginning in Dundee, Scotland about a fortnight later, so before they left for Dundee, they spent all their time and energy exploring London and attended the tennis at Wimbledon. They saw some of the greats of the day playing, and once again sighted the Queen Mother. Working as physios in Dundee, Mum and Audrey, her friend, met many interesting people from other nationalities. Audrey met the man she married a year or two later in Dundee.

Whilst there, they attended The Royal Edinburgh Military Tattoo, or the Braemar Gathering as it was known then, and it was in 1950 that the NSW Highland Regiment travelled from Australia to compete and win their section. From Dundee, they travelled all over Scotland, sometimes hiking and driving. One trip they did with an elderly local couple that had taken them under their wing was through the Scottish Highlands to the most northerly tip of Scotland, to towns like Tongue, Bettyhill and John O'Groat, with views of the Arctic Ocean and the Orkney Islands.

They worked in the Dundee Hospital for approximately 3 months and made various trips around Scotland. They had applied for positions at a hospital in Nottingham, England and were accepted to begin there in early October. While they were travelling south for their next job in Nottingham, they became mixed up in a national scandal at the time. They were searched by English police for the Coronation Stone.

The item had been removed from Westminster Abbey in London by Scottish loyalists not long before and was still unlocated. Searching the luggage of two Australian girls was a bit ridiculous as the Coronation

Stone weighed in at some 150 kilograms. However, that is another story. It was in the town of Nottingham that these two girls from the Australian bush saw their first-ever snow. They worked at the City Hospital, which was quite ironic because, in fact, it was in the country.

They worked over Christmas at the Nottingham Hospital but spent New Year in Edinburgh, Scotland, with their medical friends from Dundee and Audrey's beau. It was also a farewell dinner for a Norwegian friend, Bjorg, who they would later visit in Norway on one of their continental trips. They also visited the legendary hideout of Robin Hood, Sherwood Forest, which was by all accounts a big disappointment. By the 19th century, it had been reduced in size to about 1,000 acres, having originally been in the Middle Ages somewhere in the vicinity of over 100,000 acres. By comparison, the small holding paddocks on her father's properties, 'Terranburby' and 'Cabanda', were bigger in size than the mythical Sherwood forest.

Mum and Audrey made their first trip to the Continent for about a fortnight in February of 1951. Not very impressed with Paris, they travelled to the south of France by train visiting the areas around Marseille, Lyon, Grasse, St Tropez, Cannes, St. Raphael, St. Maxim, Cagnes and Monte Carlo. Mainly because of the difficulty of the language, they did not hitchhike on the continent. They made a very brief journey as far as Rome, but because of accommodation shortages, they only spent one day there. They returned to St. Tropez and spent a few days there before bussing back through the Swiss Alps to Lyon, then to Paris, and finally returning to England. A position for six weeks that they had applied for earlier at St. Stephen's Hospital in London was awaiting them.

Early in April 1951, Mum, Audrey and another friend sailed on a very rough passage from Newcastle, England, to Bergen, Norway, to visit their Norwegian friend Bjork, who had worked with them at Dundee in Scotland. They spent a few days in Bergen, attending the ballet and theatre and visiting local sights. They then travelled from Bergen to Bjork's family's ski hut, which was at the inland end of a winding, torturously slow, five-hour journey by train. They spent about a fortnight enjoying the snow in a number of different, small rural towns.

Mum then parted company with her friends and travelled on her own by train through Oslo, Stockholm, Copenhagen, and Odense to Cologne in Germany. From there, she caught a riverboat down the Rhine River and went to Frankfurt. Her letters contained vivid descriptions of all the sights, sounds and colours before her eyes. This was also only six years after World War 2 had ended, so structural damage to buildings and the suffering of the people was still very evident to the naked eye.

Even though they were still suffering hardship from the fallout of World War 2, the people were generally very friendly and helpful. From Frankfurt, she caught a train to Lucerne in Switzerland. She visited Basel, Zurich, Wildhaus, and Buchs before visiting and spending time in Schaan, a village in Liechtenstein, the smallest country in Europe. From here to Vienna, she passed through many towns, such as Innsbruck, Feldkirch, Zell Am and Salzburg, exploring each as time and train timetables allowed. Mum was introduced to a mutual friend in Vienna, who showed her as much of Vienna and its spectacular sights as two days allowed.

Then, it was another wait on the station platform again, to catch the train to Venice and the chance of meeting more interesting characters amongst her fellow travellers. St Mark's Square, the Grand Canal and the ducal palaces were all visited aboard a gondola. The retail outlets for the high-quality leather, lace and silver goods that Venice is noted for were all scrutinised before once again boarding the train, this time to Florence for a day and then on, ever on again, for her second visit to Rome.

The Vatican, the Forum, the Colosseum and a multitude of cathedrals, chapels and cloisters were visited, much spaghetti eaten and vino consumed while staying in Rome over the next three days. Moving again, back to Florence, then to Milan, where she spent a day before crossing the border into Switzerland again. This time to Bex, Lake

Maggiore, Montreux, and Geneva where Mum wanted to listen to one of the early United Nations debates on Human Rights.

Now, with a smattering of about five different languages, Mum could communicate to a degree with almost anybody, for directions, accommodation or support. So she was able to follow most of the debate across multiple languages. Denmark, Sweden, France, Yugoslavia, Egypt and Lebanon all had their say on Human Rights, and afterwards, Mum met Mrs Grace Rowly and Mrs Eleneor Roosevelt. Departed Geneva in the afternoon for Lucerne, where she had a long, cold and uncomfortable wait for the train back to gay Paree and once boarded it was no better than the wait. On March 17, Mum arrived back in London.

On July 10, 1951, Mum departed London by train to Holyhead in Wales, where she caught the ferry to Ireland, arriving in Dublin. Mum visited her family's ancestral homeland of Ireland for about 6 weeks for the first time. She visited relations and relations of relations 'to be sure, to be sure' in County Carlow and the surrounding counties. She worked on farms belonging to family and friends. She went on doctor's rounds with Stan O'Beirne in the countryside around Arklow. She went to Horse Shows and race meetings. She visited sites of ancient insurrections and rebellions that were seemingly still fresh in the minds of her relations as though they had happened only yesterday. She crisscrossed the picturesque, cousin-strewn countryside, attempting to fit six months' worth of visiting into the six weeks that she had.

Of course, her beloved Brigidine Nuns were in the picture as well, this being their homeland. The Brigidine Order was formed in Tullow, County Carlow, in 1807 by Bishop Daniel Delany, the same county Mum's grandfather came from. The first Brigidines came to Australia in 1883 to begin a community in Coonamble, NSW. This was the same year Mum's grandfather, John (Jack) Henry O'Brien, immigrated to Australia at the age of 21. It is no wonder her attachment was so strong. Being from the same town in a predominantly Catholic Ireland, there were possibly strong familial ties to the Brigidine Order. Coonamble was not all that far away from where Jack O'Brien settled at Warren in NSW. Forty miles in

Ireland would have been compared to living in another orbit, but in Australia, it was just right next door.

By August 17, 1951, Mum had returned to London. She started work at Lambeth Hospital and remained there for the next few months, saving money for her final trip before she returned to Australia. Whilst in London, she documented that she attended ballet, opera and theatre productions as well as attending movies of the day. And knowing her penchant for being curious, no doubt she fitted visits to places of interest in London into the rapidly shortening days.

At the end of February, she returned to Dundee for a fortnight to farewell friends and work colleagues. On March 8, 1952, she boarded the train to Glasgow to catch the overnight ferry to Ireland. She then began a week-long whirlwind tour of Ireland, farewelling relations and friends and the special place she had come to love in her two short visits. She often spoke in her letters to home about wanting to return, especially to Scotland and Ireland, but it was never to be.

On March 17, 1952, Mum posted her last letter from England from onboard the Night Ferry. The Night Ferry was an English Channel ferry ship that the train actually physically steamed onto in England and off in France. She spent a couple of days in Paris, then boarded another train en route to Portugal, Spain, Italy, and finally Malta, where she was intending to meet the ship that would take her back to Australia. She would spend almost a month touring Portugal and Spain.

She visited many interesting places, steeped in history and going back to time immemorial. She also met a wildly woven throng of fascinating people, both locals and international travellers like herself. Her letters, describing the backgrounds of people she met in Spain and Portugal, read like pages out of an Ernest Hemingway novel. Travellers through the regions of these countries in those years were few and far between, so they were something of a rarity and were treated like royalty. It seems contradictory but for those times and the places she visited, it could also be said that there were many, as she seemed to be always bumping into English, American and other Australian visitors.

She visited Salamanca en route to Lisbon. On a day trip from Lisbon, she visited the Apparitions of the Virgin Mary site in Fatima. A treasured Catholic religious head covering called a Mantilla that she bought whilst making a personal pilgrimage to Fatima was later lost to Cyclone Althea in 1971. Her faith was always front and centre of her forays during her travels. She attended Mass, if not daily, certainly as often as she could manage and, if possible, actually in the famous cathedrals, churches, and chapels she visited. She visited or made contact with various orders of priests and nuns who, in turn, gave her contacts for cities that she intended to visit. On a section of one of her train journeys in Portugal, when she could see masses of gum trees and wattles and blue hazy mountains in the distance, she felt as though she was at home in Australia.

She visited cathedrals, castles, and palaces, many of which had Moorish Muslim architectural influence because the Moors had actually invaded and controlled Spain and Portugal for about 800-odd years. There was still much evidence of the Spanish Civil War that had only occurred about 15 years earlier, with destroyed buildings and bullet-pocked walls being quite common. Whilst in Lisbon, she attended a bullfighting match with a fellow traveller who hailed from 'deep in the heart of Texas'.

While the actual bullfight was a little bloodthirsty for Mum, she enjoyed the colourful spectacle of the Toreador in action, with the crowd providing many "Ole, Ole"s in the background. Leaving Lisbon, she travelled via Seville and Cadiz to Algeciras which is on the opposite side of the bay to Gibraltar. Much of her travel through Portugal and Spain was by train with the local farmers and peasants, who had their market produce in their carriages.

The train carried vegetables, fruit, fowl, sheep and pigs, and a sprinkling of travellers such as herself. There was no better place for Mum to immerse herself in their culture and history. Then a bus trip of much the same flavour onto Malaga with a side trip to Ronda, which boasted the largest bullfighting arena in Spain. It was on "The Rapide" train trip leg of her journey to Granada that she received her first marriage proposal in French.

Fortunately, it was just a misunderstanding; it was just that her French was not quite up to scratch. The next city on her tour was Spain's capital city, Madrid, where Mum spent Easter. Then it was onto Barcelona for a short stay followed by a 36-hour train trip through to Rome, arriving in Rome for the third time on Anzac Day, 1952. This time Mum spent about a fortnight in this ancient city.

She walked the streets, visiting most of the important sights of Rome, investigating Rome most thoroughly. A priority for a Catholic visiting Rome, she attended a St Peter's Square Mass celebrated by Pope Pius XII who also blessed the crowd. During this fortnight she also had an audience with the Pope arranged but apparently for unrelated security reasons it was cancelled at the last minute. She did volunteer work for an order of nuns that operated a small community hospital in Rome for a few days.

She then travelled along the coast a little further south to spend a few days in the areas of Naples, Pompeii, Sorrento and the Isle of Capri. May 10, 1952 – her departure date from Malta – was drawing close, so wanting to spend a couple of days in Malta, she then returned to Rome for her flight over to Malta to take passage on the 'SS Largs Bay' for the return voyage to the Antipodes.

On arrival in Australia, the ship was held up by a wharf labourers strike in Adelaide, so Mum and half a dozen other travellers disembarked the boat and caught a train to Melbourne and then Sydney in June of 1952. Mum visited family and friends in Sydney and headed north to Cabanda about a month later. Shearing had commenced at Cabanda by the time the "Continental Correspondent" arrived, so it was a quick exchange of suitcases and passports for the familiar old work harness. And so doing, she slipped back into the Australian rural workforce.

Mum's determination to go the full distance with whatever she did was incredible, I thought. Even though she quite often travelled with a companion there were many times when she did travel alone. This was only about 7 years after World War 2 had ended, and Europe and England were still to large degree in chaos. Food and petrol rationing was still happening, bomb and shell damaged buildings were still very common.

The European people, while friendly, courteous and helpful, were obviously still suffering the anguish of family and friends lost to the war and of course many had become impoverished with the loss of their family homes and wealth due to the hostilities. The Germans of course also suffered guilt for the enormity of what they had caused to all their neighbouring countries and themselves.

Her parents would have been more than a "little" concerned, I believe, as their daughter travelled about in less than ideal conditions. In her letters she tried to reassure them that she was getting travel advice from the Australian Embassy in whatever country she was in. Communications then were not as instantaneous as they are today. Telephone calls were connected manually through telephone exchanges and on the Australian end, her parents living on the remote properties that they did, were even further limited on the "party line" system by not having a 24 hour service. What Mum and her friend Audrey Hardy managed to fit into their two years in England and Europe was amazing.

There was no internet, you could not google information and you could not book anything online. It was all done by old fashioned "snail mail", telegram or telephone. Absolutely amazing. Places to visit or things to do, you either read about them or heard about them by word of mouth from fellow travellers. Word of mouth was Mum's strong suit – she loved to talk to people about anything.

Their trips were self-funded by working for two or three months and then taking time off to travel. She continually mentioned in her letters that she found the countries of England, Scotland, Ireland and Europe, together with their inhabitants, so enchanting and was totally captivated by everything. She so wanted to return to the birthplace of western civilization but even though she still continued to travel in later life she never visited Europe again.

Big Ben clock tower, London

Braemar Gathering in 1950. The year Monica was there the N.S.W. Highland Regiment travelled to Scotland to participate in this event and won

Fremantle wharves. Monica looking for passage to Sth. Africa in 1948

Dr.(Nobbs) and Doreen Frost feeding the pigeons in Trafalger Square

Monica at the Collinstown Airport, Dublin. September 1951

Monica s departure onboard SS Ormonde for England in 1950. Rene O Brien, Irene O Brien, Noreen Paine, Mrs. Brown, Mr. Brown, Monica O Brien, Bob de Monchaux

On the River Rhine in 1951

Monica O Brien at Cabanda saying goodbye to her dog Steve. March 1950. Departure day for overseas trip

New Year's Dinner at Lambeth Hospital, London. Monica O Brien and Nina Malseed beside her. Rest unknown

Monica O Brien with Mr. & Mrs. Ballingall. Dundee, Scotland, 1950. (His family owned the oldest brewery in Scotland)

Mt. Lavinia Hotel, Ceylon

Queen Mother and Princess Margret.
Changing of the Guard Parade. London, 1950

Pope Pius XII blessing the crowd in St. Peters Square

Railway station at Uostosur. Norway, March 1951

Rickshaws in Colombo, Ceylon

Sheila Fitzgerald in Switzland in 1951. Monica met her in Copenhagen and they travelled together later

Skiing in Norway. Uostosur, March 1951. Bjorg Hanevik, Audrey Hardy, Liz and Leif Hanevik, Elizebeth Whitton

23

TERRYS INTO THE FUTURE

For me, three score and ten years is fast approaching, and I am thankful for having made it so far in years. But approaching that age, I am glad to be passing the baton of life on to the next generation and spectate. As a 20 year old I used to quite often look at the older generation around me and ponder that stage of life and wonder what it would be like and whether or not I would make it to where they were and in what condition. I don't have to ponder any longer, I have now recently arrived.

As any father would be, I am very proud of my children and grandchildren and their achievements in life. My only regret in life is that neither of my two marriages lasted the distance and that is an unfortunate outcome, because I still believe that the institution of marriage is the only way to raise your children. Notwithstanding, whoever is in the right or wrong, some marriages don't last the distance and you have to move on, but not with bitterness or hatred and without abandoning your children.

They need their historic backgrounds from both their mother and father, whether good or bad, to know where they have come from. If it is good they can build on that and develop other ideas for their future. If it is bad then they can, if they can see it and wish to change it, discard that which is bad to change their aspirations and create their own future free of the past. There is no need to limit your future because of your historic past. Disappearing out of your children's life because of your own misfortunes is, I believe, absolutely the 'last card in the pack' in the game of life except in some cases that have been presided over by the Family Law Courts which in a lot of cases the male has no say. Many are grossly unfair and in lots of instances biased in favour of the female.

Fortunately neither of my divorces developed into bitter animosity or open warfare and both of my exes and myself had access to spend time with our children. In the case of my first divorce with Pam in 1984, our children Joe and Dan lived with me at Elton and spent their school holidays with their Mum wherever she was living at the time. When Joanne and I divorced in 2009, Prudence, Stephen and Conroy lived with her initially, visiting me regularly, and later we had shared custody week-about. I am very appreciative of the fact that I have good relations with all of my children, which comes about I think from that continuity of relationship. Children need the diversity of perspective that comes from having input to their lives from both parents and also both sets of grandparents if they are alive and present.

Not everyone can be a scientist or an astronaut. A person with the high qualifications of a university education would often not be able to solve a simple practical problem in the paddock or even contemplate doing a 12 hour day in the hot sun. Likewise the blue collar worker that attends to perhaps the more simple, mundane matters of life would not enjoy being cooped up in the sterile surroundings of a science laboratory or even see a good reason for being in there in the first place, let alone having the qualifications to operate some of the very specialised equipment on the benches. Vive la différence!

Joe and Dan initially found employment on properties as 'ringers', Joe around the Boulia area, working on a number of different properties.

Dan worked for Dan Everingham's family at 'Oak Park Station' north of Hughenden and then also on a number of different properties around the Charters Towers area. Since then they have both held down all sorts of jobs away from the rural sector in mining, construction, truck driving, crane operating and so on, and have never been out of a job. Over the ensuing 30 years they have both married, had families and done very well for themselves.

Of course the 20 year gap between my older children and my younger children had seen many changes in the trains of thought regarding education as well. It had become conventional thinking for even a person that wanted to follow a trade career to get a Grade 12 level of education. My younger children Prudence, Stephen and Conroy followed a different path and attended school and did very well with their studies until Year 12, then went on to University courses. Of course I no longer owned a property nor lived in a rural setting, so that avenue of physical and manual hands-on work was not part of their lived experience, which probably influenced their decisions.

Joe spent about 4 years working around Boulia on various properties and eventually fell for the charms of a lovely young local lass by the name of Priscilla Schofield, whose family owned a couple of properties in the Boulia area. With all the construction work going on in north west Queensland and many huge projects looking for staff on wages that could never be matched by a station job, they decided to move to Mount Isa together to take advantage of the situation, and their first big job was at Phosphate Hill near Dajarra. They both spent the next 12 years or so working on big construction projects all over Australia on incredible money and invested wisely, and are now in a very comfortable position.

They have, since 2004, lived south of Darwin on acreage, and with a family of three youngsters they are now both retired from the FIFO construction work. Joe is working as a Franna crane operator for a crane hire company but doing work mostly in close proximity to Darwin city. Priscilla has these last few years been working as an agricultural trainer at a local high school drawing on her Cert. 3s and 4s, as well as her rural experience as a girl and a young woman, to impart knowledge to those wanting a start in the rural workforce.

They have two sons and a daughter who are all doing well with their studies. Their eldest son Jed has twice represented the Northern Territory in a school boys' Rugby League side. He has recently won a sports scholarship to attend Rockhampton Grammar School. Perhaps great things await him in the world of Rugby League; the future will reveal. His younger brother Tor is also a very keen footballer, playing both codes as well as AFL in the Rugby off season.

Motorbikes and fishing keep him occupied if he has any time to spare after footy. If he keeps up with his training and dedication to sport he might also be selected for a school boys' side and perhaps win a scholarship as well. Their younger sister Zoe is very involved with her mother's love of horses and has a strong connection to their local Pony Club, as well as a love of anything to do with Taylor Swift.

My son Dan, after working on 'Oak Park Station' for 3 years, moved to Charters Towers and worked in a motorcycle shop for a few years, doing some casual station work on the side as well as dabbling in a little bit of bull riding on the rodeo circuit. It was at the rodeos that he met his future wife Roslyn Poole who he married in 2004 and since then they have based themselves in Townsville. Dan has always been busy, working initially for contracting companies doing big road works contracting in Townsville and on Cape York Peninsula.

He did one stint in the coal fields, then returned to Townsville for a few years to work at Townsville's cattle live export yards on the city's outskirts at Julago . Since then it has been back to the coal fields at Collinsville where he remains. Ros likewise has always been a busy person, holding down clerical and receptionist positions as well as travelling to rodeo events all over North Queensland. Recently she graduated as an Enrolled Nurse after a number of years of part-time studies and she starts soon on her studies to be a Registered Nurse.

They have three daughters and two sons. Grace, their eldest, has left school and has been working for a couple of years for a new car dealership in reception. Dacey finished his education early and like a lot of young fellows went bush, working for a rural contractor in the gulf country bull catching and fencing. He has returned to Townsville temporarily and works for a concreting contractor. Next one down the line is Lily, who is still at school but has a great work ethic and keeps herself busy working after school and weekends.

She is in charge of installing the holes in donuts at a local shopping centre. She is recognised as one of their more dedicated staff members putting in more hours than most and is, she has told me, the owner of quite a healthy little bank account. She is currently applying for apprenticeships as a diesel fitter, hoping when she leaves school to follow Dad into the mining industry where the money is. Mackenna is the second last in Dan's family and this year will be her last at Primary School.

She is an avid horse rider and with her Mum attends rodeos regularly all over North Queensland as she is also a keen rodeo competitor. With her positive 'go get 'em' attitude she has won numerous ribbons and cash prizes in her age events for Barrel Racing and Bending Racing. Their youngest is Wylie, who is still at Primary School and has yet made no decisions about what career path he would like to follow.

Prudence, who is exceptionally talented with artistic skills, started studying Animation in Melbourne but this was upset by Covid-19. She escaped by the skin of her teeth from Melbourne the day before they slammed the doors shut. Returning to Townsville for about 2 ½ years, Prudence completed a Diploma of Art as well as working at Myers amongst jewellery, shoes, handbags and belts. In that time she also conducted her first solo Art Exhibition. However she is now back working at her degree, spending 2024 in Brisbane, and in 2025 she is back to the city that she loves, Melbourne (just quietly, I think it is the shoe shops).

Stephen's chosen course for a career was to do a double degree in engineering, starting at QUT in 2021, which he is completing with his usual quiet, understated efficiency. He is now half way to completion, but currently in England for 12 months furthering that path with an internship on the BMW production line in Birmingham. He will be back here in Australia at the end of July and straight back into his studies to complete his remaining 2 ½ years until graduation.

Conroy is doing a part-time Arts Degree, working part-time for the Department of Main Roads, and is also a very keen member of the Australian Army Reserves, often away attending some defence course or an exercise in the bush. He has also entered into a domestic situation with a lovely young Vietnamese lady by the name of Thu, who is also studying at University, and he did his second trip to the southern highlands of Vietnam with her over Christmas of 2024.

I am well pleased and very proud of all the dedication of my children and grandchildren in pursuing their chosen paths, as well as their work ethic and ability to get things done in what I perceive as the very complex world of modern education. I am also very thankful that I have no drug dealers, car thieves or career criminals that seem to have become a blight on all Australian communities in the space of the last couple of decades – but those sorts of outcomes I believe all stem back to parenting and the groundwork of childhood. Aspirations and dreams only come about by working at it and having respect for the other people in the community that you live in, as well as some guidance from those loved ones about you.

In this modern day and age of instant 'everything', I realise that we live in a rapidly changing world, one of climate change fear, pandemic fear as well as much-feared violent conflict and terrorism, all fueled by an unyielding and biased media influence. But as in millenia past the human race has always managed to retain that flickering flame of love, hope and resilience. I too have hope and faith. Into this mix a lot of young men and women are choosing to bring no children into this world, laying the blame at the feet of these issues. My feeling is that they are denying themselves the joy of the experience of being a parent and giving each of their parents the joy of being grandparents, and to my mind in a sense this is a selfish attitude to have. A houseful of shiny possessions will never equal the joy of having a family.

I have experienced the joy and the emotions of being a Dad twice over, albeit twenty years apart, between my two older sons at Elton and then my daughter and her two younger brothers while we were in Mount Isa, and I will say that it is something that cannot be equalled. That little helpless bundle that you went half shares in creating and is totally dependent on you for at least the next decade or so staring up at you gives you a completely different perspective on life.

In spite of the fact that they could spill some quite nasty items onto your person from either end of themselves and they could bellow for long periods of time (usually in the early hours of the morning) with wind, you soon forget those incidents when they give you a little smile or a Dad-Da for the first time. It would be equally so for Mums because they put just as much or more effort into rearing bubs as well, but I speak only for my experiences in this story.

My second family was different due to the fact that, to use that old Australian expression, "Been there, done that", but it was no less of an emotional experience with Prudence being our first and only daughter, to which we added two more boys. Each new little face, the little fingers, the little toes brings a sense of awe and delight that you and your wife have created a little person totally unique on the planet. And that little helpless person is going to develop, learning to think and act in their own right and will one day do what you are doing right now. For me personally being a father gave me a greater sense of responsibility and drove me to achieve better outcomes for my family.

At certain periods of our lives we have most likely all been a teacher in some random fashion, having demonstrated or shown someone how to do something. It may have been at work, it may have been your next door neighbour or helping someone with some roadside assistance. However when you have children you become a teacher on a different level everyday for the rest of your life. Those first steps, how to get a swing to work effectively, how to balance as they take their first bicycle ride, how to use the tools in your workshop or how to drive a car as new-found independence takes them off into the big, wide world.

Future Terry generations that I have not yet met in the ongoing and always interesting cycle of life with surprises at every turn are something that will always intrigue me. Amongst my younger children and my older grandchildren none have yet expressed an interest in marrying and having families of their own. As with Joe and Dan when they reached adulthood, my family finding their pathways through life, flourishing and moving to other areas of Australia is something that I am looking forward to.

The following quotation has been attributed to many people but no one can say with any amount of certainty who said it originally. It points out that the only certainty is that which is behind us, the rest is revealed as we move forwards but we must really appreciate what we have in the here and now.

"Yesterday is history, tomorrow is a mystery, today is a gift and that is why we call it the present."

Conroy with his mother Joanne on the day he signed up with the Australian Army Reserves

Conroy and I when he signed up with the Army Reserves

Conroy with his partner at the Grammar School Graduation

Dan & Ros Terry wedding photo

With son Dan and grand daughter Grace who is all done up for a Graduation Ball

Going for a spin with grandson Wylie

In Darwin with Joe and Cilla and their family

Jed, Tor and Zoe, my Darwin grandchildren

My daughter Prudence at her first Art Exhibition in Townsville

My son Dan *with his wife* Roslyn *nee* Poole

My son Joe with his wife Priscilla nee Schofield

Son Conroy and grandson Dacey at Westmorelands homestead

Student photo shoot while still at high school, Conroy, Prudence and Stephen

With Jed, Tor and Zoe, the Darwin grandchildren. I can do my own Rabbit Ears thank you very much

With my Townsville grandchildren, from left, Dacey, Mackenna, Lily and Wylie. Missing is their elder sister Grace

GLOSSARY

	CHAPTER	
back'o'beyond	1	way out near sunset, very remote, inaccessible, a long way away.
balloted block	1	a parcel of land requisitioned off a larger station and put up for public ballot or lucky draw. Rules apply for the successful person.
bathurst burr	6	a native of South America, it was introduced to Australia in the early 1800s. If not controlled it can contaminate the clip severly affecting its value. Also competes with crops in a field.
belly wool	6	wool on the underside of a sheep, male or female
B&S ball	9	Bachelor and Spinsters dance
bogged	4	an animal can become stuck trying to drink at the muddy edges of water hole
boggy	4	the edges of a water hole particularly in black soil country can become boggy when it gets down to a previously low level and there is a ledge of silt extending out

GLOSSARY

bore	7	a hole drilled into the earth, sometimes to a great depth to access artesian water (flows to the surface under pressure) or sub artesian water (comes close to the surface but needs a windmill for the final lift)
budgerigars	2	a small, long-tailed, seed-eating parrot native to Australia. Green, yellow and black in colour.
bulliman	3	aboriginal term for a policeman.
butts	6	are wool packs conveniently placed along the board and around the wool table for wool other than fleece wool. They may be for locks, bellies, dags, skirtings or whatever the classer designates
camaraderie	1	a position of mutual trust and friendship, a long association.
cast	3	fallen over and unable to get up from that position
CAT scans	15	a computed tomography scan, formerly called computed axial tomography scan, is a medical imaging technique used to obtain detailed internal images of the body
cherabin	14	a large freshwater prawn
classer	6	makes sure in classing the lines of wool are even. Is responsible for overseeing the entire preparation of the clip. Shed preparation to overseeing how the bales are pressed
coachers		a small group of quite, well handled cattle into which you add the wild cattle you have mustered making for easier containment.
cockies	6	slang term that refers to the owners of the stations

contractor/ expert	6	the boss of the shearing team. He signs the shearers on at the start, he is everywhere attending to problems to ensure the pace does not slacken and all runs smoothly
crutching	5	is done a few months before shearing. Removes wool from the crutch area and the upper rear legs of male and female sheep. Helps prevent fly blow and significantly reduces staining of the fleece when you shear
dags	6	dried feaces adhering to the wool.
dam	4	a man made water storage facility, earth from a deep excavation is used to build the banks
delver/delving	2	to clear a stock water drain so that the water flows the full length of the drain.
dib-dib-dib	3	do your best, which is an Australian Scouts saying, originally dyb but became over time, dib
donga	9	portable building
drafting	6	is the owners responsibility. The sheep are drafted primarily by gender so teats on females and pizzles on males do not get cut off. Also cancerous sheep, black wool sheep and strangers are drafted off
dray	1	a heavy duty two wheeled horse drawn vehicle
drover	1, 2	a person that is part of a team shepherding animals along a stockroute.
droving	1	taking a mob of sheep or cattle along a stock route
fettlers	21	workers that inspect and maintain a railway line to a safe standard

GLOSSARY

flinders grass	6	is a smaller and finer type of perennial or a seasonal grass that grows from the seeds of last seasons plants.
fly	4	refers to the blow fly not the harmless but annoying native bush fly
fly strike	5	usually early in the year, during or just after the wet season. The anus/pizzle area of the sheep with six months wool on them become stained with urine or faeces which then become fly blown. Maggots can kill a healthy animal in two or three days
gestation	4	the length of a pregnancy for any type of female
governess	1	usually a young woman teaching children school lessons on remote properties
great australian salute	4	when you have to continually wave at least one hand in front of your face to prevent flies from entering your mouth, nose or eyes. Usually only during or immediately after the wet season
grog		an alcoholic beverage whether it be spirits, wine or beer
hides		referring to a group of animals, usually cattle
jackaroo	5	a station hand that works on a property with a view to assuming a managerial career. Eats with the owners family and not in the kitchen with the other men
joining	4	when the rams are put in with the ewes to get them pregnant
kemp	6	extremely low grade of wool, very coarse and usually only found on the lower legs or around the face

lambing	4	the time of year when the ewes deliver their lambs. Can be adjusted by when you join the rams to suit your location and season in Australia
lamb marking	5	usually done at about two or three months old. The lambs get an ear mark, tail removed, mulsed and the male portion castrated
large lizards		colloquial term for crocodiles
larrikins	2	a funny person, quite often plays pranks on his friends
let go pens	6	the pens that each shearer lets his shorn sheep go into. They are counted out at the end of each run by the contractor and entered into the run tally book.
lumbar puncture	15	also known as a spinal tap, a needle is inserted into the space between two lumbar bones of the spine and a sample of cerebrospinal fluid is removed for testing.
marking cradle	5	a steel cradle that the lamb is secured in by the rear legs, face up.
macadamisation		sealing a road with tar and gravel to develop it into an all weather road
mickey	6	to mock or ridicule someone but in a teasing or playful way, or a male animal that has not been castrated
mill	5	a steel tower with a wind harnessing wheel on top, connected by rods to a pump hundreds of feet down the bore hole. Brings water to the surface

GLOSSARY

mitchell grass	6	a coarse grass found over most of inland Australia. Grows from deep rooted tussocks and is able to be dormant for extended periods.
MND	15	Motor Neurone Disease, a degenerative neurological condition
mob		referring to a group of animals or people. Aboriginals refer to extended family as 'our mob'
MRI scans	15	stands for magnetic resonance imaging and refers to a medical imaging scan that creates detailed images (or pictures) of your body's soft tissues, bone and fat
MS	15	Multiple Sclerosis, a degenerative neurological condition
mulesing	5	is the removal of skin from around the tail and upper back legs, reduces fly strike by up to 90%. Properly done it is over in seconds, heals quickly and is far prerferable to being eaten alive by maggots not if but when they get blown
murder	1	a group of crows
mustering	1	gathering stock together from the paddock for either animal husbandry or for sale
noogoora burr	6	a native of America it is widespread in Queensland. If not controlled, it contaminares wool severely affecting its value. Also competes with crops in a field.
navvies	21	manual labourers, another term for fettlers in the railway
on the wallaby		travelling or on a journey. Old time term used by swagmen during the Depression years but still used on occasion

packhorse	1	a draught animal, sturdier style of horse suited to carrying heavy loads.
paddocks	5	the divisions on a property by fencing to control animal husbandry or to control grass or water useage
pannikin	10	a steel cup sometimes coated with enamal
paraway	3	Aboriginal for faraway
perishables	1	milk, butter, fresh fruit and vegetables.
perrenial	4	an annual or seasonal grass that grows afresh from the seeds of last years grass
pizzle	5	a male sheep's penis
pizzling	5	part of the crutching process takes the wool off around the pizzle of the male sheep. Helps prevent fly blow and significantly reduces staining of the fleece when you shear
polled/polys	1	It is a ram or bull that is bred without horns
prickly acacia/algeroba	6	a very hardy and invasive species of mesquite tree that has become a listed pest over much of inland Queensland.
presser	6	puts similar fleeces into the press and bales the wool. Records bale weight, bale number and property name, fleece type in the bale tally book and stencils each bale accordingly.
raconteur	3	a person with good people skills, loves telling a story.
railway siding	1	an area where rail wagons can be shunted off the main line to be loaded or unloaded
ringer/ringing	9	station hand employee, derived from the early days of stopping running cattle by turning the

GLOSSARY

		lead in on themselves and ringing them around in a circle
ringer/ringing	6	can also refer to a shearer who regularly shears more than 200 sheep per day, thereby 'ringing' the shed
roly-poly	4	a grass tumble weed
rouse abouts	6	collect the shorn fleeces and spreads it onto the wool table for classing. Keeps the board clear of dags, locks and bellies etc. Sometimes helps with penning up but the priority is on the board
runs	6	each day is divided up into four runs of two hours duration with a half hour break between each. Usually a shearer will shear at least fifty sheep in each run.
rushes		when a large group of animals get a fright (usually when sleeping) and run uncontrollably. American term is stampede
scalie	9	Department of Main Roads/ weights and measures officer
scone	11	a baked dough snack, can also be a colloquial term for a persons head
scour	5	Diarrhoea
shearing	6	is done anually and involves removing the entire fleece, classing it for quality and putting it in bales
shore	5	the past tense for shearing sheep
showies	2	people that follow the Australian show or carnival circuit around with rides or amusements
smoko	5, 6	Morning or afternoon tea

spell		to have a rest, recuperate or rejuvenate
spiders	16	hobbles restrict the movement of a horses front legs. Spiders restrict the movement of all four legs by connecting all four legs to a central ring usually used on an unruly horse that is being broken in. Prevents striking or kicking
stock route	1	an area of land designated for travelling stock. The travelling mob had to complete a certain distance each day in a forwards direction
supplements	4	mineral lick blocks come in all shapes and sizes. Used when the natural grass is low in nutritional value
swing a bag		a person that is officially registered to take bets on a race course, known as a bookie or swinging a bag with all the tickets and betting paraphernalia in it
tar branding	6	an easy and very visible means of applying a liquid paint to identify a sheeps origins. It is faded and spread but still visible at the next shearing
the board	6	is the shearers work area between the catching pens and the let-go shute. Between sheep, shearers, rouse abouts, fleeces and butts it is a very narrow, confined and busy space
the track	13	refers to the north/south road in the Northern Territory before it was sealed, a lot of people still use the term even though it is now a sealed highway
tucker	6	refers to food or meals
turkeys nest		an earthen above ground water storage facility filled by a wind mill from a bore, to a gravity fed trough

GLOSSARY

vermin	2	animals that prey on domesticated animals, foxes, pigs, dingoes, eagle hawks, crows.
water runs	4	driving around (at the end of year, usually every day) and checking each and every dam on the property to remove bogged sheep from the waters edge.
wagon	20	a heavy duty four wheeled oxen drawn vehicle potentially carrying up to 14 tonnes
Weaners	2	A young animal that's been weaned off its mother, either sheep or cattle
Wethers	5	castrated male sheep
wide comb	6	is the portion of the shearers hand piece that is pushed through the wool. There is absolutely nothing wrong with them but unionised shearers being what they are, there was an many reasons as there were Aussie shearers for outlawing them.
wigging	5	part of the crutching process, takes the wool off aroung the eyes and cheeks of the male and female sheep to enable their vision to feed and water properly. A sheep that can't see does not do as well
wiggled	5	involuntary movement, usually associated with happiness or delight
willy-willy	4	a circular gust of air
wool table	6	the table on which each and every fleece is skirted of impurities and classed before going into a wool bin with similar fleeces.
wool roller	6	the classers helper, skirting the fleeces of dags and grass seed impurities. Rolls the fleece for

		inspection by the classer. May be called on to assist with other jobs around the wool table
yakaying	6	Shouting, making a noise

www.ingramcontent.com/pod-product-compliance
Lightning Source LLC
Chambersburg PA
CBHW080601170426
43196CB00017B/2873